TARGETING IMMIGRANTS

TARGETING IMMIGRANTS

Government, Technology, and Ethics

JONATHAN XAVIER INDA

Blackwell
Publishing

BLACKWELL PUBLISHING

350 Main Street, Malden, MA 02148-5020, USA
9600 Garsington Road, Oxford OX4 2DQ, UK
550 Swanston Street, Carlton, Victoria 3053, Australia

First published 2006 by Blackwell Publishing Ltd

1 2006

Library of Congress Cataloging-in-Publication Data

Inda, Jonathan Xavier.
Targeting immigrants : government, technology, and ethics / Jonathan Xavier Inda.
p. cm.
Includes bibliographical references and index.
ISBN-13: 978-1-4051-1242-0 (alk. paper)
ISBN-10: 1-4051-1242-5 (alk. paper)
ISBN-13: 978-1-4051-1243-7 (pbk. : alk. paper)
ISBN-10: 1-4051-1243-3 (pbk. : alk. paper) 1. United States—Emigration and immigration—Government policy. 2. Immigrants—Government policy—United States. 3. Emigration and immigration—Government policy—Moral and ethical aspects. I. Title.
JV6483.I62 2006
325.73′09′.045—dc22
2005013066

A catalogue record for this title is available from the British Library.

Set in 11/13.5pt Bembo
by Graphicraft Limited, Hong Kong

For further information on
Blackwell Publishing, visit our website:
www.blackwellpublishing.com

CONTENTS

ACKNOWLEDGMENTS

Special thanks go to Gerardo Aldana, Ralph Armbruster-Sandoval, Edwina Barvosa-Carter, Leo Chavez, Ramon Gutiérrez, David Horn, Rudy Torres, the anonymous reviewers at Blackwell, and my colleagues in Chicana/o Studies at the University of California, Santa Barbara. They all, in different ways, contributed greatly to this project. I would also like to thank audiences at the various institutions where I presented portions of the book: the Latina/o Studies Program at the University of Illinois, Urbana-Champaign; the Center for the Study of Race and Ethnicity at the University of California, San Diego; the Department of Anthropology at the University of California, Santa Barbara; and the Department of Comparative Studies at the Ohio State University. Many thanks go to Jane Huber and Emily Martin at Blackwell for their enthusiastic support of the project. Finally, I owe a great debt to the Rockefeller and Ford Foundations. I started writing the book while on a Rockefeller Postdoctoral Fellowship at UC San Diego and continued to work on it as a Ford Postdoctoral Fellow at UC Irvine.

INTRODUCTION: GOVERNMENT AND IMMIGRATION

The Problem of Illegality

Let us begin with the following scene.

The date is October 1, 1994, the setting a 14-mile stretch of the US–Mexico border running from the Pacific Ocean to the rugged canyons east of San Ysidro, California. This stretch is the busiest illegal border-crossing zone in the nation. As dusk draws near, over 150 Border Patrol agents, more than twice the usual number, fan out in an array of vehicles (horses, bicycles, sedans, all-terrain vehicles, military helicopters, and small high-speed boats) along the fields, canyons, riverbanks, and beaches of this tract of border. They are arranged tactically in three lines of defense, each half a mile apart. From these strategic positions, using a host of sophisticated surveillance devices (including ground sensors, night scopes, and video cameras), the agents survey the stadium-light-illuminated terrain along the 10-foot metal fence that separates San Diego from Tijuana, scanning for illegal crossers bent on eluding them. At the first signs of incursion, the agents spring into action and give chase to the rush of trespassers. Before the night is over, the US Border Patrol will have made over 800 arrests in this area, more than three times the number registered at the same time the previous year (Sanchez 1994).

This scene depicts day one of Operation Gatekeeper, an ambitious rational-technical program developed by the Immigration and Naturalization Service (INS), and now under the auspices of US Customs and Border Protection (CBP) in the Department of Homeland Security (DHS), to reduce the flow of illicit immigration from Mexico into the

San Diego, California area.[1] Gatekeeper is part of a larger, systematic federal government effort to strengthen control of the Southwest border. As articulated in the *Border Patrol Strategic Plan: 1994 and Beyond, National Strategy*, this comprehensive border control scheme is based on a strategy of "prevention through deterrence." The objective is to increase fencing, lighting, personnel, and surveillance equipment along the main gates of illegal entry – such as San Diego, California and El Paso, Texas – in order to raise the probability of apprehension to such a high level that unauthorized aliens would be deterred from crossing the border. The rationale here is that such localized practices of govern-mental intervention disrupt traditional illegal crossing patterns, forcing migrants to consider passage through more arduous, remote locations. Potential border crossers are thus either dissuaded from ever attempting to cross, or those who do try, given that they fail repeatedly, eventually give up out of sheer frustration and/or from exhausted resources (Andreas 2000). The INS/CBP's utopian vision aims for nothing short of the sweeping "restoration" of the integrity and safety of the Southwest border; the vision is of a border that works to arrest the flow of immigrants.

Significantly, Operation Gatekeeper's goal of curtailing illegal immig-ration to the United States is directly connected to the ways undocu-mented immigrants have been problematized over the last few decades – to the manner in which particular knowledges or regimes of truth have constructed the "illegal alien" as a problem. More specifically, this goal is related to how a host of knowledges, stemming from a variety of "experts" such as social scientists, politicians, INS/DHS bureaucrats, policy analysts, and the public, have represented "illegal" immigrants as threats to the well-being of the social body. For example, these immig-rants have been associated with such cultural, social, and economic maladies as overpopulation, crime, deteriorating schools, urban decay, energy shortages, and national disunity. Moreover, they have been accused of displacing American workers, depressing wages, spreading diseases, and burdening public services. Programs such as Operation Gatekeeper, then, have been formed in connection with particular assemblages of knowledge and the expertise of numerous authorities. They have sought to ground their conduct and objectives in the pos-itive knowledge of the objects to be governed.

The purpose of this book, to put it briefly for now, is to explore this conjunction between knowledge and governmental practice. More precisely, the study focuses on the post-1965 government of "illegal" immigration. It is concerned, on the one hand, with the kinds of knowledge, the specific problematizations, and the various authorities that have constructed "illegal" immigrants as targets of government; and, on the other, with the specific tactics, techniques, and programs that have been deployed to manage this population, particularly at the US–Mexico border. The book, in short, is concerned with how "illegal" immigrants have been problematized as objects of knowledge and governmental intervention.

Government and Governmentality

The conceptualization of this project in terms of the relation between knowledge and government draws from and is meant to contribute to the growing body of interdisciplinary literature that has developed since the late 1980s or so around the theme of governmentality. This work has emerged out of Michel Foucault's (1988, 1991) scattered writings and lectures on the arts of government. In these pieces, the term "government" refers generally to the conduct of conduct – to the more or less calculated and systematic ways of thinking and acting that propose to shape, regulate, or manage the conduct of individuals and populations toward specific goals or ends (Rose 1996a; Dean 1999). Understood this way, government points our attention very broadly to any rational effort to influence or guide the comportment of others – whether these be workers in a factory, inmates in a prison, wards in a mental hospital, the inhabitants of a territory, or the members of a population – through acting upon their hopes, desires, circumstances, or environment. The term thus designates not just the activities of *the* government and its institutions but, more generally, the practices of all those bodies whose aim is to shape human conduct. From this perspective, then, the state is only one element, albeit an important one, in the multiple networks of actors, organizations, and entities that exercise authority over individuals and populations.

Scholars working with this notion of government have been most concerned with exploring those practices that take as their target the wealth, health, security, and happiness of populations. More specifically, they have been occupied with studying all those strategies, tactics, and authorities that seek to mold conduct individually and collectively in order to safeguard the welfare of each and of all. They have thus drawn attention to the intrinsic links between strategies for knowing and directing large-scale entities and schemes for managing the actions of particular individuals – to how the conduct and circumstances of individuals are connected to the security and well-being of the population as a whole. Focusing along these lines, scholars of governmentality have produced important studies on a broad range of subjects, including: space and urban planning (Rabinow 1989); psychiatry, medicine, and psychology (Castel 1981; Ong 1995; Rose 1998); poverty and insecurity (Dean 1991; Procacci 1993); social insurance and risk (Ewald 1986; Defert 1991); the regulation of pregnancy and reproduction (Horn 1994; Weir 1996; Ruhl 1999; Greenhalgh 2003); programs for self-esteem and empowerment (Cruikshank 1999); crime control (O'Malley 1992; Rose 2000b); globalization (Ong 1999; Ferguson and Gupta 2006); colonialism (Kalpagam 2002; Scott 2006); and the regulation of unemployment (Walters 2000). The perspective of these studies does not amount to a formal methodology or a unifying theory of government. It is actually a perspective that draws attention to government as a heterogeneous field of thought and action – to the multiplicity of authorities, knowledges, strategies, and devices that have sought to govern conduct for specific ends. Nonetheless, it is possible to single out at least three closely related analytical themes along which their analyses are organized. A review of these themes will help better establish the aims and limits of this book.

The first analytical theme involves the political rationalities (or mentalities) of government. According to Nikolas Rose and Peter Miller, two of the foremost proponents of the governmentality approach, this domain designates: "the changing discursive fields within which the exercise of power is conceptualized, the moral justifications for particular ways of exercising power by diverse authorities, notions of the appropriate forms, objects and limits of politics, and conceptions of the proper distribution of such tasks among secular, spiritual, military and familial sectors" (1992: 175). Political rationalities may thus be generally conceptualized as intellectual machineries that render reality thinkable in such a manner as to make it calculable and governable. They point to the forms of political reasoning ensconced in governmental discourse, the language and vocabulary of political rule, the constitution of manageable fields and objects, and the variable forms of truth, knowledge, and expertise that authorize governmental practice (Dean 1995: 560).

Political rationalities, in short, name that field wherein lies the multiplicity of endeavors to rationalize the nature, mechanisms, aims, and parameters of governmental authority.

With respect to this first analytical theme, governmentality scholars generally have a couple of important concerns. One concern is with the epistemological character of political rationalities (Miller and Rose 1990; Rose and Miller 1992; Dean 1999; Walters 2000). They are interested in how these rationalities both foster and rely upon assorted forms of knowledge and expertise – such as psychology, medicine, sociology, public policy, and criminology. Knowledges of this kind embody specific understandings of the objects of governmental practice – the poor, the vagrant, the economy, civil society, and so forth – and stipulate suitable ways of managing them.[2] Moreover, such forms of knowledge define the goals and purpose of government and determine the institutional location of those authorized to make truth claims about governmental objects. Governmentality scholars, then, are occupied with how the practices of government are intertwined with specific regimes of truth and the vocation of numerous experts and authorities. They show that the activity of governing is possible only within particular epistemological regimes of intelligibility – that all government positively depends on the elaboration of specific languages that represent and analyze reality in a manner that renders it amenable to political programming.

The other important concern of governmentality scholars is with the problem-oriented nature of political rationalities (Rose and Miller 1992; Dean 1999). They note that government is inherently a problematizing sphere of activity – one in which the responsibilities of administrative authorities tend to be framed in terms of problems that need to be addressed. These problems are generally formulated in relation to particular events – such as epidemics, urban unrest, and economic downturns – or around specific realms of experience – urbanism, poverty, crime, teenage pregnancy, and so on. The goal of governmental practice is to articulate the nature of these problems and propose solutions to them. Guided by this perspective on government, the governmentality literature tends to explore how certain events, processes, or phenomena become formulated as problems. Moreover, it is often concerned with investigating the sites where these problems are given form and the various authorities accountable for vocalizing them. To focus on government, then, is to attend, at least on some level, to its

problematizations – to the ways intellectuals, policy analysts, psychi-
atrists, social workers, doctors, and other governmental authorities conceptualize certain objects as problems. It is to focus on how government
is bound to the continual classification of experience as problematic.

The second analytical theme of the governmentality literature involves the programs of government – that is, how government is
conceptualized into existence in programmatic form (Miller and Rose
1990; Rose and Miller 1992; Dean 1999; Walters 2000). Government
is programmatic in the sense that it assumes that the real can be programmed – that it can be made thinkable in such a manner as to make
it amenable to diagnosis, reform, and improvement. This programmatic
character manifests itself most directly in specific programs of government – that is, in more or less explicit knowledgeable schemes for
reforming reality, for rendering the world intelligible and susceptible to
rational administration. Governmentality scholars tend to train a good
deal of their attention on these programs of government. They focus
on how such governmental schemes conceptualize, manage, and
endeavor to resolve particular problems in light of specific goals. They
attend to how such plans attempt to shape the environment and circumstances of specific actors in order to modify their conduct in very
precise ways. All in all, this emphasis on the programmatic calls attention to the eternally optimistic disposition of government – to its firm
belief that reality can be managed better or more effectively.

Finally, the third analytical theme of the governmentality literature
concerns the technologies of government – that is, how government
takes on a technological and pragmatic form (Miller and Rose 1990;
Rose and Miller 1992; Dean 1995; Rose 1996a, 1998; Walters 2000;
Ong and Collier 2005). The technological is that domain of practical
mechanisms, devices, calculations, procedures, apparatuses, and documents through which authorities seek to shape and instrumentalize
human conduct. It is that complex of techniques, instruments, and agents
that endeavors to translate thought into practice and thus actualize
political rationalities and abstract programs. Governmentality scholars'
concern with the technological domain reveals itself best in the attention
paid to specific technical instruments. These instruments encompass
such things as: methods of examination and evaluation; techniques of
notation, numeration, and calculation; accounting procedures; routines
for the timing and spacing of activities in specific locations; presentational
forms such as tables and graphs; formulas for the organization of work;

standardized tactics for the training and implantation of habits; ped-agogic, therapeutic, and punitive techniques of reformation and cure; architectural forms in which interventions take place (i.e., classrooms and prisons); and professional vocabularies. Particularly important tech-nical instruments are what Bruno Latour (1986) calls material inscrip-tions. These are all the mundane tools – surveys, reports, statistical methodologies, pamphlets, manuals, architectural plans, written reports, drawings, pictures, numbers, bureaucratic rules and guidelines, charts, graphs, statistics, and so forth – that represent events and phenomena as information, data, and knowledge. These humble technical devices make objects "visible." They render things into calculable and pro-grammable forms. They are the material implements that make it pos-sible for thought to act upon reality. The governmentality literature's concern with technologies of government, then, draws attention to the technical means for directing the actions of individuals and populations. Without these technologies the government of conduct cannot take place.

In line with these emphases of the governmentality literature, the present study has three objectives. First of all, it aims to explore how certain mentalities and intellectual machineries – those that might be called post-social (see below) – have constituted "illegal" immigration as an object of government: how they have rendered it thinkable, calculable, and manageable. Part of this exploration entails looking into how the phenomenon of "illegal" immigration has been constructed as a problem to be addressed and corrected. More specifically, it involves scrutinizing the precise ways in which this phenomenon has been problematized: most notably as an issue of criminality, job theft, and welfare dependency. Another part entails paying close attention to the assorted forms of knowledge and expertise – specifically those of social scientists, politicians, INS/CBP bureaucrats, policy analysts, and the public at large – that claim to set forth facts about "illegal" immigra-tion. It involves, in other words, analyzing the specific regimes of truth and the various authorities with which the practice of governing immig-ration is intertwined. The concern here is thus to explore the constitu-tion of "illegal" immigration as a problem object, as well as the variable forms of truth, knowledge, and expertise that render it intelligible and governable.

The second objective of this book is to explore the programmatic aspects of governing "illegal" immigration. More precisely, it is to study a number of more or less explicit knowledgeable schemes for reforming the circumstances of "illegal" immigrants in order to direct their conduct in very specific ways. These schemes include Operation Gatekeeper and Operation Hold the Line, both of which aim to secure the US–Mexico border against illicit entry. This focus on border control has to do with the fact that, over the last few decades, it has been the primary way through which political and other authorities have sought to manage undocumented immigrants.[3] The goal here is to detail how boundary enforcement programs have attempted to resolve the problem of "illegal" immigration.

The third objective of this study is to examine the technological dimensions of managing "illegal" immigration. In other words, there is a strong focus on the actual mechanisms or technical devices – such as border architecture, military know-how, pamphlets, policy reports, and INS/DHS statistics – through which governmental authorities actualize particular political mentalities and abstract programs. One of the aims here is to draw attention to the material tools that make "illegal" immigration "visible."

The book as a whole, then, just as the literature of governmentality more generally, is concerned with how assorted forms of knowledge, modes of calculation, kinds of governing authorities, and technical means intertwine to construct particular objects – in this case "illegal" immigrants – as targets of government. The book can thus be read as an attempt to examine the art of governing "illegal" immigration – art in the sense that the activity of governing "requires craft, imagination, shrewd fashioning, the use of tacit skills and practical know-how, the employment of intuition and so on" (Dean 1999: 18). Such an examination consists, on the one hand, of empirical description: it depicts how particular regimes of knowledge have produced truths about "illegal" immigrants and, consequentially, how various entities in positions of authority have sought to regulate them.[4] And on the other, the examination entails critical diagnosis: it is diagnostic to the extent that it seeks to establish a critical connection to practices of government, attending to their exclusions, presuppositions, assumptions, naivetés, oversights, and costs (see Rose 1999a). Overall, then, this analysis consists of describing and diagnosing the assemblage of mechanisms and devices for producing knowledge about and intervening upon the problem of "illegal" immigration. The book can thus also be read as an exploration of how the practice of government is inextricably tied to the activity of thought. It is intimately concerned with the connection between thinking and acting, representing and intervening, knowing and doing. It deals, in essence, with the modern operations of power/knowledge.[5]

The Post-Social Arts of Government

An important concern of the governmentality literature has also been to analyze what have been called post-social (or advanced liberal) rationalities and technologies of government. It is within such post-social strategies for governing conduct – particularly within their repressive side – that I would like to situate the contemporary management of illegal immigration. Let me begin with a brief articulation of the meaning of "the social." Then we can move on to consider the "post-social" domain. In the discussion of "the social," I roughly follow the work of Gilles Deleuze (1979), Mitchell Dean (1999), Pat O'Malley (1996), and Nikolas Rose (1996a, 1999a, 2000a).

From the perspective of governmentality scholars, the social is not an adjective that designates the class of phenomena which sociology takes as its object. It does not refer to an existential fact about humanity – that people are social animals enmeshed in webs of human relations, institutions, conviviality, and so forth. Rather, the social has a more particular meaning. It refers, according to Gilles Deleuze,

> to a *particular sector* in which quite diverse problems and special cases can be grouped together, a sector comprising specific institutions and an entire body of qualified personnel ("social" assistants, "social" workers). We speak of social scourges, from alcoholism to drugs; of social programs, from repopulation to birth control; of social maladjustments or adjustments, from predelinquency, character disorders, or the problems of the handicapped to the various types of social advancement. (1979: ix)

The social is thus best conceptualized as a zone of governmental action and technical intervention (see Horn 1994). It represents a particular way of constructing and managing the objects of government – of posing questions concerning the conduct of individuals and populations.

This social mode of constituting the terrain of government has its roots in mid-nineteenth-century Europe and North America. In the wake of its emergence, as Pat O'Malley notes, the principal objects of rule and the ways of engaging with them were constituted in terms of a collective entity with emergent properties that could not be reduced to the individual constituents, that could not be tackled adequately at the level of individuals, and that for these reasons required the intervention of the state. Social services, social insurances, social security, the social wage were constituted to deal with social problems, social forces, social injustices and social pathologies through various forms of social intervention, social work, social medicine and social engineering. (Quoted in Walters 2000: 8)

Over the course of the nineteenth century, then, the social emerged as an integrative and collective domain of rule inasmuch as political leaders came to accept the responsibility of managing the negative effects of urban life, industrial work, and wage labor. The government of the social came to be embodied in an array of programs formulated to deal with specific problems arising in a variety of places inside the social body.

During the twentieth century, social government was most notably instantiated in a distinct political rationality that has come to be called welfarism (Dean 1999; Rose 1999a). Welfarism was grounded in the belief that the state should maintain a realm of collective security in order to safeguard the life of each and every member of the population. It was based on the idea that the situation of all social groups within society – workers, employers, professionals, and managers – could gradually be improved. Programmatically, this rationality of welfarism came to be articulated around a range of distinct problem domains: the living and working conditions of the laboring classes; the sexuality, health, and education of children; the norms of family life; the role of women as mothers and housewives; poverty and squalor; prostitution and immorality; delinquency and anti-social behavior; and so forth. The goal of administering these domains was to ensure collective security through curtailing the risks to individuals and families that resulted from the craziness of economic cycles, alleviating the harmful consequences of unrestrained economic activity by interceding directly into the conditions of employment, and more generally through promoting the betterment of the social life of individuals. Highly significant to these administrative endeavors were the truth claims of experts – doctors, social workers, psychologists, probation officers, welfare workers, the career public servant, and so forth. These experts – working within a variety of institutional spaces such as public (state) schools, juvenile courts, workplaces, baby health and family planning clinics, and unemployment offices – produced bodies of social knowledge concerning normality, pathology, urban unrest, social stability, and so forth, and proposed ways to direct and control events and persons in light of such understandings. The securing of the population thus involved a multitude of strategies that were shaped taking into account the assertions of experts as to what was righteous, healthy, normal, moral, or beneficial. Expert knowledge and professional skills stimulated and authorized the "complex social bureaucracy of pedagogy and care" that came to characterize the social state (Rose 1999a: 133).

Social insurance was one of the most important elements of this bureaucracy of pedagogy and care. We can use it to highlight a distinctive characteristic of welfarism: how it sought to socialize individual citizenship. Mechanisms of social insurance – accident insurance, health and safety legislation, unemployment benefits, and so forth – aimed to secure the life of the population from the risks associated with such phenomena as poverty, old age, sickness, unemployment, accidents, crime, and ill health (see Dean 1999). As such, social insurance was essentially an inclusive and solidaristic governmental technology: "it incarnate[d] social solidarity in collectivizing the management of the individual and collective dangers posed by the economic riskiness of a capricious system of wage labor, and the corporeal riskiness of a body subject to sickness and injury, under the stewardship of a 'social' State" (Rose 1996a: 48). Social insurance, in other words, was deployed as a mechanism of solidarity that translated accidents, sickness, unemployment, and other afflictions into insurable risks that were individually remunerated but collectively borne. It provided a certain measure of individual and collective security against the uncertainties of social life. This allocation of social provisions to individuals on the basis of their membership in a collectivity embodied a particular conception of the subject. The subject of government was conceptualized here as a social citizen – as a social being whose security was guaranteed through collective dependencies and solidarities. The individual was ordained into society in the figure of a citizen with social rights and needs, "in a contract in which individual and society had mutual claims and obligations" (Miller and Rose 1990: 23). Welfarism, then, conceived of the subject as an individual who was to be governed through society – within a nexus of collective responsibility. It constructed citizenship in terms of contentment, solidarity, and welfare.

The social, as a terrain of thought and action, has been kind of an *a priori* of governmental schemes and tactics for more than a century now. For a long time, to govern well signified governing in the name of the social: in the interests of social cohesion, social justice, and social promotion. Since the mid-1970s, this social rationality of government has come under severe attack from a variety of political forces. Neoliberals asserted the necessity of moving away from the excessive governing characteristic of the welfare state to a more frugal form of governance – one which would foster the mechanisms of the market and thus allow economic processes to operate naturally; civil libertarians expressed concern about the incompatibility between the discretionary powers of social government and the rights of individuals; and those on the left questioned the social state's effectiveness in minimizing ill health, poverty, and insecurity. All seemed to agree, whatever their other incongruities, that the role of the state as the guarantor of steadfast and progressive social advancement had become deeply problematic. The social state – with its large bureaucracies, extravagant welfare programs, and interventionist social engineering – had simply grown too excessive. It not only hindered the market, created costly and inept bureaucracies, and generated exorbitant taxes, but also, worst of all, instead of fostering social responsibility and citizenship, actually created dependency and a client mentality, thus heightening the very problems of delinquency, immorality, and ill health that it meant to remedy (Rose 2000a: 157).[6]

One of the consequences of this critique of social government, according to governmentality scholars (see O'Malley 1992; Dean 1999; Rose 1999a), has been the gradual reshaping of the terrain of government itself. This reshaping, it should be noted, has not been a matter of the simple replacement of one governmental style by another. Indeed not. For the social mentality of government continues to have sway. Nonetheless, the ideal of the social state has generally given way to that of what could be called the post-social state. This new ideal is such that political government is no longer obligated to tackle all the ills of social and economic life. It is no longer required to plan, know, and direct from the center in order to address society's desire for health, security, and welfare. The responsibility for dealing with these problems is therefore largely displaced from the state to a multitude of specific actors: individuals, schools, communities, localities, hospitals, charities, and so forth. Market rationalities – contracts, consumers, competition – play a crucial role here. For it is through the market that individual actors are expected to secure their well-being. The market is seen as the perfect mechanism for assuring the life of the population – for averting the risks linked to old age, ill health, poverty, accidents, and so forth. Its rationalities are thus extended into all kinds of domains – welfare, security, mental health – previously governed by social and bureaucratic logic. Post-social rule, then, entails new modes of apportioning the work of government between the political apparatus, communities, economic actors, and private citizens. It seeks to govern not by means of society but through managing the choices of the citizen, constructed now as a being who aspires to be self-actualizing and self-fulfilling (Rose 1996a: 41). Here the state, instead of being a provider – the ultimate guarantor of security – comes to exercise only limited powers of its own when it comes to social security; and thus public provision of welfare and social protection ceases to appear as a necessary part of governing the well-being of the population.

There are two key characteristics of post-social modes of government that are important to signal out for further discussion here: the fragmentation of the social into a multitude of markets and the new prudentialism. Let us deal with them in that order. The social state, as I have noted, was firmly rooted in the idea that politicians, through calculated government interventions, could act upon social life in order to optimize it, in the belief that political strategies could allay the most harmful individual consequences of capitalism – job insecurity, unemployment, poor working conditions – without destroying the spirit of private enterprise. As a result of the metamorphosis of government into a post-social form, what one sees as Nikolas Rose notes is "a detaching of the center from the various regulatory technologies that, over the twentieth century, it sought to assemble into a single functioning network, and the adoption instead of a form of government through shaping the powers and wills of autonomous entities: enterprises, organizations, communities, professionals, individuals" (Rose 1996a: 56). This detaching of the center can best be seen in the disarticulation of numerous governmental activities from the formal political apparatus: in the fragmentation of the social domain into a series of quasi-markets. There has indeed been a proliferation of market-based, semi-autonomous non-state organizations whose role is to administer areas of social life formerly only under the direct sway of the state. The functions for which these bodies have taken responsibility include such things as: planning the regeneration and government of urban locales; managing formerly public utilities such as water, gas, electricity; regulating investment and securities in the financial sector; and providing welfare, prison, and police services (Rose 1996a: 56). This reconfiguration of governmental practices along market lines has been closely associated with the development of an assemblage of technologies for managing these new semi-autonomous bodies. Such technologies of performance, as Mitchell Dean (1999) calls them, are designed to submit the workings of governmental entities to formal calculation. They include such things as monitoring, evaluation, indicators, contracts, performance measures, audits, and output targets. Governmental entities are thus managed not through direct intervention in their everyday operations but indirectly through monitoring their performance. They are governed in a manner that allows them a certain decision-making power while making them accountable for their conduct. The post-social reconfiguration of government, then, is not to be understood as entailing a simple opposition between the state and the market. Political authorities do not simply step aside to permit the market to function "freely." They actually govern it from afar through regulating its autonomy (Rose 1996a: 57). They program and shape not the market but all kinds of technologies of performance, utilizing these to bring the activities of a diverse range of organizations in line with political ends. What the post-social transformation of government does, in short, is reinscribe the formal political apparatus within the social body in such a way as to generally produce a distance between it and other governmental entities.

The second key characteristic of post-social rule has to do with the specification of a new subject of government. As I have noted, social mentalities of government constructed the political subject as a social citizen whose capacities and obligations were expressed in the idiom of collective solidarity and social responsibility. The individual was consequently integrated into society as a social being with social needs – under a compact in which the individual and society had reciprocal rights and duties. For post-social regimes of government, the political subject is less a social citizen whose security is guaranteed through the bonds of collective social life and the receipt of public largesse than an individual whose citizenship is derived from active self-promotion and the free exercise of personal choice. The post-social citizen is thus to be an entrepreneur unto him- or herself: "each person [is] to conduct his or her life, and that of his or her family, as a kind of enterprise, seeking to enhance and capitalize on existence itself through considered acts of initiative, and through investments – of time, money, emotion, energy – that are calculated to bring future returns" (Rose 2000a: 162); each individual is to maximize the quality of his or her life – and give meaning and value to it – through acts of responsible choice in relation to an increasing range of things from the education of one's children to the disposal of one's income. Within this form of governance, the citizen is consequently to meet his or her civic commitment to the well-being of the national body not through relations of dependency and obligation, but through seeking to realize him- or herself as a free, autonomous subject (see Rose 1999a). And s/he is to be linked to society not through social devices that depend on the direct calculations of political authorities, but through a range of technologies existing outside the formal control of the state. These technologies of agency, as Dean (1999) names them, aim to develop and deploy one's possibility of agency. They seek to shape, guide, and mold the will and competencies of individuals so as to make them capable of acting as free and active citizens. These technologies encompass not only basic nation-forming devices as a common language and skills of literacy, but also such things as techniques of empowerment and self-esteem – which can be found in all kinds of activities from health promotion campaigns and social impact studies to teaching at all levels and community development – and the mechanisms of the mass media, advertising, and marketing – all of which have a hand in shaping the habits and dispositions of individuals through the dissemination of an ethics of responsibility linked to pleasure and lifestyle maximization (Rose 2000a: 62). Post-social forms of rule, then, govern not through collective solidarity but through the directed and responsible actions of self-governing agents (Rose 1993: 298). They rest upon the reconstitution of the political subject from a social being with rights and needs to a post-social citizen with choices and yearnings to self-fulfillment.

This reconstitution of the subject of government is perhaps most apparent in the domain of risk management. Here social insurance, as a socializing and collectivizing principle of solidarity, has largely given way to the privatized administration of risk. Citizens are now exhorted to take upon themselves the principal responsibility for managing their own security and that of their loved ones. They are asked to adopt a calculative and prudent disposition toward risk and not to rely on socialized securities. For example, active citizens are to provide for their retirement through private pension plans, secure themselves against the vicissitudes of ill health, unemployment, and accidental loss through private insurance, and generally play a big part in safeguarding themselves from anything that could potentially endanger the safety of their freely chosen ways of life (Rose 1999a: 159). Pat O'Malley (1996) has dubbed this style of risk management the new prudentialism.[7] It is a style in which insurance against the possibilities of job loss, old age, sickness, and so forth becomes primarily a matter of private responsibility. It is an approach, in other words, where active citizens are to procure formerly more "socialized" benefits through purchase in the marketplace.

There is more to this new prudentialism, however. For it is not simply that one is asked to be prudent with respect to previously "social" risks, but also in relation to a host of other insecurities. According to Nikolas Rose, this new prudentialism "uses the technologies of consumption – advertising, market research, niche marketing and so forth – to exacerbate anxieties about one's own future and that of one's loved ones, to encourage each of us to invest in order to master our fate by purchasing insurance designed especially for us and our individual situation" (1999a: 159). What this does is put into motion a practically endless spiral of both risk amplification and risk management, such that the continual identification of new problems is steadfastly matched by the production of new solutions to deal with them. Significantly, this process has led to the sizable expansion of the private market for security, which now encompasses not just health insurance and pension plans but also all kinds of practices and devices, from health and fitness programs and burglar alarms to training for community policing, home testing kits for cholesterol levels, and fetal monitoring. Moreover, it has meant that active citizens must now be responsible for an increasing range of risks: from the risk of sexually acquired disease and dependency on drugs, alcohol, or welfare to the risk of physical/mental ill health, insufficient resources in retirement, and being a casualty of crime (Dean 1999: 166).

The new prudentialism, then, can be thought of as a technology of governance that responsibilizes individuals for their own risks – of unemployment, sickness, mental health, poverty, crime, and so forth. It can be seen as a practice that produces individuals who are responsible for their own destiny and make calculations about their future with the aid of a multiplicity of independent experts and private enterprises – in short, that engenders rational, calculative, responsible, and knowledgeable human beings. As such, the new prudentialism is essentially about making ethical subjects (see Part One). The term "ethical" here refers not so much to moral practices as to how persons conduct themselves and comprehend their existence. It speaks to the duty of individuals to take proper care of themselves. In a post-social context, ethical beings are ones who assume charge of their own well-being and adopt a prudent disposition toward the future. They are persons who comport themselves rationally and responsibly.

Summing up, the post-social domain is best conceived as a reconfigured zone of governmental thought and action. It designates the broad ensemble of mentalities, agencies, and technologies that make up the prototypical ways of conceptualizing and administering the targets of government in contemporary liberal democracies. These are ways that envision securing the life of the population not through strategies directed and financed by the state, but through the instrumentalization of a desire for self-reliance – through the production of prudent, self-managing, ethical political subjects. They are styles that constitute citizens not "as members of an overarching social whole, to which they owe allegiance, and to which they can make a legitimate call for social assistance," but "as autonomous individuals, responsible for their own fate, invested with personal agency and thus with a purely personal responsibility for their status and actions" (O'Malley 1999: 95). The characteristic elements of this post-social reconfiguration of government thus include a downscaling of the state, the privatization of numerous services formerly part of the state apparatus, the devolution of power to communities and localities, the extension of market rationalities – consumers and contracts – into the remains of the state machinery, and generally the increasing separation of the formal political apparatus from other governmental agencies – that is, the expansion of government at a distance (Osborne and Rose 1999: 751; Rose 1996b: 12). Post-social regimes of rule, then, seek to place a limit on what the state can do for individuals. They endeavor to govern not through a beneficent state, but through the responsibilization of individuals and communities – making them accountable for their immediate and coming well-being.

Race and the Technologies of Exclusion

While the governmentality literature's emphasis on the individualiza-
tion of responsibility goes a long way in identifying the moral imperatives of post-social regimes of rule, it has left relatively unexplored one
important element of such regimes: their technologies of exclusion –
especially their racial technologies of exclusion, those practices and
techniques through which racially marginalized subjects are constructed
and managed. The way to understand these practices is to think about
them in relation to the responsibilization of the subject. For what the
responsibilizing imperatives of contemporary government have done is
created a realm of abjection – composed of debased and stigmatized
subjects deemed impervious to the demands of prudentialism. Post-
social regimes of rule, in other words, have produced a division between active citizens and anti-prudential, unethical subjects, between a
majority who can and do secure their own well-being through judicious self-promotion and those who are judged incapable of managing their own risks: the criminals, the underclass, the homeless, the
vagrants, the truly disadvantaged. And this is very much a racialized
division: the subjects most often deemed irresponsible – African Americans, Latinos, Native Americans, Asian Americans – are those whose
phenomenal/cultural characteristics serve to distinguish them from the
dominant "white" population.[8] The argument here, then, is that the
figure of the prudential subject needs to be understood in relation to its
antipode: the oft-racialized anti-citizen unable or reluctant to exercise
responsible self-government. For post-social regimes have been involved not just in the responsibilization of citizens but also in their
irresponsibilization. They have not just produced communities of prudential subjects but also made visible throngs of individuals who putatively do not quite measure up to the demands of prudentialism. In
short, it is necessary to understand not just the inclusions of contemporary governmental technologies and political rationalities but also their
exclusions – to grasp how post-social regimes have been actively involved
in producing and naturalizing a highly racialized division between the
prudent and the anti-prudent, the autonomous and the dependent, the
citizen and the anti-citizen, and the ethical and the unethical.

The importance of paying heed to such dividing practices cannot be
overstated. For the construction of particular individuals as irresponsible
has radical implications for the way they are governed. There seems to

be a twofold strategy for managing such subjects (see Rose 2000b). On the one hand, there are technologies – following Barbara Cruikshank (1999), we can call them technologies of citizenship (see Part One) – that endeavor to reinsert the excluded into circuits of responsible self-management, to reconstitute them through activating their capacity for autonomous citizenship. We can see these technologies at work in the government of welfare. Contemporary programs of welfare reform, such as the Personal Responsibility and Work Opportunity Reconciliation Act of 1996 (Welfare Act), take the ethical reconstruction of the welfare recipient – most often constructed as a young, black, single mother – as their primary task. Such programs have a tendency to underscore the demoralizing effects of receiving welfare: how it leads to the formation of a culture of dependence, to a situation in which welfare subjects lose their capacity to perform the functions of ordinary citizens, including work. Welfare recipients are thus basically constructed as non-prudential subjects existing outside the circuits of civility and responsible self-management. What these programs endeavor to do – through a multiplicity of quasi-autonomous agencies – is regulate the conduct of welfare subjects in order to remoralize them. They emphasize the importance of making the reformation of habits a condition for receiving benefits. Pragmatically, this means that access to monetary aid has become largely contingent upon having a job or searching for one. For example, the Welfare Act imposes work requirements on those receiving welfare. Recipients can only receive federally funded Temporary Assistance for Needy Families (TANF) for two years. After that they must be taking part in work-related activities in order to obtain such assistance. And then they can only receive it for a total of five years during their lifetime. The philosophy here is that the most effective way to get recipients off welfare is to require them to find a job as swiftly as possible and acquire work skills through hands-on experience. The overall goal is to end dependency. It is to nourish and reconstruct autonomy and self-sufficiency. The idea of such post-social schemes is thus to govern the excluded in a way that prepares them to take upon themselves the responsibility for managing their own well-being and that of their kin. Should the project of ethical reconstruction fail, however, and it does fail, people are nevertheless cut off from aid and left to their own devices.

On the other hand, there are post-social technologies – we can call these anti-citizenship technologies (see Part One) – that deem the exclusion of certain anti-citizens to be unavoidable, and endeavor to regulate these individuals and sectors of society – most notably young African American and Latino males but others as well – through operations that seek to contain the threats they and their actions pose. These technologies include policies such as "zero tolerance" and "three strikes," the preventive detention of unmanageable individuals, and the increasing use of the death penalty (see Rose 2000b; Stenson 2000). What has happened, according to Jonathan Simon, is that "crime and punishment [have] become the occasions and the institutional contexts in which we undertake to guide the conduct of others (or even of ourselves)" (1997: 174). He refers to this development as "governing through crime." At the forefront of this development are sentencing regimes of just desserts, deterrence, and retribution that place a high premium on the notion of individual responsibility. Part of the idea here is that offenders must be held accountable for their actions: that they must bear the burden of their lifestyle choices. The calculus of punishment thus serves to press upon the offending (or potentially offending) party the need to be responsible and govern oneself ethically. Part of the idea is also that normal people must be protected from all those who threaten their security and quality of life – unreconstructable welfare subjects, muggers, prostitutes, the homeless, pimps, gang members, petty criminals, drug offenders, murderers, and the like. The confinement of the few thus becomes a requirement for the freedom of the many. The result of all this – of governing through crime – has been a rather dramatic increase in the prison population and the general upsizing of the penal complex. Indeed, those who cannot manage their own risks have increasingly become subject to imprisonment: not as a mechanism of remoralization, however, but simply as a method of containment. An image thus takes form – one that is very much racialized – "of a permanent underclass of risky persons who exist outside the normal circuits of civility and control and will therefore require permanent and authoritarian management in the name of securing a community against risks to its contentment and its pursuit of self-actualization" (Rose 2000a: 164). The other side of the post-social coin is thus the increased use of law and order measures to govern the marginal and the excluded.

What is taking place, then, under post-social forms of rule, is that while political government might have been downscaled and the responsibility for dealing with society's need for health, security, and welfare largely displaced to a multiplicity of specific agencies (individuals, communities, schools, localities, charitable organizations, the market, and so forth), this does not mean that the state is simply withering away. And while it may be that under such rule the government of conduct generally works through fostering the self-managing capacities of individuals, it does not mean that harsh, despotic measures have no relevancy at all. We thus find that inasmuch as the government of the majority – of those who can secure their own well-being through active self-promotion – by and large takes place through the mechanisms of market and outside the formal political apparatus, the regulation of those who cannot manage their own risks occurs increasingly through the widening reach of the repressive arms of the state. To be sure, the post-social state does make some effort to remoralize and reinsert risky individuals into circuits of civility – those of family, work, and consumption. But on the whole, it seems to favor governing them through crime – through harsh punitive measures. The price paid for the entrepreneurial and individualist autonomies of the majority thus appears to be a growing dependence on crime and punishment to contain the hordes of racialized anti-citizens. What we are witnessing, then, just to sum up, is the unfolding of a particular relation between the penal and welfare complexes such that while welfare budgets are trimmed, penal budgets expand: while the social state is deliberately allowed to wither, a kind of post-social police state flourishes as a penal dragnet comes to blanket and demarcate racialized zones of exclusion. We are seeing, in short, a police and criminal shadow cast over the marginal sectors of society as the responsibilizing imperatives of post-social government come to rely on punitive institutions to make up for the downscaling of social protection.

It is within this exclusionary and neglected side of post-social government that I would like to situate the contemporary problematization of illegal immigration. The book will thus explore, on the one hand, how a variety of experts – social scientists, INS/DHS officials, policy analysts, immigration reform organizations, and the public at large – have constructed illegal immigrants – typically imagined as Mexican – as imprudent, unethical subjects incapable of exercising responsible self-government and thus as threats to the overall well-being of the social body. This problematization of illegal immigrants as anti-prudent has taken a number of specific forms. The most visible form has undoubtedly been that of illegal immigrants as lawbreakers. The idea here is that such immigrants are, to put it plainly, illegal. These are people who have flagrantly violated US immigration laws, either by crossing the border clandestinely or by overstaying their visas. They are thus by definition criminals. Illegal immigration is a crime. A second important form is that of illegal immigrants as public burdens. The thinking here is that these immigrants come to the United States primarily to get on welfare and take advantage of the state's social services. Indeed, they are commonly seen as bent on sponging off the American people. And a final important form is that of "illegal" immigrants as job takers. The general feeling appears to be that the undocumented take away or steal jobs from (at least some) American workers. For many citizens, then, illegal immigrants – as criminals, welfare dependents, job stealers – simply cannot be proper subjects. They are uncommitted to personal responsibility and the rule of law. They are not capable of proper self-management. And it is the social body that is harmed as a result.

On the other hand, the book will examine how the programs that have been formulated to govern illegal immigrants and contain their threat have been rather restrictive, exclusionary, and punitive. The aforementioned Operation Gatekeeper, for instance, has brought together an impressive array of policing technologies – personnel (Border Patrol agents), material structures (fences and lights), and surveillance devices (helicopters, ground sensors, TV cameras, and infrared night-vision scopes) – at the San Diego–Tijuana border in order to keep undocumented immigrants out of the United States. The result has been to cast an ever-densening web of control and surveillance over the US–Mexico border and those migrants who attempt to cross it illicitly. Put otherwise, as vast amounts of resources have been poured into boundary enforcement, this southern border, along with numerous marginalized subjects, has become ensnared in a police and criminal dragnet. The gist here is thus that insofar as illegal immigrants have been constructed as anti-prudential subjects who harm the well-being of American citizens, the measures employed to govern them have become extremely exclusionary and punitive. So much like the government of racialized anti-citizens more generally, illegal immigrants have increasingly been regulated through police and punitive measures. Indeed, crime and punishment have become the occasions and the institutional contexts in which we undertake to govern illegal immigration. Illegal immigrants have effectively been criminalized and treated as a criminal class.

This book, then, while firmly grounded in the governmentality literature, also seeks to address and remedy one of its major shortcomings: the failure to deal substantially with the racially exclusionary practices of post-social government. It addresses and remedies this failure through placing the management of illegal immigration – read Mexican immigration – primarily within the repressive side of post-social government. It handles it through exploring how such government tends to deal with racialized subjects, illegal immigrants in this case, through draconian measures. The main contribution the book makes to the governmentality literature is thus to expand its purview. It is to bring within its range of vision those subjects deemed averse to the exigencies of prudentialism: those reckoned to threaten the welfare of the population.

Charting the Terrain Ahead

To make clear the material included in the pages that follow, I want to put in a nutshell what the book is about and provide a conceptual map of its parts.

Most broadly, this book deals with the modern workings of power/knowledge. It is about how the exercise of government is inextricably bound to the activity of thought. It is concerned with the intimate link between knowing and doing, thinking and acting, representing and intervening. The idea here is simply that knowledge is necessary for effective rule. It is that government needs to "know" reality in order to act upon it. More specifically, the book is about the post-1965 government of illegal immigration in the United States. It is concerned, on the one hand, with how post-social rationalities have rendered illegal immigration thinkable, calculable, and manageable: with how they have problematized it as a target of government. And on the other, it is preoccupied with the specific tactics, technical devices, and programs that have been deployed to govern illegal immigration, particularly at the US–Mexico border. Methodologically, the book relies principally on printed source materials – including government publications, social scientific journals, archival documents, proceedings of scholarly conferences, newspapers, and popular magazines. The approach I take to these materials is ethnographic (see Escobar 1995; Horn 1994; Rabinow 1989).[9] I use them at once to pay close attention to the languages and voices of those authorized to make truth claims about illicit immigration and to explore the concrete practices through which government seeks to regulate the conduct of illegal immigrants. Altogether, then, the book explores how variegated forms of knowledge, types of governing authorities, styles of calculation, and technical mechanisms have intertwined to construe illegal immigrants as governmental objects. It analyzes the assemblage of mechanisms and devices for generating knowledge about and acting upon the problem of "illegal" immigration.

The trajectory of the book is as follows.

Part One elaborates on the post-social arts of government. It proposes that we think of the politics of prudentialism in terms of what Nikolas Rose (1999b) has called ethopolitics. Ethopolitics is fundamentally a politics of life. It is concerned with how persons comprehend themselves and manage their existence. It emphasizes treating one's life prudently as a kind of rational planning enterprise – one that requires constant work on the part of the political subject. Key to ethopolitics are two broad governmental strategies. On one side, there are multifarious tactics that endeavor to activate the self-ruling capacities of the general population. These tactics work largely through calling upon individuals to self-monitor and to conduct themselves prudently in the face of social insecurities. Here I will concentrate primarily on how such ethopolitical strategies instantiate themselves in the areas of health care and crime control. On the other side, we find a number of more specific tactics that seek to work on those individuals who have failed to conduct themselves ethically and manage their own well-being. Some of these techniques – what were earlier called technologies of citizenship – attempt to activate the self-governing aptitudes of these troublesome individuals and stimulate them to take active care of their selves. I will explore practices of this kind as manifested in contemporary projects of welfare reform. Other tactics – what I earlier dubbed anti-citizenship technologies – judge the ethical betterment of difficult subjects unlikely and thus concentrate on containing and incapacitating them. We will see practices of this sort at work in the administration of illegalities and delinquencies. This part, then, will basically focus on how subjects are regulated as ethical beings – on how post-social government entreats individuals to take responsibility for the care of their selves. It will become clear that ethopolitics is very much a racialized politics.

Part Two examines the "making up" of the illegal immigrant. Part of the goal here is to explore how the social identity "illegal immigrant" came to be fabricated and given the categorical visibility that it now holds. Key to this making up of "the illegal," I argue, have been technologies of enumeration. Such technologies – statistics, averages, probabilities – occupy a privileged position in modern styles of social description. They are uniquely authoritative ways of knowing and producing truths about the social body. They slice up the population in "a myriad of ways, sorting and dividing people, things, or behaviors into groups, leaving in their wake a host of categories and classifications" (Urla 1993: 820). Here I will be concerned with how technologies of enumeration have elevated immigration standing to the status of signifier and measure of identity. In particular, I will look at the role that an avalanche of printed numbers in the 1970s and 1990s played in the formation of "the illegal immigrant" – the Mexican "illegal" in particular – as a highly visible social category. Part of the goal in this part is also to examine how illegal immigrants have been made up as problems to be addressed and rectified. I will note that they have been constructed in numerous discourses – political, social scientific, and so forth – as unethical, imprudent subjects who pose a threat to the social body: as beings who have failed to take responsible care of their selves and therefore represent a burden to the population. In particular, I will be concerned with how illegal immigrants have been problematized as welfare dependents who come to America principally to take advantage of its generous social services, as people who have brazenly violated US immigration codes and are thus indifferent to the rule of law, and as subjects who take jobs away from Americans.

Finally, Part Three shifts the focus from the general making up of illegal immigrants to the specific punitive strategies, tactics, and programs that have been deployed to contain their threat. More specifically, it concentrates on one ethopolitical way of managing illegal immigration: this being through crime. Governing unauthorized immigration through crime has most notably taken the shape of enhanced law enforcement and border management. This is reflected in such anti-citizenship technologies as Operation Gatekeeper. This operation, as I noted earlier, is essentially a quasi-military endeavor that has amassed fences, lights, manpower, and high technology at the San Diego–Tijuana border in order to deter illegal entry into the United States. The idea here is that if one prevents "illegals" from crossing the border, they cannot pose a risk to the population and threaten their well-being and contentment. I will argue that while Operation Gatekeeper and related border measures have been effective in stemming the flow of illegal immigration through San Diego and other urban areas, they have done little to reduce the overall number of illicit entries (see also Cornelius 2001). What has happened is that the movement of immigrants has simply shifted to less patrolled mountain and desert locations. Moreover, I will note that if enhanced border policing has had a significant effect on illegal immigrants, it has been to put them in harm's way (see also Eschbach et al. 1999). The argument here is that as migrants have responded to the blockading of familiar urban crossing points by attempting to cross through desolate terrains, the trip north has become much more dangerous. The result: a radical increase in the number of immigrant deaths. So in effect, the border has become a place where immigrant life is being disavowed to the point of death.

PART ONE

Ethopolitics and the Management of In/security

THE ETHOS OF
RESPONSIBILITY

In the introduction, I noted that, over the last thirty years or so, there has been a gradual reconfiguration of the territory of government. The ideal of the social-welfare state, dominant for much of the twentieth century, has generally yielded to that of the post-social state. This new ideal is such that the political apparatus no longer appears obligated to safeguard the well-being of the population through maintaining a sphere of collective security. Instead, individuals are now asked to take upon themselves the primary responsibility for managing their own security and that of their families. I also noted, however, that while post-social forms of government generally work through fostering the self-managing competencies of individuals, they routinely resort to despotic measures – such as imprisonment – to manage those subjects deemed immune to the exigencies of prudentialism. So while the state might have been downscaled when it comes to the social protection of the population, it has significantly expanded with regards to its repressive apparatuses. The responsibilizing demands of contemporary government have thus given visibility not simply to the prudential citizen but also to its antithesis: the anti-prudential subject unwilling or unfit to exercise competent self-government. They have rendered intelligible not just communities of responsible citizens but also droves of irresponsible ones.

In this part, I would like to elaborate on this post-social politics of responsibilization. I propose that we think of such politics in terms of what Nikolas Rose has called ethopolitics:

> Ethos here is for "ethos" – the sentiments, moral nature or guiding beliefs of persons, groups or institutions. By etho-politics I mean to

characterize ways in which these features of human individual and collective existence – sentiments, values, beliefs – have come to provide the "medium" within which the self-government of the autonomous individual can be connected up with the imperatives of good government. Etho-politics seeks to act upon conduct by acting upon the forces thought to shape the values, beliefs, moralities that themselves are thought to determine the everyday mundane choices that human beings make as to how they lead their lives. In etho-politics, life itself, as it is lived in its everyday manifestations, is the object of adjudication. (1999b: 477–8)

Ethopolitics is thus a politics of life and of how it is to be lived. It is concerned with how individuals understand themselves and conduct their existence – with the ways in which they give form and meaning to their lives. It emphasizes making corporeal existence and the vitality of the self a privileged space of government and thus treating one's life responsibly as a kind of rational planning project – one that demands continuous work and effort on the part of the political subject. Ethopolitics, in short, is about pressing upon individuals the need to be prudent and to conduct themselves ethically.[1]

Pragmatically, ethopolitics manifests itself in two broad governmental strategies (see Rose 2000b). On the one hand, there are a host of general technologies that aim to animate the self-governing capacities of the population at large. These technologies work through delineating certain mores, standards, and practices that individuals can adopt to actively craft a self and deal with the insecurities of social life. They call upon individuals to undertake the activity of self-government by engaging freely in processes of continuous self-monitoring, self-care, and self-improvement. Here we will be primarily concerned with how such ethopolitical mechanisms play themselves out in two important social domains: health care and crime control. With respect to the former, we will show how responsible individuals are expected to take rational steps to dodge and to insure against health risks and insecurities, acquiring a personal prophylactic capacity in relation to the event of their infirmity; with regard to the latter, we will highlight how prudent subjects are counted upon to become knowledgeable and skilled about crime risks and crime prevention, and thus to take upon themselves the charge of securing their home, person, and property.

On the other hand, there are multitudes of more specific (and often despotic) techniques that seek to deal with those individuals who have somehow failed to comport themselves ethically. Some of these mechanisms endeavor to reactivate the autonomous capabilities of such anti-citizens and reinsert them into circuits of responsible self-management. Put otherwise, they are designed to transform the habits of individuals and populations seen as vulnerable to particular risks or who have some sort of deficiency (for instance, lack of power or self-esteem), the goal being to empower these people and turn them into responsible subjects capable of properly governing themselves. Barbara Cruikshank (1999) has called these mechanisms "technologies of citizenship." We can see technologies of this sort at work in the government of welfare. Here we will concern ourselves specifically with how contemporary programs of welfare reform, such as the Personal Responsibility and Work Opportunity Reconciliation Act of 1996, accentuate the demoralizing effects of welfare receipt and thus take the ethical reconstitution of the welfare subject – portrayed conventionally as a young, black, single mother – as their principal chore. Other mechanisms, however, deem improbable, if not impossible, the ethical reconstruction of certain anti-citizens and therefore endeavor to regulate these individuals and sectors of society through strategies of containment. I call these mechanisms "anti-citizenship technologies." I name them thus because they focus not on empowering or activating the self-governing capacities of marginalized subjects but instead on incapacitating them. Indeed, these are technologies bent on disempowerment: on the abjection (that is, casting out) and exclusion of particularly troublesome individuals and populations. We can see technologies of this kind at play in the government of crime and illegality. Here we will deal primarily with how tactics such as "zero tolerance" policing, "three strikes" policies, and preventative detention are employed to check unmanageable individuals – typically represented as young, black (or Latino), and male.

All in all, ethopolitics underscores approaching one's life as an enterprise of sorts. The emphasis is on individuals taking responsibility for the care of the self; it is on their obligation to conduct themselves in a manner that seeks to guard against insecurities and to capitalize on life through acts of initiative and investment calculated to bring future benefits. Our concern here will be to explore just such politics. It will be on specifying some of the technologies through which human beings are governed as (un)ethical subjects. In exploring such post-social ethopolitics, I will draw largely on the research of others.

MAKING ETHICAL SUBJECTS

Let us begin with a closer look at the ethopolitical strategies concerned with encouraging the self-managing capacities of the general population. These technologies, as I have noted, call upon citizens to conduct themselves ethically and take upon themselves the responsibility of managing their own well-being. They operate through impressing upon individuals the necessity of adopting a calculative attitude toward life and guarding against the many risks – of ill health, crime, unemployment, old age, and so on – that could potentially endanger their chosen mode of existence. The two risk domains that we will deal with here are health care and crime control. We will see that the making of ethical subjects is not primarily achieved in relationship to the state but instead results in large part from active engagement with a diverse range of market-based, nonstate (or quasi-state) institutions and practices. Such is the way post-social forms of government work to activate the capacities of the contemporary citizen. The post-social citizen, as I suggested in the introduction, is one who fulfills his or her civic obligation to the national polity not through relations of dependency, but through seeking to realize him- or herself as a free, self-reliant subject. S/he is one who endeavors to maximize the quality of his or her life – and give import and value to it – through active self-promotion and acts of responsible choice in the marketplace.

The Duty to Be Well

A principal territory in which the ethopolitics directed at the population at large manifests itself is undoubtedly that of health care. Indeed, a duty to be healthy and well has become a central element in the contemporary care of the self. "Lose weight!" "Eat right!" "Sleep well!" "Stop smoking!" "Drink responsibly!" "Practice safe sex!" "Just say no to drugs!" Such are the popular injunctions to be healthy that we hear today. This duty to be well is an ideology that sociologists have come to describe as healthism. According to Robert Crawford, healthism

> is defined . . . as the preoccupation with personal health as a primary –
> often *the* primary – focus for the definition and achievement of well-
> being; a goal which is to be attained primarily through the modification
> of life styles, with or without therapeutic help. The etiology of disease
> may be seen as complex, but healthism treats individual behavior, atti-
> tudes, and emotions as relevant symptoms needing attention. Healthism
> will acknowledge, in other words, that health problems may originate
> outside the individual, e.g. in the American diet, but since these prob-
> lems are also behavioral, solutions are seen to lie within the realm of
> individual choice. Hence, they require above all else the assumption of
> individual responsibility. (1980: 368)

Healthism, in other words, takes the pursuit of good health to be a necessary part of a person's welfare. And it posits that the upkeep of such a state of health is the responsibility of the individual, insisting that human beings can and should develop a personal preventative capacity in relation to the event of their illness (Greco 1993). A key aspect of healthism is thus the expectation that individuals will adopt a calculative and prudent disposition toward health risks and insecurities. It is that people will police their behavior in such a way as to minimize their exposure to health dangers and therewith maximize their life opportunities. For healthism, then, health is something that individuals must rationally think about and act upon in relation to their current and future well-being. It is something that they must treat ethically as a strategic enterprise to be monitored, safeguarded, and cared for. For healthism, in short, health is essentially an ethical substance: something that individuals are obligated to work on and improve as self-actualizing subjects (Foucault 1990).

This emergence of the duty to be well as a basic element in the care of the self can be attributed to what might be called the health promotion complex. This complex is composed, on the one hand, of the state's public health apparatus, whose general responsibility is to oversee, assess, regulate, and better the public's health. The apparatus is itself made up of an array of actors, principally health promoters, medical workers, health economists, bureaucrats, and epidemiologists working directly for the state in public health agencies, but also academics who conduct research on public health matters and either train public health workers or act as consultants for the state. And on the other, the health promotion complex is composed of a multitude of private establishments and agents, whose goal is similarly to foster the health of the population (or at the very least of individuals). Here we can locate such institutions as private health care services, community health advocacy groups, private insurance companies, commodity culture, and the commercial mass media, as well as place numerous private expert and lay authorities: medical practitioners, psychologists, support groups, Internet discussion groups, health advice columnists, and so forth. The health promotion complex, then, is a vast network dispersed across a multitude of social sites – sites that encompass both the private and public domains. As such, the government of health takes place neither simply through the state nor merely through private schemes but via a co-operative relationship between the two spheres (although, to be sure, the state plays only a small role in providing actual health care, as we will see). Indeed, it takes place through joint action – through a partnership between state institutions and bureaus, private sector agencies and enterprises, and voluntary associations (Petersen and Lupton 1996: 3–6).

The health promotion complex plays two important and interrelated functions with respect to the government of health. One of them is to track down and identify risks. Risks are things that pose hazards; they are sources of danger or threat. Here medical, scientific, epidemiological, and social scientific understandings (both private and state) play a crucial role. These expert knowledges are counted upon to produce truths as to what constitutes a danger to the population's health. They are charged, that is, with the responsibility of defining, classifying, documenting, and evaluating health risks. Expert knowledges generally group health risks into two broad categories (Lupton 1995: 76). One category is composed of those risks deemed to result from environmental conditions. Here we can include such hazards as pollution, radiation, nuclear waste, and toxic chemical residues. These risks are generally classified as *external* since the individual is perceived to have little or no control over them. The other category – this being the one that has received the most attention – is composed of those risks judged to eventuate from the lifestyle choices of individuals. Here we can include a number of personal practices that experts have identified as having an adverse effect on an individual's well-being: alcohol consumption, smoking, poor diet, consumption of certain foods, drug use, lack of exercise, poor sleep habits, unbridled sexual behaviors, and the like. These risks are typically classified as *internal* since the individual is assumed to have the capacity to manage them. The main effect of this expert identification of health risks has been to make contemporary societies generally more and more risk conscious. Health risks thus now appear to loom around every corner, confronting us no matter where we turn. They seem to be everywhere in the social body, constantly threatening our well-being. Indeed, it looks as though there is no limit to where risks can be found and hence no place to hide from them. For the individual, then, a basic fact of living in contemporary society is having to perpetually deal with risk.

The other function of the health promotion complex is, of course, to actually promote individual and collective health. The purpose of calling attention to the riskiness of everything is not to create a climate of fear and insecurity – although this has in a sense been the practical effect given the mass media's tendency to overstate expert findings on risk – but to render dangers and insecurities predictable and thus avoidable. It is to make reality calculable and therefore amenable to intervention. The approach to life here is a rational one: things do not just transpire without warning, but can be prognosticated (Ewald 1991). There are at least three important roles the health promotion complex performs in fostering the health of the population. One of these is that of pedagogue. What the complex strives to do is instruct individuals as to how to be healthy – to educate them with respect to how to conduct their lives in order to secure a hearty existence. This aim is accomplished through delineating standards and norms as to what constitutes good health; and, more generally, through providing individuals with the information they need in order to monitor and regulate themselves so as to eliminate comportment and avoid conditions deemed risky.

A related role is that of moralist. For the instruction the complex dispenses is generally framed in an ethical mode. The underlying assumption of this framing is that the individual is an ethical being who is directed at self-government, self-care, and anxious for self-knowledge. The self that is privileged and normalized here is that of the rational, prudent, and entrepreneurial self actively making decisions about his or her conduct in the pursuit of self-improvement (Lupton 1995: 61).

The expectation is thus that individuals, as ethical subjects, should build the appraisal of health risks into their life planning. It is that people, as rational and responsible individuals, should think about the future and take sensible measures to protect themselves against ill health.[2] One such measure, among the more important ones, is the pursuit of fitness: "Fitness is widely promoted as an opportunity to avert several of the risks to selfhood present in modern society; it is a way to protect oneself from characteristic ills of modern culture such as drug abuse, depression, eating disorders, and cardiovascular disease" (Petersen 1996: 52–3). This kind of pursuit requires that individuals exercise regularly; constantly check their consumption of unhealthy goods such as tobacco, alcohol, and fatty foods; and routinely visit medical experts to monitor such things as blood pressure and cholesterol level. A self-care lifestyle, then, is seen as the best avenue for dodging the maladies that perpetually menace the welfare of the individual in a climate of risk and insecurity.

The third role of the health promotion complex is that of health care and healthy lifestyle provider. While the state and the private spheres work as partners in the first two roles, here the state generally takes a back seat to the market. The post-social state sees itself primarily as a health educator – furnishing people with the information they need to be self-reliant – and only marginally as a provider. The market is thus left as the principal mechanism through which individuals can insure and ensure their health. Striving after a risk-fee existence has therefore come to depend on consuming a range of goods and services, not only medical care proper but also a host of products that are marketed for their health-fostering properties: exercise machines, individualized fitness programs, weight loss centers, nutritious foods, and so forth (see Petersen and Lupton 1996). So as health risks have proliferated, so have the private enterprises to manage them, and the care of the self has come to mean purchasing health and happiness in the marketplace.

The health promotion complex, and its articulation of healthism as a dominant ideology, has no doubt had a wide-reaching effect. Today, we are all, in one way or another, conscious of our duty to be well. But the complex has not targeted everyone equally. There are certain populations that have received a disproportionate amount of attention and thus hyper-embody this sense obligation to be healthy. The most poignant case is perhaps that of the pregnant woman (Lupton 1999a, 1999b; Ruhl 1999; Oaks 2001). This woman is today encircled by, and constituted through, a surfeit of expert and lay knowledges. These knowledges tend to construct the pregnant body, along with the fetus, as a fragile entity immanently at risk, as perpetually vulnerable and susceptible to a host of ailments. At the same time, however, they seek to advise women as to how to avoid risks and maximize the health of their babies-to-be. Much of this advice is directed at the conduct of pregnant women – at how they should regulate their bodily comportment. For example, in one best-selling handbook for pregnant women, as Deborah Lupton notes, "women are told that as well as avoiding any consumption of alcohol and tobacco (and illicit drugs such as marijuana and cocaine), they should avoid spending time in rooms with people who smoke, give up tea, coffee and cola drinks, avoid certain sugar substitutes, . . . be careful in using household cleaning products and insecticides and not take prescription or over-the-counter therapeutic drugs (even headache pills) if possible" (1999b: 65). Other important advice concerns such things as the need for women to attend prenatal classes and read diligently about childbirth so as to better understand what the pregnancy process entails and thus be more equipped to handle any complications that may arise; and the indispensability of women paying regular visits to the (private) doctor in order to receive prenatal care – care that should include, among other things, tests that monitor the normality of the fetus (e.g., amniocentesis, chorionic villus sampling, and ultrasound) (Lupton 1999a: 89; 1999b: 65).

Pregnant women are in effect located in a tight mesh of observation, calculation, and authoritative knowledges that demands endless labor on their part. Consequently, the onus of responsibility for the success or failure of the pregnancy is placed squarely on their shoulders. The message is that only the woman's hard work and judicious self-care can ensure the well-being of the fetus. This is no doubt a hefty responsibility. However, it is not one that women are generally forced into accepting: nobody makes them go to the doctor, avoid health spas, or control their consumption of food. Rather, it is a responsibility that women generally take up willingly. They embrace it willingly because they themselves want to give birth to a healthy child. The goal of the health promotion complex to have pregnant women adopt a risk-minimizing mode of existence thus intersects nicely with the desire of women to do whatever is necessary to enhance the health of their babies (Lupton 1999a: 90). The expectation that pregnant women behave ethically, in short, is matched by their general willingness to adopt a prudent disposition toward their health – to accept the duty to be well.[3]

All in all, then, the ethopolitics of health is part of a political and ethical field in which subjects are compelled to treat their lives as planning projects and look for ways to augment their life possibilities. It is part and parcel of a post-social politics of citizenship that places a great emphasis on individual responsibility. Good citizens are ones who manage their own relationship to risks through self-monitoring and self-assistance. They are ones who police their own conduct in order to maximize the quality of their lives. The ethopolitics of health, in sum, underscores approaching one's life and health as an enterprise. The stress is on individuals taking upon themselves responsibility for the care of their health; it is on their duty to assume the norms of prudent and self-actualizing personhood.

Practices of Security

Another important territory in which ethopolitics directed at the general population manifests itself is that of crime control. Over the last three decades, elevated crime rates have become a normal social fact in the United States.[4] Tell-tale signs of this political reality abound. Incidences of property theft and violent crime, for example, are now as much as ten times those of the pre-World War II period. Numerous social sites – from city streets to public schools – have become witness to more and more crime and disorder, in the form of drug use and abuse, graffiti and vandalism, the "insolence" of uncontrolled youth, and so forth. And an increasing number of people have reported being victims, or knowing someone who has been a casualty, of a variety of crimes: assault, rape, battery, housebreaking, larceny, car theft, and the list goes on. From being chiefly an issue that touched the marginal and the poor, crime has thus become a routine preoccupation for anyone who uses public transportation, owns a vehicle, walks in urban spaces at night, or leaves their home unattended during the daytime.[5] Normal, too, have become such phenomena as the marketing of fear and the extensive media coverage of criminal happenings. Just consider the prevalence of security and insurance advertisements informing us that an assault occurs every so many seconds or that a rape takes place every few minutes. Such advertisements attempt to sell safety through generating and fostering anxiety about crime. Or consider the enormous publicity given to everyday offenses such as crack cocaine and heroin use, to the petty criminal behavior of the deinstitutionalized mentally ill, or to more atrocious misdeeds such as the periodic mass shootings at high school campuses. All told, then, over the last few decades, crime has come to occupy an increasingly important place in modern culture. It has come to represent not an anomalous event but an ordinary danger. It has come to be experienced, in short, as an inescapable fact of modern existence – as a taken-for-granted element of daily life (Garland 2001: 106–7, 152–4).

Over this same period, the government of crime has come to be broadly framed in ethopolitical terms. For social rationalities, crime control was an integral part of the state's obligation to secure the welfare of the population. It was one of the principal benefits of social citizenship. The ruling assumption for most of the twentieth century was thus that the government of crime should be kept almost exclusively in the hands of the state; that security against disorder and violence ought to be principally the responsibility of specialized governmental institutions (e.g., the police) working in the public's interest. Social mentalities felt no need for programs to animate private energies, nor for policies that involved the public and emphasized social prevention. The only thing they deemed necessary "was a framework of legal threats and a reactive [state] response" (Garland 2001: 34). For post-social rationalities, on the other hand, while crime control continues to be an important political obligation, it is no longer seen as something for which just the state should bear responsibility. The persistent message of such mentalities is that public institutions must not be counted on to be the primary and only veritable purveyors of security against crime. It is that citizens should not expect the state to be liable for meeting all of their safety needs. The pragmatic objective of post-social rationalities has thus been to spread responsibility for regulating crime to institutions, organizations, and individuals outside the state apparatus. David Garland has characterized this mode of crime control as a responsibilizing strategy:

> It involves a way of thinking and a variety of techniques designed to change the manner in which governments act upon crime. Instead of addressing crime in a direct fashion by means of the police, the courts and the prisons, this approach promotes a new kind of indirect action, in which state agencies activate action by non-state organizations and actors. The intended result is an enhanced network of more or less

directed, more or less informal crime control, complementing and extending the formal controls of the criminal justice state. Instead of imagining they can monopolize crime control, . . . state agencies now adopt a strategic relation to other forces of social control. They seek to build broader alliances, enlisting the "governmental" powers of private actors, and shaping them to the ends of crime control. (2001: 124)

The responsibilizing strategy, then, entails animating the commitments, choices, energies, and moralities of a multitude of private agencies and actors. Individual citizens, town planners, school officials, families, employers, corporations, communities, and the list goes on, are all expected to take on the responsibility of controlling and preventing crime. They are counted upon to adopt a prudent and calculative attitude toward crime risks and insecurities – to comport themselves in a manner that helps reduce criminal opportunities. The post-social government of crime thus takes place not just through the state but also through a number of other active agents. The emphasis is on advancing self-government, self-monitoring, self-reliance, and self-actualization. It is on the ethical duty of individuals, communities, and organizations to take care of themselves and assume a certain responsibility for their own risk management.

The main consequence of the government's responsibilizing strategy, not surprisingly, has been the general production of a responsibilized, crime-preventing, and security-conscious populace.[6] This state of affairs is clearly visible on at least two planes: the individual and the collective. With respect to the individual, there is no doubt that, over the last few decades, individuals have come to adopt more and more routine measures to protect themselves against crime risks. These measures can be roughly divided into two groups. One group has to do with public security. Included here are such practices as keeping off the streets (or not walking alone) at night, avoiding parks and squares after dusk, skewing public transportation, not parking in unsupervised lots or garages, carrying restricted amounts of cash, driving one's children to school as opposed to letting them walk, circumscribing one's comportment in public spaces so as not to draw attention to oneself as a possible victim, and just generally being aware of one's surroundings (Garland 2001: 162). The other group of measures deals with domestic security – with turning the home into a safe, private sanctuary. The practices of domestic security involve making the home impenetrable to potential intruders through the use of mechanical devices (alarms, security cameras, movement-sensitive lights, doors, locks, fences, bolts, and so on) and other means (the elimination of screening bushes and shrubbery, the use of guard dogs, and so forth); rendering portable items harder to steal (for instance, hiding jewelry and other valuables, keeping records of appliance identification numbers, marking property, etc.); "controlling the production of signs" (for example, leaving the lights or television on while away in order to create the appearance of habitation); purchasing firearms as defense against attack; and insuring the contents of the residence (O'Malley 1991: 175).

Important in inducing individuals to take up risk-avoiding practices has been the publicity campaign. The state has used this simple but wide-ranging technique of persuasion to target both the general public and specific groups of possible victims – students, women, shoppers (Garland 1996: 452). Publicity campaigns, which are generally conducted through radio and television advertising and the mass leafleting of businesses and private homes, have two basic aims. One is broadly ethical: to raise the public's consciousness about crime – to get individuals to realize that they have a duty to become knowledgeable about and to protect themselves against criminal risks. The other is pragmatic: to furnish citizens with the practical information they need to become prudent subjects – information "about local crime rates, about how to recognize suspicious persons, how to make the home and its contents secure, how to recognize and avoid high-crime-risk situations, about the value of insuring and marking property, and so on" (O'Malley 1996: 201). The publicity campaign thus seeks at once to persuade individuals to assume responsibility for crime risks and to give them the knowledge they need to accept such an obligation. Generally, then, the state's responsibilizing strategy, through techniques such as the publicity campaign, has engendered individuals who exercise caution and take steps against victimization. It has produced subjects who are highly reflexive about the threat of crime.

With respect to the collective, the public's crime consciousness has come to be most visibly displayed in the mobilization of "community" as a primary territory of security. Key to this mobilization has been the post-social state's more general identification of community as an essential terrain for the management of individual and collective life.[7] For the post-social state, indeed, the community has become an important context through which a wide variety of government is to be effected. Consider, for example, the management of metropolitan areas. Programs of urban renewal often conceptualize the problems of the inner city in terms of a lack of community spirit – implying a paucity of entrepreneurialism, collective pride, and capacity for self-sufficiency (Rose 1996c: 336). The way they seek to regenerate the economic and human foundation of these zones is through constituting and empowering the people who reside there precisely as a community. It is through instrumentalizing, fostering, and encouraging the connections, bonds, energies, authorities, and affiliations of each particular locale. Or consider the administration of AIDS and any number of other problem domains. The programs that have been developed to deal with these similarly tend to work through the ties and bonds of community, whether it be those of gay collectivities or other groupings.[8]

The form this post-social state politics of community takes with respect to crime control (or at least one of the forms) is the enabling of communities to take responsibility for their own risk management and for the protection of their members – be these the students and staff of a university, the workers and management of an organization, or the inhabitants of a neighborhood. We can clearly see this enabling at work in such programs as neighborhood watch. These types of programs, as Pat O'Malley explains, "are distribution centers for security material. Television cassettes under the subtle and evocative title of 'Secure Living' are made available to such groups, and newsletters are funded that give information of local crime profiles, information about domestic security practices and how to identify 'suspicious behavior'" (1991: 181–2). Added to this, the police periodically attend local neighborhood watch meetings in order to provide members with information about crime and security, often pertaining to burglary and related crimes. The neighborhood watch scheme is thus basically an endeavor that seeks to harness the commitments and forces of individuals for the purposes of crime prevention within a community setting. It is a police–community partnership designed to enhance the security of the community – harm reduction, fear reduction, loss reduction – through animating the self-governing capacities of its members. Community here is imagined as an ethospatial zone through which responsibilized individuals can defend themselves and pursue their interests. What political authorities have sought to do, then, through programs such as neighborhood watch, is "make up communities of active citizens committed to the securitization of their habitat" (Rose 2000b: 329).[9] They have sought to build responsible communities primed to invest in themselves and take precautions against victimization. The government of security operates here through the instrumentalization of personal loyalty and responsibility inside a self-governing community (Rose 1999a: 249–50).

Central as well to the mobilization of community as a prime terrain of security – within a post-social context that values government through community – has been the commercial sector's exploitation of the fear of crime to market and develop an array of what Teresa Caldeira (2000) has called fortified enclaves. These enclaves are segregated spatial enclosures designed to provide a safe, orderly, and secure environment for those who dwell within them. They stress the worth of what is private and sheltered while devaluing what is public and exposed. They are oriented inwards, away from the putatively chaotic life of the public streets outside. The most notable instantiation of the fortified enclave is perhaps the gated community. Such communities have sprung up all over the United States in the past few decades. They can be found anywhere from the inner city to the suburb, from rich neighborhoods to very poor ones. Gated communities, according to Edward Blakely and Mary Snyder, are "residential areas with restricted access in which normally public spaces [such as streets, sidewalks, parks, beaches, rivers, trails, and playgrounds] are privatized. They are security developments with designated perimeters, usually walls or fences, and controlled entrances that are intended to prevent penetration by nonresidents" (1997: 2). In other words, the gated community is basically a private enterprise that seeks to prevent crime and ensure the safety of its residents through carefully controlling who passes through (and lives within) its portals. It is a self-governing venture designed to enhance security through the exclusion of those who might threaten the population's quality of life: namely, anyone coming from the public spaces outside.[10] As such, what the gated community offers is safety, privacy, stability, and peace of mind. Here prudent subjects can be free to live out their reveries of "lifestyle maximization" (Rose 1999a: 249). They can walk the streets at night, linger in parks after dusk, park their cars in safety, let their children roam freely, walk their dogs in peace, not worry about controlling the production of signs, and dispense with dealing with strangers, intrusions, and disruptions. In essence, here behind the community walls, responsible individuals can better control their environment, prevent intrusions into their private domains, improve their quality of life, and find happiness. What the commercial sector has done, then, through the gated community, is styled localities responsible for the management of their own risks and for the security of their residents. It has brought together individuals into unions willing to take care of themselves.

While the gated community is the most widely recognized manifestation of the fortified enclave, it is certainly not the only important one. Another significant manifestation is the fortress city – with Los Angeles being the paradigmatic example (Davis 1992; Rose 1999a). This type of city, particularly its downtown, is best described as an archipelago of fortified and protected spaces, of normalized enclosures designed to protect individuals and communities from the hazards of ordinary life (Soja 2000: 299). It is a place where a "corporate citadel" of shopping malls, offices, arts centers, and gourmet restaurants, along with their accompanying amenities such as walkways and parking garages, is segregated from the surrounding poverty-stricken neighborhoods (Rose 1999a: 250). Like the gated community, one of the main ways the fortress city ensures the safety of its inhabitants (e.g., consumers and office workers) is through securing its entry points. These are generally gated and watched over by private security guards and/or surveillance cameras. Sometimes proof of identity – for example, ID cards or security codes – is required for access. For the most part, however, particularly when it comes to shopping centers and eating establishments, "where the illusion of openness with security is a commercial requirement," entry is left up to the discretion of the private security forces (Rose 1999a: 251).

There are other ways, too, that the fortress city ensures security. Where total enclosure is not feasible or undesirable, as in the case of open malls, security is structured into the contours of space and the environment. Grassy areas, for example, are designed so that street persons cannot use them as sites for setting up camp. Street furniture is built to discourage undesirable conduct: sleeping, sitting too long, and so on. And things such as water fountains, street sculptures, and flowerbeds "are both aesthetic objects, designed to manifest and induce civility in those who pass, and control objects, designed to direct people to or from certain locations, to secure against the formation of crowds, to turn them instead into disciplined and well-ordered multiplicities" (Rose 1999a: 252). The fortress city, then, has combined gates, architecture, urban design, and private policing to produce privatized enclaves of business and consumer contentment. It has programmed space in such a way as to "ensure a seamless continuum of middle-class work, consumption and recreation, without unwonted exposure to Downtown's working-class street environments" (Davis 1992: 231). So here the commercial sector has made up communities (using the term loosely) responsibilized for their own security. It has constructed privatized enclaves accountable for regulating the spaces and subjects under their domain.

All told, what the ethopolitics of crime control has meant is the increased responsibilization of individuals and communities for controlling and preventing crime. The former, as upright citizens, are expected to assume a judicious disposition toward crime risks and insecurities, while the latter are counted upon to be self-governing and ensure the security of their members. The emphasis here, indeed, is on the ethical duty of active agents and agencies to watch out for themselves and assume some responsibility for their own risk administration. It is on their obligation, in short, to embrace the post-social norms of prudentialism. None of this should be taken to suggest though that the state has given up the business of crime control. Indeed not. Rather, what has happened is that policing has become a mixed economy – with the state keeping primary responsibility for securing public spaces and the warehousing of marginalized subjects, and individuals, communities, and the commercial security industry assuming the duty of protecting private spaces. We will detail the state's involvement in policing shortly.

THE GOVERNMENT OF
THE MARGINAL

So much for the governmental strategies aimed at activating the self-governing capacities of the general population. Now let us turn to the ensemble of more specific technologies concerned with those individuals who have, for whatever reason, failed to conduct themselves ethically and take responsibility for managing their own well-being. These technologies, as I have noted, can be divided into two families: one, which we have called technologies of citizenship, endeavors to reanimate the independent capacities of unethical citizens and reintroduce them into networks of prudent self-management, while the other, dubbed anti-citizenship technologies, deems the ethical reconstitution of such citizens unlikely and therefore seeks to govern them through strategies of containment. The former family of technologies is best exemplified in the government of welfare, the latter in the management of delinquency and illegalities. What we will find here is that, while under post-social forms of rule the government of conduct generally takes place through promoting the autonomous competence of individuals, it does not signify that despotic practices have no pertinence at all. Indeed not. For the regulation of the marginal – of the poor, the underclass, the homeless, the vagrant, the disadvantaged – often occurs through the repressive apparatuses of the state. This too is part of the contemporary politics of citizenship. The post-social state, along with a variety of private agencies, will make an effort to remoralize risky individuals and turn them into ethical, self-governing subjects. However, for the recalcitrant who refuse, or for whatever reason fail, to comport themselves ethically, the use of law and order measures is deemed entirely fitting (Rose 2000b: 335).

Welfare Dependencies

Let us begin our analysis with a closer look at those strategies that seek to reactivate the autonomous capabilities of anti-citizens. These technologies of citizenship, as I just noted, are most clearly instantiated in the post-social government of welfare. During the last few decades of the twentieth century, the War on Poverty and the Great Society programs – such as Aid to Families with Dependent Children (AFDC) and food stamps – came under increasing attack from all sides of the political spectrum for having worsened, instead of ameliorated, the problem of poverty. "We tried to provide more for the poor," asserted conservative academic Charles A. Murray, "and produced more poor instead. We tried to remove the barriers to escape from poverty, and inadvertently built a trap" (1984: 9). The basic problem with welfare programs, according to their detractors, was that they had induced the poor into a state of "dependency." For many critics, indeed, "dependency" was the crux of the welfare quagmire.[11] Democratic Senator Daniel Patrick Moynihan, for example, noted that

> the issue of welfare is the issue of dependency. It is different from poverty. To be poor is an objective condition; to be dependent, a subjective one as well. . . . Being poor is often associated with considerable personal qualities; being dependent rarely so. [Dependency] is an incomplete state in life: normal in the child, abnormal in the adult. In a world where completed men and women stand on their own feet, persons who are dependent – as the buried imagery of the word denotes – hang.[12] (Quoted in Fraser and Gordon 1994: 309)

The term "dependency" here has two important registers, one economic, the other ethical. From an economic standpoint, "dependency" simply points to how the poor – impoverished unwed mothers in particular – had come to rely on the state, instead of work, as their primary source of subsistence. The contention was that welfare programs, AFDC in particular, had made it possible and acceptable for the poor to "choose" the road of unemployment. The poor were thus imagined as rational economic actors who had calculated they could use the welfare complex for their own benefit and earn a living without having to work (Rose 2000b: 331). From an ethical standpoint, "dependency" refers to how relying on the state for one's subsistence turned out to be a habit-forming practice that in the long run stripped the poor of their self-discipline and of their competence to function as responsible adults. It points to how welfare receipt inculcated the poor with a client mentality and turned them into passive, lazy individuals who had no capacity for work or ethical self-management. Far from helping the poor, then, what welfare programs did, according to critics, was create a class of economically and ethically suspect citizens locked into poverty. They produced an underclass of dependent subjects bereft of moral character, lacking dignity and autonomy, and unwilling or unable to be self-sufficient and take responsibility for their own care. The archetype of this new class was the welfare mother (also known more derogatorily as the welfare queen), imagined as a licentious young, black, single, inner-city woman prone to bearing babies she could not support (Fraser 1993: 13).

Given the general consensus that welfare programs had failed the poor, especially black single mothers, political authorities devised numerous schemes to reform the welfare system. These schemes or technologies of citizenship generally took the ethical reconstitution of welfare subjects as their primary task (see Rose 1999a). They sought to reactivate the autonomous capabilities of such anti-citizens in order to get them off welfare and reinsert them into circuits of responsible self-management. The most significant technology of citizenship was undoubtedly the Personal Responsibility and Work Opportunity Reconciliation Act of 1996 (the Welfare Act). The ambitious objective of the Welfare Act was essentially to eliminate welfare dependency, or as former President Bill Clinton so famously put it, to end "welfare as we know it." The way it sought to accomplish this aim was primarily through making the reformation of conduct a condition for receiving benefits. Pragmatically, this entailed dismantling AFDC and replacing it with Temporary Assistance for Needy Families (TANF). AFDC was an entitlement program that guaranteed cash assistance to poor, female-headed families whose incomes and assets fell below a preestablished threshold. There were generally no other stipulations – such as work participation or time limits – attached to the receipt of such aid. Families could obtain assistance in perpetuity as long as they met the income eligibility requirements. TANF, on the other hand, is not an entitlement program. This means that poor families are no longer automatically entitled to receive aid if their income falls beneath a certain level. They now have to satisfy several additional conditions. Two are particularly important to highlight here. One has to do with behavior.

TANF makes the receipt of aid conditional upon work. Poor families can obtain assistance without any reciprocal obligations for two years. After that, the parent must be taking part in work-related activities in order to continue receiving benefits. The other has to do with time. TANF imposes temporal limits on the receipt of aid. Citizens can be on welfare for a total of no more than five years during their lifetime. The idea behind imposing these new conditions is that the most effective way to end welfare dependency is to require recipients to find a job as rapidly as possible and develop work aptitude through hands-on training. Work is key because it is assumed to confer independence, both in economic and in ethical terms. With respect to the former, work is seen as allowing welfare subjects to become financially autonomous, while as regards the latter, it is believed to capacitate welfare recipients with the self-esteem they need in order to more generally take charge of their lives (Abramovitz 2000: 31). The goal here is thus to nurture and restore self-sufficiency and autonomy. It is to handle welfare subjects in a way that prepares them to assume responsibility for their own well-being and turns them into productive members of society.

Crucial to the execution of welfare's responsibilizing strategy is the careful monitoring of welfare subjects (Schram 2000: 59–88). This monitoring occurs principally through intensive case management. Such micro-administration entails at least three important activities. The first, and perhaps most important, one is the screening of welfare applicants. The main purpose of screening is to ascertain the job readiness of individuals seeking benefits. The focus here is not so much on assessing their specific job skills and training needs as on determining their behavioral and psychological capacity to function in the workplace. For it is personal deficiencies – habits, behaviors, and personal characteristics – and not a lack of job skills that are defined as the primary impediment to being job ready. Significant screening practices accordingly include checking for alcohol abuse, mental disorders, drug use, and other conditions presumed to hamper an individual's ability to self-govern. Should claimants be deemed incapable of self-sufficiency, the charge of welfare management is to determine what kinds of collateral services – counseling, psychological, and so forth – they need in order to help them deal with their personal lacks and thus become ready for the world of work. Should welfare-seekers be judged competent, however, the job of the welfare administration shifts to pushing them immediately into the labor market and deflecting them from getting benefits.

The second case management activity entails making welfare recipients sign individual responsibility plans. These plans, known in some states as contracts of mutual responsibility, essentially amount to social contracts whereby society agrees to aid the individual in her time of need on the condition that she promises to take measures that will lead her toward a paying job. The fact that they are contracts is not accidental. The idea here is that requiring welfare recipients to enter into a binding agreement will likely make them more accountable for carrying through with programs for achieving self-sufficiency.

The final case management activity entails tracking the welfare recipient's headway toward accomplishing the goals articulated in their mutual responsibility contracts. This activity is not as advanced as the other two. Most states, for example, lack data as to how welfare recipients are succeeding (or not) in working their way through the job assignment process. There are, however, numerous projects being developed – such as new information systems – that will allow states to continuously monitor the welfare subject as she makes her way from welfare to paid employment. The actualization of welfare's responsibilizing strategy, then, depends essentially on caring through watching (Schram 2000: 77).[13] It hangs on helping welfare recipients primarily through keeping tabs on them, the hope being that such vigilance will oblige them to reform their conduct and become responsible citizens.

The effects of this caring through watching, and of welfare reform generally, have been rather significant. On the one hand, there is no doubt that some welfare recipients (it is not clear exactly how many) have been empowered to reconstitute themselves ethically: to enter the labor market, successfully take up the care of themselves and their loved ones, and leave behind a life of dependency. "[W]elfare reform," notes Tommy G. Thompson, former Secretary of the Department of Health and Human Services, "is moving more people into work so that they can support themselves and their families. . . . [It] has helped an unprecedented number of people on welfare to become self-supporting" (Jackson 2001: A14). The main indication of this empowerment is the falling welfare rolls (which is not to say that all of this dropoff is due to women having found jobs, as I will discuss below). In California, for instance, the number of individual welfare recipients dropped from about 2.58 million in August of 1996 to a little more than 1.27 million in June of 2000 (US DHHS 2000). Nationwide, the numbers dropped from 12.24 to 5.78 million over the same period (US DHHS 2000). It did not hurt, of course, that the United States experienced an economic boom and enjoyed a thriving labor market during the late 1990s.

On the other hand, however, it is also clear that not every person who has "left" welfare has become empowered and triumphantly self-supporting (Abramovitz 2000; Mink 1998; Schram 2000). A case in point are the numerous women who have been expelled from the welfare rolls for failing to meet the goals set out in their individual responsibility plans (King 1999: 281). Their specific infractions range from simple offenses such as skipping appointments with caseworkers to more serious transgressions such as failing to take steps to find, procure, and hold a job (Schram 2000: 73). From the perspective of welfare reformers, the punishment these women received was well deserved. For they failed to show that they could become responsible individuals. From the viewpoint of welfare advocates, though, the castigation was overly severe. For it was not necessarily the case that these women deliberately sought to be "irresponsible." There were actually numerous objective barriers that blocked their path to self-sufficiency. For example, employers were often unwilling to hire them (Berrick 2001: 138). One reason for this reluctance had to do with the general stereotyping of welfare women as lazy and unreliable; another with the unfortunate reality that such women generally lacked the vocational skills necessary to make them attractive to employers. Other barriers included such things as a lack of jobs in the inner city, the absence of good public transportation to shuttle women to areas where jobs are more readily available, insufficient access to the training and schooling needed for social advancement, and the dearth of affordable child care (Schneiderman and Schneiderman 2001: M2).

Whether the punishment was just or harsh, though, the fact remains that many women have been summarily dismissed from welfare. Their fate: to join the ranks of the homeless (King 1999: 283), survive on informal businesses – such as providing in-home child care and braiding hair – that previously supplemented welfare income (Abramovitz 2000: 33), and exist on the charity of family members, churches, community organizations, and so forth (Rose 1999a: 265).[14] While caring through watching may have helped a good number of welfare women become self-sufficient, then, it has left plenty of others – those deemed unwilling to become responsible and govern themselves ethically – out in the cold. Indeed, while welfare reform might have empowered some, it has confined numerous others to lives of continued, and even more severe, poverty.

Such, then, is one family of ethopolitical technologies for governing the marginal. These technologies of citizenship take the ethical reformation of subjects as their principal objective. They aim, that is, to reconstitute the habits of independence, capacity for life planning, and ability for self-improvement of marginal individuals (Rose 2000b: 335). The goal here is to reinsert such anti-citizens – poor women, members of the underclass, inhabitants of the ghetto – into circuits of civility and prudent self-management. It is to morally rearm them with the fundamental virtues of honesty and self-reliance so that they can be reinscribed within circuits of work and consumption. Should this ethical project fail, however, marginal subjects are left to their own devices. They are abandoned to fend for themselves.

Illegalities and Delinquency

Now let us turn to those governmental technologies that deem the ethical reconstruction of marginal subjects unlikely and therefore work principally through practices of containment. These anti-citizenship technologies are most clearly manifested in the post-social government of illegalities and delinquency. Since the 1970s or so, as I noted in the introduction, crime and punishment have become a primary means through which political authorities seek to govern the conduct of populations. Jonathan Simon (1997) refers to this development as "governing through crime." What has happened is that, in placing such a strong emphasis on individual responsibility, post-social modes of government have not simply drawn attention to conduct deemed irresponsible; they have also tended to criminalize and punish it. This punitive turn in contemporary rule is most clearly visible in the widespread popularity of sentencing regimes of just desserts, deterrence, and retribution. These regimes include such measures as: quality of life campaigns and zero tolerance policing; harsher penalties and the extensive utilization of imprisonment; "three strikes" and compulsory minimum sentencing policies; austere and no frills prisons; redress in juvenile court and the incarceration of minors; the resurrection of corporal punishment and chain gangs; supermaximum prisons and boot camps;

the increased frequency of judicial executions; community notification laws and pedophile registers; and more extensive parole restrictions (Garland 2001: 12). The rationale for governing through crime and punishment is that irresponsible individuals must be held accountable for their misdeeds: that they must be made to shoulder the burden of their lifestyle decisions. The calculus of punishment thus serves to press upon the offending (and potentially offending) agent the importance of being prudent and governing oneself ethically. The thinking too is that responsible citizens must be protected from the hordes of anti-citizens who threaten their security and contentment: petty criminals, muggers, prostitutes, pimps, the homeless, gang members, drug offenders, unreconstructable welfare subjects, murderers, and the like. The containment of the few therefore becomes a prerequisite for the freedoms of the many. The image that takes shape here, then, is of an undeserving mass of anti-citizens who have failed to embrace their responsibilities as subjects of "moral community" and must consequently be subject to permanent and despotic administration in the name of protecting the public's safety (Rose 2000b: 337). The archetype of this anti-citizen is the young, urban African American or Latino male, envisioned typically as a dangerous street gang banger – as the embodiment of an "explosive mix of moral degeneracy and mayhem" (Wacquant 2001: 118).

The contemporary prominence of governing through crime is perhaps best instantiated in three widely utilized punitive tactics or anti-citizenship technologies: quality of life (or zero tolerance) policing campaigns; mass incarceration; and post-detention surveillance. Let me elaborate on each tactic in turn. Quality of life policing campaigns are basically endeavors to intensively monitor misdemeanors, incivilities, and disorder (McArdle and Erzen 2001). Their aim is to sweep public spaces clean of deviance and bedlam – to deal aggressively with beggars, the homeless, squeegee men, loiterers, drunks, drug offenders, pimps, prostitutes, and other nuisances. The premises underpinning such campaigns appear to be two. The first premise is that the assertive prosecution of low-level rule breaking leads to the prevention of more serious crime. The thinking here is as follows: while public drinking, vagrancy, and other petty offenses may appear to be benign, they are actually the disorderly material upon which major criminal activity feeds; actively dealing with such transgressions thus helps to forestall (and resolve) graver problems.[15] The second premise is that the intensive policing of public spaces improves the quality of life for decent citizens: it makes them feel safer and thus better able to enjoy the freedoms – of association, consumption, and so forth – that undergird a liberal polity. These quality of life campaigns have been implemented in numerous localities around the United States (e.g., Baltimore, San Francisco, and Sacramento). But undoubtedly their most notable realization has been in New York City. Since 1994, Mayor Rudolph Giuliani and subsequent administrations have vigorously waged a quality of life crusade as part of their effort to foster public order and forge a safe and sterilized urban aesthetic (Erzen 2001; McArdle 2001). This crusade has taken place largely through the New York Police Department's (NYPD) zealous policing of public spaces, with stop-and-frisk campaigns (whereby plainclothes policemen stop and search individuals suspected of, for example, carrying drugs), the deployment of task forces to deal with specific incivilities, and other such tactics. The initial low-level offenses targeted were window washing (approaching vehicles in traffic, or about to stop in traffic, for the purpose of washing windshields), petty drug dealing, and prostitution. The list has now expanded to encompass more than twenty offenses, including panhandling in public places, streets, roadways, and transit facilities; abandoning property such as mattresses, shacks, or structures on public streets; disorderly behavior on park department property; public consumption of alcoholic beverages; operation of a sound-reproduction device without proper authorization; the removal of residential trash; disorderly behavior in transit facilities; street vending without a permit; public lewdness; open fires; unreasonable noise; and loud motorcycles.

The effects of New York City's order maintenance and crime-control program have been rather significant. On the one hand, there is little doubt that this program has helped to clear the streets of unwanted incivilities, particularly in business and shopping districts. Places such as Time Square, for example, have been "cleaned" up and transformed into "safe," theme-park-like spaces of consumption. On the other hand, however, there is also little doubt that certain classes of people have become subject to increased police harassment. Foremost among the harassed are the homeless. These people are not explicitly named as targets of the quality of life campaign. But it is obvious that many of the offenses being prosecuted – for example, drinking and urinating in public – are the by-products of life on the streets. Also heavily harassed are racialized subjects. In November 1999, a report of the New York State attorney general's office showed that the NYPD used racial profiling in its stop-and-frisk campaigns: Latinos, for example, were stopped four times more frequently than whites, and blacks six times as much (McArdle 2001: 6). While New York City's quality of life campaign may have helped to make the city orderly, then, it has done so at the expense of banishing ill-fitting people from public space. It has done so through watching, surveying, policing, and controlling those whose street presence offends the public's sensibilities. The same goes for quality of life campaigns more generally: they have created public order through criminalizing every minor transgression, every act of unruly conduct – particularly if is perpetrated by the poor and racialized minorities (Garland 2001: 181).

The second punitive tactic, mass incarceration, refers to the increasing practice of dealing with illegalities and delinquencies through institutional warehousing. The idea here, in part, is that imprisonment has become a rather highly favored mode of punishment. From 1973 to 1997, for example, there was a 500 percent increase in the number of people incarcerated in the United States; also rising during this period were the average duration of prison terms and the relative number of custodial, as against non-custodial, sentences (Garland 2001: 14). Part of the idea, too, is that the prison has become much more thoroughly an apparatus of exclusion and control. To be sure, the "Big House" has always been a highly punitive, confining, and exclusionary institution. For much of the twentieth century, though, it also had a rather strong rehabilitative mission. Its goal was not just to punish offenders but also to resocialize them – to turn them into law-abiding, if not productive, members of society (Wacquant 2001: 111–12). This rehabilitative ideal has generally gone by the wayside. The prison is nowadays by and large more narrowly concerned with simply neutralizing offenders. Its purpose is principally to incapacitate – to physically sequester law-breakers as long as possible in order to prevent them from harming the public. It functions, in short, as a warehouse of sorts, as a repository for troublesome people, both the dangerous (e.g., murderers and rapists) and the merely annoying (e.g., the mentally ill, drug addicts, and the poor).

This general move toward warehousing and incapacitating delinquents can be seen in a number of contemporary policies. Foremost among these are the mandatory sentencing laws popularly grouped under the label "three strikes and you're out." These laws, which took root throughout the United States during the 1990s, are aimed at keeping habitual offenders, or what are often called "career criminals," off the streets. California's "three strikes" policy, for example, dictates that felons found culpable of a third serious offense be imprisoned for twenty-five years to life. The law specifies the following: "Although the first two 'strikes' accrue for serious felonies, the crime that triggers the life sentence can be *any* felony. Furthermore, the law doubles sentences for a second strike, requires that these extended sentences be served in prison (rather than in jail or on probation), and limits 'good time' earned during prison to 20 percent of the sentence given (rather than 50 percent, as under the previous law)" (Greenwood et al. 1994: xi). Other public policies signaling the salience of warehousing include the "War on Drugs" – a massive effort to criminalize drug consumption and incarcerate users – and the increasing tendency to prosecute minors charged with violent crimes as adults (Pratt 1999: 150; O'Malley 2001). The most dramatic consequence of warehousing delinquents, other than radically increasing the number of men and women behind bars, has been the transformation of the prison into a ghetto of sorts. For the people most subject to imprisonment have been African Americans. "They" are the ones most often associated with criminality. They are the primary group from whom the public is envisioned as needing protection. According to Jonathan Simon: "In the mid-1990s nearly one in nine young African American males was in prison at least some of the year, and one in three was in prison, on parole or on probation. However, in big cities with large zones of concentrated poverty, the penal custody rate is closer to half the population of young African American men. In the course of a lifetime, nearly one-third of African American men will serve time in jail or prison" (2000: 1122). Warehousing, then, is targeted at not just any subjects but principally the racially abject. It functions, in other words, as a racial technology: as a practical mechanism for managing the conduct of "unruly" racialized populations. The goal here, of course, is not reform or rehabilitation but incapacitation and punishment.

The third punitive tactic, post-detention surveillance, refers to the increasing practice of extending the reach of penal sentencing through subjecting convicts to ever-lengthier and more encompassing post-prison modes of social control. As Loïc Wacquant notes,

All but two states require *postprison supervision* of offenders and 80 percent of all persons released from state penitentiaries are freed under conditional or community release; the average term spent on parole has also increased steadily over the past two decades to surpass 23 months in 1996 – nearly equal to the average prison term served of 25 months. . . . With fully 54 percent of offenders failing to complete their term of parole in 1997 (compared to 27 percent in 1984), and parole violators making up a third of all persons admitted in state penitentiaries every year (two-thirds in California), parole has become an appendage of the prison which operates mainly to extend the social and symbolic incapacities of incarceration beyond its walls. With the advent of the Internet, corrections administrations in many states . . . have put their entire inmate data bases on line, further stretching the perimeter of penal infamy by making it possible for anyone to delve into the "rap sheet" of prisoners via the World Wide Web, and for employers and landlords to discriminate more broadly against ex-convicts in complete legality. (2001: 113)

The most extreme manifestation of this trend toward enhanced post-prison surveillance is found undoubtedly in the administration of re-leased sex offenders (see Simon 2000). Since the mid-1990s, every state in the nation has enacted some measure or another to monitor their conduct. The most common move has been to require local authorities to maintain a registry of every former sex offender within their domin-ion and to alert the populace – via media announcements, mailings, posters, and the like – of their whereabouts (Wacquant 2001: 113). A related move has been to mandate that ex-sex offenders themselves apprise local communities of their penal status. In Louisiana, for in-stance, they are expected to give written notification of their situation to neighbors, landlords, and local school and park officials. They must also announce their presence in a local newspaper within about a month of their arrival. The effect of these practices of disclosure and notification has been to permanently mark sex offenders with the blemish of their conviction. No matter where they may settle, judicial stigma follows them, often along with public harassment, insults, attacks, and humiliation. The message that community-notification, and other post-detention, measures send is thus that there is no such thing as a former offender – "only offenders who have been caught before and will strike again" (Garland 2001: 180–1). It is that once a criminal, always a criminal.

Such, then, is the other family of ethopolitical technologies for managing the marginal. They are technologies of anti-citizenship that judge the ethical reconstruction of irresponsible subjects unlikely and consequently seek to govern them through routines of containment. The goal here is not to reinsert these anti-citizens into networks of civility and responsible self-management but to incapacitate them – to subject them to continuous and authoritarian administration. It is to envelop them in a wide net of control and surveillance. The result: the anathematization of whole communities – African Americans, the poor, and so forth – as criminal and undeserving. Indeed, the outcome has been to render specific populations, particularly racialized minorities, highly suspect and vulnerable.

RACING THE UNETHICAL

In this part, I have suggested that we think of the post-social politics of responsibilization in terms of what Nikolas Rose has called ethopolitics. Ethopolitics is a politics of life. It is preoccupied with how persons comport themselves and comprehend their existence. It stresses making the welfare of the self a primary terrain of government. Central to ethopolitics, I also indicated, are two broad strategies of rule. On one side, there are numerous technologies that seek to activate the self-managing capacities of the general population. These technologies work largely through inculcating individuals with the necessity of being prudent and conducting themselves ethically in the face of social insecurities. Here we dealt principally with how such ethopolitical techniques manifested themselves in relation to health care and crime control. And on the other side, there are a host of more targeted technologies that attempt to deal with those individuals who have failed to take up the call of prudentialism and adequately manage their own contentment. Those we called technologies of citizenship seek to animate the independent capacities of these troublesome individuals and encourage them to take responsibility for the care of their selves. We saw practices of the sort at work in the administration of welfare. Those we called anti-citizenship technologies consider the ethical reformation of troublesome subjects improbable and thus propose to govern them through despotic measures of containment and incapacitation. We saw practices of this kind at play in the management of illegalities and delinquencies. This part, then, has basically dealt with how post-social government exhorts individuals to treat their lives responsibly as rational planning projects and to conduct themselves in a manner that guards against risks and insecurities. It has focused, in short, on how individuals are governed as ethical beings.

One thing that has become clear here is that ethopolitics is very much a racialized politics. For the subjects most often deemed unethical – that is, unable or unwilling to take care of their selves – are those whose phenomenal/cultural attributes differentiate them from the dominant "white," European American population. Consider, for example, the case of welfare dependency. The prototypical welfare subject is the young, black, single, inner-city mother prone to "spawning" children she cannot adequately care for. Or take the case of illegalities and delinquency. The exemplary criminal is the young, urban African American or Latino male bereft of moral qualities and lacking dignity and responsible autonomy. The post-social tendency is thus to disproportionately manage racialized minorities through harsh punitive measures. It is they who are most vigorously being forced off the welfare rolls. It is they who are the main targets of quality of life campaigns. It is they who are increasingly warehoused in America's prisons. What is happening here, then, is that while post-social government might generally work through promoting the self-managing capacities of individuals, it does not hesitate to take despotic steps against those subjects – namely, racialized minorities – deemed to threaten the well-being and safety of the population. The price of maintaining the entrepreneurial and individualist freedoms of the majority thus seems to be a growing reliance on crime and punishment to neutralize the throngs of racialized anti-citizens. What we are seeing, in sum, is a police and criminal shadow cast over the racially marginal sectors of society as ethical government has come to depend on punitive institutions to protect the welfare of responsible citizens. It is in this repressive underbelly of ethopolitics that we will locate the contemporary management of illegal immigration.

PART TWO

Producing "the Illegal," or
Making Up Subjects

GOVERNMENT AND NUMBERS

In Part One, I proposed that we think of the post-social politics of responsibilization in terms of what Nikolas Rose has called ethopolitics. Key to ethopolitics, I suggested, are two general strategies of government. On one side, there are numerous tactics that take as their target the general population and work largely through inculcating individuals with the necessity of being prudent and conducting themselves ethically in the face of social insecurities. And on the other, there are a host of more targeted, often repressive, technologies that attempt to deal with those individuals – often racialized minorities – who have failed to take up the call of prudentialism and adequately manage their own contentment. I would like to suggest that it is in this latter, despotic and racialized underbelly of ethopolitics that we must locate the post-1965 government of "illegal" immigration. My analysis of what could be called the ethopolitics of immigration will be concerned, on the one hand, with how "illegal" immigrants have chiefly been problematized as unethical and, on the other, with how the programs that have been deployed to manage them have consequently been rather exclusionary, restrictive, and punitive. We will tackle the programmatic aspects of government in Part Three. Here we will deal in the main with its problematizing side.

To elaborate a bit, the concern of this part is to look at how the post-1965 problematization of "illegal" immigrants has largely taken place in ethical terms – at how the "problem" of "illegal" immigration, that is, has on the whole been rendered understandable as an ethical problem. To be more precise, this part is concerned with investigating how a variety of immigration "experts" – social scientists, INS/DHS bureaucrats, policy analysts, immigration reform organizations, and the popular press – have constructed "illegal" immigrants – typically imagined as Mexican – as anti-citizens incapable of exercising responsible self-government and thus as threats to the overall well-being of the social body. This ethical problematization of "illegal" immigrants has taken a number of specific forms. One important form we will be concerned with here is that of "illegal" immigrants as lawbreakers. The idea is that such immigrants are, to put it plainly, illegal: that they are by definition criminals. For these are people who, by virtue of having overstayed their visas or crossed the border clandestinely, have flagrantly violated US immigration laws. A second important form we will deal with is that of "illegal" immigrants as job takers. The general belief seems to be that the undocumented take away or steal jobs from (at least some) Americans. And a third form of ethical problematization we will be interested in is that of illegal immigrants as public burdens. The thinking here is that these immigrants come to the United States primarily to get on welfare and take advantage of the government's generous social services. Indeed, they are commonly seen as bent on sponging off the American state and people. For many experts, then, "illegal" immigrants – to the extent that they are imagined as criminals, job takers, and welfare dependents – simply cannot be proper subjects. They are uncommitted to personal responsibility and the rule of law. They are not capable of proper self-management. The putative consequence of this immigrant irresponsibility is the cultural and economic wounding of the social body.

Central to the problematization of "illegal" immigrants as unethical beings, I suggest, have been a variety of numerical technologies: statistics, population counts, economic forecasts, and the like. The centrality of these technologies in the constitution of "illegal" immigration as a problem domain is intimately linked to the general place that numbers occupy in the relationship between government and knowledge. I noted in the introduction that the exercise of government is inextricably connected to the activity of thought – that all government depends on the elaboration of specific languages that represent and analyze reality in a manner that renders it intelligible and amenable to political programming. The idea here is simply that knowledge is necessary for effective rule. It is that government needs to "know" reality in order to act efficaciously upon it. Numerical technologies have perhaps been the most potent scientific instruments for knowing reality and for enabling interventions into social processes (Urla 1993; Appadurai 1996; Poovey 1998; Rose 1999a; Kalpagam 2000). Indeed, it is primarily through numbers that we come to know the problem domains (e.g., unemployment, crime, poverty) and objects (e.g., the unemployed, the criminal, the poor) upon which government operates. Numbers produce at least two kinds of knowledge in relation to these object domains. One kind is enumerative: numbers, at the most basic level, simply generate information about the size and scale of governmental objects (Cohen 1982: 43). The other kind is what could be called surveying: numbers – in the form of rates, averages, percentages, probabilities, and the like – create a general map or picture of given governmental domains. The combined effect of these numerical knowledges or calculative practices is the creation of a bond of uniformity around the targets of government. It is the mapping of their limits and the delineation of their internal features. What numbers do, then, is basically make up governmental object domains (Rose 1999a: 197): they single out a certain segment of existence, identify its properties and processes, and give it categorical visibility.

The argument that I would like to make in this part is that, like governmental domains more generally, it is largely through numerical technologies that "illegal" immigration has been made up as a problematic dimension of experience. This argument will have two strands. One strand will focus on how practices of enumeration have largely been responsible for the production of the "illegal" immigrant as a socially significant category. This strand will concentrate, that is, on how the "illegal" immigrant is fundamentally an effect of the efforts to count him/her. The second thread will deal with how surveying routines, through the countless "facts" they generate about "illegal" immigration, have fashioned a domain with very specific qualities and features. To be more specific, this thread will note how, through numbers, "illegal" immigration has largely been constituted as an ambit littered with subjects who imprudently depend on the social body for their well-being. Important to this analysis will be what I earlier referred to as material inscriptions (Latour 1986; Rose 1998). These are the mundane technical instruments – surveys, reports, pamphlets, manuals, architectural plans, written reports, drawings, pictures, bureaucratic rules and guidelines, charts, graphs, and so forth – that translate reality into documentary form. Such devices will be key because it is via them that political and other authorities accumulate numerical facts about "illegal" immigration: it is through them, indeed, that "the illegal" is written down, counted, measured, and tabulated. The specific inscriptions that will concern us here include INS/DHS policy documents, reports to Congress, Census statistical returns, policy think-tank reports, immigration advocacy group pamphlets and manuals, government-sponsored investigations, and scholarly papers. In the end, I will suggest that, above all, what calculative practices and the devices that inscribe them have made visible is the "illegal" immigrant as unethical subject: the "illegal" immigrant as criminal, job taker, and welfare dependent. The analysis will focus on the post-1965 period up to the September 11, 2001 "terrorist" attacks on the United States. However, by way of conclusion, I will briefly lay out what has happened since.

LEGISLATING ILLEGALITY

Before detailing the steadfast and often zealous post-1965 problematization of "illegal" immigration, I would like to provide a brief historical backdrop to the issue. I want to suggest that the genesis of the contemporary concern with immigrant "illegality," especially as it relates to Mexicans, can be traced to two sets of legislative measures. The first set consists of the Immigration Act of 1917 and the Immigration Act of 1924. These Acts, through their legislation of substantive restrictions on Mexican immigration and via their enhancement of deportation procedures and mechanisms, essentially gave birth to what we have come to know as the "illegal alien" (Ngai 1999, 2001, n.d.). The second set is made up of the Bracero Program (1942–64) and Immigration Act of 1965. These measures, through opening up and closing off avenues for legal immigration, in effect set in motion the "considerable" flow of unauthorized immigration that we find in the post-1965 period. The case that I will make, then, is that US immigration law has been instrumental in giving shape to immigrant "illegality" in its present-day form (De Genova 2002).

Immigration Restrictions and Deportation Policy

The origins of Mexican immigrant "illegality" can be traced to two important early twentieth-century immigration laws: the Immigration Act of 1917 and the Immigration Act of 1924. What these two Acts did was usher in a restrictionist regime in immigration policy that ended the era of more or less free-flowing movement of people from

Mexico and Europe to the United States. This regime came to fruition in a context of intense anti-immigrant sentiment – sentiment directed particularly at the "undesirable races" of Asia, Latin America, and eastern and southern Europe (Ngai 1999; Nevins 2002). A primary effect of putting an end to "open" immigration was the birth of the Mexican "illegal" immigrant.

To be more precise, the birth of Mexican immigrant "illegality" resulted from a couple of specific policies put in place by the Acts of 1917 and 1924. The first policy entailed the imposition, for the first time, of substantive restrictions on immigration from Mexico.[1] These restrictions initially included a head tax ($8), a medical examination, a literacy test, and the establishment of investigative procedures to determine whether an individual was likely to become a public charge; then, in 1924, law-makers added a visa requirement and fee ($10) (Sánchez 1993: 55, 57). So whereas prior to 1917 immigrants were able to cross the border relatively unfettered (to work in such jobs as railroad construction, mining, and agriculture), those crossing afterward increasingly had to go through a host of cumbersome procedures. For many, these procedures proved too taxing. The biggest headaches for would-be immigrants were the head tax and visa fee. Many could simply not afford to make the required payments. Problematic as well were the medical examinations. These typically involved a variety of procedures that immigrants found rather humiliating: bathing, delousing, and medical line inspection (where immigrants would walk in a single line before a medical officer) (Ngai 2001). The consequence was that some would-be immigrants were discouraged from crossing the border altogether, while others were compelled to avoid formal admission and thus cross it surreptitiously. What the imposition of substantive restrictions did, then, was cause a drop in legal immigration, from an average of 58,747 a year in the late 1920s to 12,703 in 1930 (Ngai 1999), and induce a concomitant rise in entry without inspection (Sánchez 1993: 57).

The second policy implicated in the birth of Mexican immigrant "illegality" entailed the institution of enhanced procedures and mechanisms of deportation (see Ngai 2001). Prior to the Act of 1924, deportation practice was rather limited in scope and means. For example, mere entry without inspection was not sufficient cause for expulsion. Deportation measures were instead more narrowly reserved for a variety of undesirable classes that Congress had barred from entering the United

States but had somehow managed to get through. These classes included the mentally retarded, the insane, persons with dangerous contagious diseases, prostitutes, paupers, polygamists, Chinese laborers, and anyone who was likely to become a public charge.[2] Furthermore, there was a statute of limitation on deportation. In 1891, Congress set the period of deportability at one year. This meant that excludable aliens could normally only be deported if they were detected within twelve months of their arrival. Then, in 1917, the period of deportability was extended to five years. Finally, there were no real mechanisms for enforcing deportation laws. There were procedures in place to identify and deny admission to excludable persons at points of entry. But if these persons avoided notice and successfully entered the country, there were virtually no means to track them down. It was typically only as a result of being hospitalized or imprisoned that excludable aliens were ever discovered. With the passage of the 1924 Act, the practice of deportation changed dramatically. First of all, the law expanded the categories of deportability to include all persons entering without inspection or lacking a valid visa.[3] Second, it did away with the statute of limitation on deportation for virtually all types of illicit immigrants. And third, the Act created, for the first time, a genuine enforcement mechanism to tackle unauthorized entry. This mechanism was the Border Patrol. Its general charge was to apprehend "illegal" immigrants and expel them from the country. The importance of these augmented deportation procedures and mechanisms is that without them there would have been no Mexican "illegal" aliens.[4] It might have been the restrictions on immigration that propelled immigrants to avoid formal admission and enter the United States on the sly. But it was the making of entry without inspection (or without proper documentation) a deportable offense that actually turned these people into "illegals." For without the possibility of deportation, it was rather immaterial whether or not an immigrant had proper documentation. So what technically gave life to the Mexican "illegal" immigrant was the fact of deportability (Ngai 2001).

It was in this way, then, with immigration restrictions spurring immigrants to enter the United States without proper documentation and enhanced mechanisms of deportation making undocumented status matter, that Mexican immigrant "illegality" was born. This was an "illegality" destined to become an increasing object of governmental concern. As the 1920s wore on, for example, the Border Patrol progressively became more zealous in tracking down and apprehending "illegal" aliens. Its routine practices came to include the indiscriminate stopping and interrogation of Mexican laborers, as well as the execution of massive "sweeps" in Mexican communities along the border. The latter would often ensnare hundreds of "illegal" immigrants at a time. A main effect of these patrolling practices was to dramatically increase the number of Mexican immigrants subjected to deportation.[5] The figure jumped from 1,751 in 1925 to over 15,000 in 1929 (Ngai 2001). This concern over Mexican "illegality" would only get more intense during the decade that followed. It would in fact reach a fever pitch. With the country in the throes of the Great Depression, Mexican immigrants became targets of extreme hostility. They were accused of offenses ranging from the spreading of disease and the displacement of American workers to the inundation of local welfare agencies. A trend that consequently developed in American communities across the country was the organization of campaigns to repatriate Mexican nationals.[6] The largest campaign took place in Los Angeles. Executed in 1930 and 1931, this operation forced tens of thousands of Mexican immigrants to return to Mexico. Nationally, the number of repatriated averaged approximately 80,000 persons per year between 1930 and 1937. Researchers estimate that as many as 600,000 individuals of Mexican descent were sent back "home" during the 1930s (Gutiérrez 1995: 72). After these mass deportations, Mexican immigration slowed down to a trickle. Consequently, the concern with Mexican "illegality" diminished as well. However, the figure of the Mexican "illegal" immigrant had already been born. And it would only be a short time before s/he would again became an object of governmental concern.

The Bracero Program and the Immigration Act of 1965

While the Immigration Acts of 1917 and 1924 gave genesis to Mexican immigrant "illegality," it was two other legislative measures that more immediately produced the post-1965 concern with "illegal" Mexican immigration. One measure was the Bracero Program, the other the Immigration Act of 1965. The former measure generated an avenue for temporary legal immigration from Mexico and then closed it off, while the latter put numerical restrictions, for the first time, on permanent legal immigration from the Western Hemisphere. The effect of reducing avenues for legal immigration was to engender a "substantial" flow of unauthorized entry.

Perhaps the more significant of the two measures was the Bracero Program. The mass deportations of the 1930s, as I have noted, slowed down Mexican immigration to a negligible level. The onset of World War II would dramatically reverse this trend. With millions of able bodies off to war, the United States developed a severe labor shortage, particularly in agriculture. The federal government would turn to its southern neighbor to help satisfy the country's labor needs. In 1942, the United States and Mexico signed a bilateral agreement that established the foreign contract-labor measure that would become known as the Bracero Program (Calavita 1992; Carrasco 1997). Under the terms of the agreement, Mexican laborers were to be brought to work in the United States for temporary, renewable periods. The program began in September 1942 with the importation of several hundred Mexican migrants to work in the sugar beet fields just outside Stockton, California. It would then grow steadily during the war years, so that by 1947 almost 220,000 Mexican laborers had been contracted to work in the United States (Gutiérrez 1995: 134). The Bracero Program was ostensibly an emergency measure meant to remedy wartime labor shortages. After the war, however, the agricultural industry was disinclined to giving up bracero labor. Consequently, it pressured Congress to keep the program going. It was kept alive until December 1964. The total number of braceros recruited over the lifetime of the program was more than 4.6 million (García y Griego 1998: 1215).

A key side-effect of the Bracero Program was the generation of a "considerable" flow of "illegal" immigration (Gutiérrez 1995; Carrasco 1997; García y Griego 1998). We can get a crude glimpse of the size of this flow from INS expulsion figures. While the INS apprehended only an annual average of 7,203 "illegal" aliens between 1940 and 1943, it generally seized in the neighborhood of more than 500,000 between 1947 and 1954 (Gutiérrez 1995: 142). There were at least two crucial factors that contributed to this surge in "illegal" immigration. One factor was the infrastructure that the Bracero Program created to facilitate the legal movement of people from Mexico to the United States. Composed of transportation, communication, human, and other networks, what this infrastructure did was connect the interior of Mexico to work sites and communities across the United States. Once in place, it would serve as conduit not just for legal immigration but also for unauthorized population movements as well. The other crucial factor was the penchant of many employers for hiring undocumented workers. These immigrants were often preferred over braceros because it was less cumbersome and not as expensive to hire them. Significantly, the surge of "illegal" immigration would not go unnoticed. State officials, unions, and others would begin to argue that "illegal" immigrants depressed wages, caused numerous social problems, and generally represented a threat to the stability of society at large. Consequently, on June 9, 1954, the US Attorney General, Herbert Brownell, ordered a massive offensive against "illegal" immigration. The aim of this offensive, known as "Operation Wetback," was to deter immigrants from entering the United States without inspection and to apprehend and deport those already in the country "illegally." The operation resulted in the deportation of close to 4 million Mexican immigrants (Carrasco 1997: 197). Moreover, it virtually brought to a standstill undocumented immigration from Mexico.[7] Predictably, as this immigration stream came to a halt, the concern with Mexican immigrant "illegality" abated as well.

The halt in "illegal" immigration, as well as the decline in concern over it, would be short-lived, however. One of the things the Bracero Program did, as I noted above, was create an infrastructure that connected the interior of Mexico to US labor markets. When the Bracero Program ended in 1964, this infrastructure, along with the demand for immigrant labor, was left firmly in place. Consequently, those immigrants who had been migrating legally as braceros, rather than ceasing to migrate, simply started to enter the United States "illegally."[8] A major effect of ending the Bracero Program was thus to rekindle the flow of "illegal" immigration. Indeed, how could it have been otherwise? With a central avenue for legal immigration closed but with the need for Mexican immigrant labor still strong, it was to be expected that "illegal" immigration would flourish. Contributing to this rekindling of immigrant "illegality" would be the Immigration Act of 1965. Earlier in the century, with its enactment of the Immigration Act of 1924, Congress had put in place a restrictionist system of immigration based on national origins quotas. Under this system, the number of admittances from any one country was limited to 3 percent of that nation's US population in 1890 – later changed to 1920. Given the makeup of the US populace in 1890 and 1920, this quota system was considerably biased in favor of immigration from western and northern

Europe. One important exception to the national origins quotas rules concerned immigration from the Western Hemisphere. Largely in deference to US policy concerns (the wish to keep good working relationships with the countries of the Western Hemisphere) and agricultural interests (the desire to provide growers with a steady supply of labor), there were no numerical restrictions placed on immigration from this part of the world. The Immigration Act of 1965 put an end to this system of immigration. Gone were the national origins quotas with their partiality toward northwestern European immigration. And gone as well was the exemption of the Western Hemisphere from numerical restrictions. The new immigration system that was put in place allotted immigrant visas on a first-come, first-served basis within a structure of hemispherical numerical limits: the Eastern Hemisphere was given a ceiling of 170,000 visas, with each nation permitted a maximum of 20,000, while the Western Hemisphere was allotted 120,000 slots, with no upper limit per country.[9] This new system was celebrated as egalitarian since it did not privilege certain areas of the world over others. Its effects on Mexico would be deleterious, however. For in putting limits on immigration from the Western Hemisphere, it severely restricted yet another legal avenue for Mexican immigration. The result was that even more Mexican immigrants who would have migrated legally wound up having no choice but to migrate without proper documentation.

Taken in concert, then, what the termination of the Bracero Program and the implementation of the 1965 Immigration Act did was basically "illegalize" the flow of Mexican immigrants. For in closing the door to legal passage, these actions simply succeeded in opening up a space for illegal movement to flourish. Set in motion were thus the flows of undocumented immigration that would become the objects of governmental concern in the post-1965 period.

PRACTICES OF
ENUMERATION

Now let us turn to the resolute and often fervent post-1965 problematization of "illegal" immigration. This problematization has largely turned, I have suggested, on the question of numbers. Indeed, it has appreciably been through figures that the "illegal" immigrant has been constituted and made visible as a problem object. There are two types of knowledge that numbers have generated with regard to undocumented immigration. One I have called enumerative, the other surveying. In this section, I would like to concentrate on the former. This type of knowledge has taken two basic forms. One form is that of the apprehension statistics of the INS/DHS. These statistics record the number of aliens arrested in violation of US immigration laws. The other form encompasses the statistical estimates of demographers, academics, statisticians, and the INS/DHS concerning the number of people residing "illegally" in the United States. The importance of these enumerative practices cannot be overstated. At the most basic level, these practices have rendered the "illegal" immigrant categorically visible. The idea here is simply that to make a count of something, especially if it is an official count, is to confer recognition upon it (Starr 1987). What these practices have done, moreover, is given "illegal" immigration visibility as a phenomenon of "great" magnitude. Words such as "flood," "out of control," and "invasion" have routinely been used to characterize the flow of "illegal" immigrants. Particularly important in this regard has been the way that politicians and the mass media have picked up and reported on the enumeration of "illegal" bodies. Given the patent importance of counting practices, what I would like to do in this section is delve into the specifics of how they have made up the "illegal" immigrant. We will begin with a general look at these practices: at the calculating authorities, forms of enumeration, and documentary procedures involved.

Calculating Authorities

Important in enumerating "illegal" immigration and producing truths about the size and scale of the phenomenon have been a number of entities. One of these is the Immigration and Naturalization Service (INS). Until March 1, 2003, when it was officially abolished and its duties transferred to various agencies within the newly created Department of Homeland Security (DHS), this federal agency of the US Department of Justice had, among other duties, primary responsibility for enforcing the country's immigration laws. Crucial among its enforcement activities were the detection and apprehension of deportable (or illegal) aliens. A deportable alien is someone who has violated US immigration laws. Included among the deportable are aliens who entered the United States without inspection, as well as persons who entered legally but subsequently lost their lawful status (e.g., tourists who overstayed their visas). Two INS units bore foremost responsibility for carrying out the work of locating and arresting such aliens: the US Border Patrol and the Investigations Division.[10] The principal mission of the former was (and still is) to safeguard the land and water borders of the United States between official entry ports, its chief goals being "to prevent illegal entry into the United States, interdict drug smugglers and other criminals, and compel those persons seeking admission to present themselves legally at ports of entry for inspection" (US INS 2002: 230). The Investigations Division concentrated on enforcing immigration laws within the interior of the country. Its duties included investigating "aliens involved in criminal activities" and inspecting "work sites to apprehend unauthorized alien workers and to impose sanctions against employers who knowingly employ them" (US INS 2002: 230). Aliens apprehended by these INS units were typically expelled from the country. Some underwent formal removal or deportation proceedings. This was typically the case with aliens implicated in serious criminal doings. Most deportable aliens, however, were offered what is called voluntary departure. Under this procedure, an alien admits to illegal status, waives his/her right to a hearing, and is removed under INS supervision. This practice was common with aliens appre-hended while attempting to enter the United States without inspection.

An attendant aspect of the INS's enforcement activities entailed keeping statistics about apprehensions. From 1933 through 1977, these statistics, as well as others dealing with more general immigration issues (e.g., asylees, temporary admissions, naturalizations), were documented in the *Annual Report of the Immigration and Naturalization Service*.[11] Then from 1977 through 2001, they were published in the *Statistical Yearbook of the Immigration and Naturalization Service*. (Now they appear in the *Yearbook of Immigration Statistics*, which is printed under the auspices of the DHS.[12]) Apprehensions, as noted above, measure the number of aliens picked up for violating US immigration laws. We are dealing here not with individuals but with events. For instance, if an alien were apprehended two times during a fiscal year, that person would show up twice in the apprehensions statistics. The *Annual Report* and the *Statis-tical Yearbook* typically present apprehension figures, as well as all other numbers, in table form. Apprehensions tables essentially amount to historical pictures of alien arrests. Each furnishes a tally of the total number of deportable aliens located from 1925, when apprehension figures were first recorded, through the present of a given report/ yearbook; a decade by decade breakdown of the aggregate number; and annual totals for most years (see Figure 2.1).[13] Significantly, the two INS statistical books also normally contain a section – variously titled "Border Patrol and Investigations," "Domestic Control," and (most recently) "Enforcement" – that gives a narrative overview of apprehensions data together with a re-presentation of arrest figures in chart form. The charts generally take the shape of either bar or line graphs. These serve to highlight how apprehension figures change from one year to the next as well as to illustrate long-term arrest trends. The narrative overviews typically contain a statement about the number of aliens apprehended during a given fiscal year. They also generally pro-vide information about the number of Mexican nationals found in illegal status. If not, then they will normally note how many appre-hended aliens were arrested along the Southwest (US–Mexico) border. Additionally, the overviews sometimes compare one year's figures to those of the previous year; at other times, they discuss how apprehen-sions numbers have changed over time.

A second attendant aspect of the INS's enforcement activities in-volved making estimates of the number of aliens living "illegally" in

Deportable aliens located: Fiscal years 1925–2000

Year	Deportable aliens located[1]	Year	Deportable aliens located[1]
1925–2000	**41,732,881**	1977 _____	1,042,215
		1978 _____	1,057,977
1925–30 _____	128,484	1979 _____	1,076,418
1931–40 _____	147,457	1980 _____	910,361
1941–50 _____	1,377,210		
1951–60 _____	3,598,949	**1981–90** _____	**11,883,382**
		1981 _____	975,780
		1982 _____	970,246
1961–70 _____	**1,608,356**	1983 _____	1,251,357
1961 _____	88,823	1984 _____	1,246,981
1962 _____	92,758	1985 _____	1,348,749
1963 _____	88,712	1986 _____	1,767,400
1964 _____	86,597	1987 _____	1,190,488
1965 _____	110,371	1988 _____	1,008,145
1966 _____	138,520	1989 _____	954,243
1967 _____	161,608	1990 _____	1,169,939
1968 _____	212,057		
1969 _____	283,557	**1991–2000** _____	**14,667,599**
1970 _____	345,353	1991 _____	1,197,875
		1992 _____	1,258,481
1971–80 _____	**8,321,498**	1993 _____	1,327,261
1971 _____	420,126	1994 _____	1,094,719
1972 _____	505,929	1995 _____	1,394,554
1973 _____	655,968	1996 _____	1,649,986
1974 _____	788,145	1997 _____	1,536,520
1975 _____	766,600	1998 _____	1,679,439
1976 _____	875,915	1999 _____	1,714,035
1976,TQ[2] _____	221,824	2000 _____	1,814,729

[1] Aliens apprehended were first recorded in 1925. Prior to 1960 data represents aliens actually apprehended. Since 1960, figures are for total deportable aliens located, including nonwillful crewmen violators.

[2] The three-month period – July 1 through September 30, 1976 – between fiscal year 1976 and fiscal year 1977.

Note: See Glossary for fiscal year definitions.

FIGURE 2.1 Example of Immigration and Naturalization Service apprehension figures table.
Source: US INS 2002.

the United States. This aspect, however, was not as thoroughly developed, at least not until later years, as that of apprehensions. It was only with the publication of the 1995 *Statistical Yearbook* that the INS began consistently calculating and publishing information on the size of the "illegal" immigrant population. This yearbook and a number of others afterward contain a section entitled "Estimates."[14] These sections as a rule present estimates data in table form together with a brief narrative rundown. The tables provide information on the size of the "illegal" immigrant population at a particular point in time, as well as data on the top twenty countries of origin and states of residence. The narrative descriptions re-present many of these statistics along with a few other figures: for example, the annual growth level of the "illegal" immigrant population, the number of "illegal" immigrants estimated to have entered the United States without inspection (as opposed to the number believed to have entered legally on a temporary basis and then failed to depart), and the percentage of the US population living in "illegal" status. These INS estimates of the "illegal" alien population are generally considered to be analytical. This means that they are empirically based and statistically sound. Prior to the 1995 *Statistical Yearbook*, the INS's efforts at calculating and documenting the size of the "illegal" immigrant populace were rather sporadic. The earliest effort dates back to the early 1970s. A handful would follow later in the decade. Then there is nothing until the 1990s. These efforts were also somewhat on the speculative side. This means that the estimates they produced were not methodologically reliable. At their simplest, these speculative estimates amounted to little more than impressionistic guesses. At their best, they were the outcomes of methodological techniques employing "a combination of fragmentary data, reasonable assumptions, informed guesses from experienced people, simple arithmetic, and logic" (Corwin 1982: 244). The documentary forms in which these estimates were circulated varied. Some were published in special reports; others simply appeared in prepared statements delivered by INS commissioners before various Congressional committees.

Also important in enumerating "illegal" bodies and producing facts about them have been an array of demographers, statisticians, and academics. Like the INS, these technicians of numbers have been intimately involved in estimating the scale of the "illegal" immigrant population residing in the United States. The estimates these individuals have produced have tended to be analytical. Although, to be sure, there has been a fair share of speculative ones. They have also tended to be of two types (Van Hook and Bean 1998). One type measures the stock of the "illegal" immigrant populace. "Stock" is a demographic term used to indicate the size of a population at a given moment in time. The other kind gauges the flow of the "illegal" immigrant stream. "Flow" designates the amount of entries into (in-flow) or exits from (out-flow) a population during a specific time interval. Some attention has been given here to what is called net flow (in-flow minus out-flow). This measure is generally taken as an indicator of population growth. A special concern of investigators has been to quantify the Mexican component of the "illegal" immigrant population. Indeed, there are very few studies that do not on some level deal with Mexican immigrants. Many even focus exclusively on them. This extraordinary preoccupation with Mexicans is largely due to the perception that they make up a significant portion of the deportable population. The estimates produced of the "illegal" Mexican immigrant populace, as well as of the "illegal" population more generally, have been published in a wide variety of forums. They range from demography and immigration journals to policy documents and conference proceedings. These estimates have also been carried out under the auspices of a wide assortment of institutions: research universities, immigration think-tanks, the Mexican government, the Bureau of the Census, and various US governmental commissions and groups established to study the "problem" of illegal immigration (e.g., the Select Commission on Immigration and Refugee Policy and the US Commission on Immigration Reform).

Making Visible

The importance of these enumerative practices, as I briefly noted above, is that they have made the "illegal" immigrant visible. Indeed, they have brought him/her into visibility. At the most basic level, this visibility has been categorical. What counting practices have done, in effect, is produced the very category of the "illegal" immigrant. They have singled out individuals who have violated US immigration laws, divided them off from other people, and classified them together under various labels ("illegal immigrants," "illegal aliens," "deportable aliens," and so forth). The general idea here, one that Ian Hacking has alerted us to, is that "counting is hungry for categories" (1982: 280). It is that processes of enumeration generate the very categories they add up. It is that counting practices as a rule sort up and divide things, people, and conduct into classes, creating all sorts of groupings and classifications (Urla 1993: 820). At this basic level, what enumeration has also done is conferred recognition upon illegal immigrants. The general claim here is that to categorize and make a count of some phenomenon is to grant it authenticity (Starr 1987; Porter 1995). This is especially true if the count is an official one. For official statistics, as Paul Starr notes, are "cognitive commitments of a powerful kind" (1987: 53). Once particular categories have been operationalized in government data, they enter not only the language of administration but also generally that of society at large (i.e., the mass media, academia, the public, and so forth). Thus it is that phenomena become socially recognized. In the case of "illegal" immigration, the count has certainly been official. This official count has principally taken the form of INS statistics. Indeed, these have noticeably operationalized the category of the "illegal immigrant." From there, this category has entered other domains of social life and the phenomenon of "illegal" immigration has been made recognizable.

At another level, this one being perhaps more important, practices of enumeration have made illegal immigration visible as a phenomenon of "vast" scale. This process of visibilization has involved three interconnected elements. One element has to do with apprehension figures and the way they have been presented in INS statistical books. These books have consistently highlighted how, in the post-1965 period, apprehensions of deportable aliens have generally climbed from one year to the next, often quite dramatically. Moreover, they have tended to strongly link the problem of "illegal" immigration with Mexican nationals surreptitiously crossing the US–Mexico border. A second element involves the expert enumerations of the stock and flow of "illegal" bodies. These have generally shown that the "illegal" immigrant population has consistently numbered in the millions, the range being from 1 to 12, and that it has generally grown from year to year. Here too there has been considerable attention placed on "illegal" immigrants from Mexico. The final element in this process of visibilization has to do with the way politicians and the mass media have taken up and couched the various enumerations of the "illegal" immigrant population. Their tendency has been to dramatize the numbers and associate "illegal" immigration with such terms as "out of control," "invasion," and "flood." Mexican immigrants and the US–Mexico border, not surprisingly, have once again figured prominently in the picture. At this other level, then, what has happened is that immigration experts, politicians, the mass media, and the INS have come together, although not necessarily wittingly, to visibilize "illegal" immigration as a massive phenomenon.

Body Counts

It is on this other, more important, level that I want to focus the rest of my remarks as regards practices of enumeration. Two time periods have been particularly important in the visibilization of "illegal" immigration, especially that from Mexico, as an event of considerable magnitude: the 1970s and the early to mid-1990s. Let us first consider the former. This period is significant because it witnessed the initial post-1965 problematization of "illegal" immigration as out of control.

Central to this incipient problematization were INS apprehension figures. These figures were important because they signaled that "illegal" immigration was a rapidly growing phenomenon (at least in terms of the number of aliens entering the country illicitly).[15] The 1970 *Annual Report* proves instructive here. Consider, for example, the following quote from the narrative section of the report:

> Service officers located 345,353 deportable aliens during the year, an increase of 61,769 or 22 percent over fiscal year 1969. An increase of 75,741 Mexican aliens located this year coupled with a decrease of 15,125 in the number of nonwillful crewman violators nearly compensates for this year's increase. Since the termination of the Mexican Agricultural Act [the Bracero Program] at the end of 1964, the number of illegal entries over the Mexican border continues to soar. This year's total is more than triple the 1965 figure. (US INS 1971: 11)

Now look at this related extract:

> Since the expiration of the Mexican Agriculture Act on December 31, 1964, the number of deportable aliens located has continued an upward climb. For the 6-year period, fiscal years 1965–70, 71 percent of the 1,251,466 total deportable aliens located were of Mexican nationality. Year by year, the annual percentage of this nationality group has risen, from 50 percent in 1965 to 80 percent this year. (11)

Finally, consider this next citation:

> Of the total deportable aliens located, 244,492 or 71 percent entered illegally at other than ports of inspection – 77,318 or 46 percent more than last year. . . . Ninety-eight percent of the surreptitious entries were by Mexican aliens. (12)

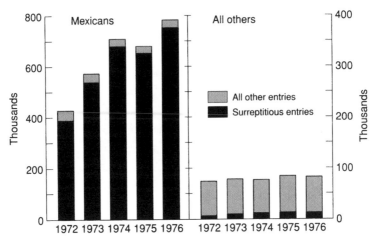

Deportable aliens found in the United States, 1972–1976

FIGURE 2.2   INS chart of deportable aliens found in the United States each year from 1972 through 1976.
Source: US INS 1978.

Revealed in these passages are at least three things. First of all, there is little doubt that apprehensions grew significantly, at least threefold, from 1965 to 1970.[16] Second, it is quite evident that a rise in Mexican apprehensions accounted for much of this growth. And third, it is clear that most apprehended aliens, above all Mexicans, entered the United States clandestinely. At the beginning of the 1970s, then, apprehension figures showed that "illegal" immigration was a growing "problem" – one primarily due to the increasing number of Mexican bodies crossing the US–Mexico border on the sly.

Moving ahead in the decade, we find that apprehension figures just kept on climbing. Consider, for instance, the 1976 *Annual Report* (US INS 1978). This report contains a chart that graphs the number of deportable aliens found in the United States each year from 1972 through 1976 (see Figure 2.2). The chart is split in two: one half focuses on "Mexicans," the other on "All others." For each grouping, we get details on the number of aliens apprehended during a given year, as well as on these aliens' status at entry (e.g., surreptitious). The chart indicates that overall apprehension figures continued to march upward, solidifying the trend begun in the mid-1960s. Moreover, it shows that the "problem" of illegal immigration became more decidedly a Mexican one: the number of Mexican apprehensions nearly doubled from 1972 to 1976 (beginning just above 400,000 and ending just below 800,000), while the figure for all other nationalities went up only slightly (remaining below 100,000 for the entire period). Finally, the chart reveals that surreptitious entry continued to grow as the primary way that apprehended aliens were entering the United States.

Significantly, the *Annual Report* also contains a narrative overview of the apprehension figures presented in the chart. This overview reinforces, augments, and dramatizes the visual data. Note the following quotes, for example:

> The steady increase of illegal entries continues to overrun Service defenses on the Mexican border which, coupled with the accompanying increase in other immigration violations, gave rise to an unprecedented volume of undocumented aliens. (US INS 1978: 13)

> After a brief decline in mid-year 1975, apprehension of deportable aliens resumed the rising trend evidenced in the previous decade. The location of 875,915 deportable aliens during fiscal year 1976 depicts an increase of 109,315 or 14 percent over 1975; 87,770 or 11 percent over the previous decade high in 1974; and well over 5 times the number located during fiscal year 1966. This year's increase was largely attributed to the location of 101,082 Mexican nationals by Service officers for a total of 781,474 deportable Mexican aliens – representing 89 percent of the total of all nationalities located. (13)

> During fiscal year 1975 [*sic*], Service officers apprehended more than three-quarters of a million deportable aliens surreptitiously entering the country between ports of entry. Of these, 769,271 or 99 percent came across the Mexican border; 3,431 over the Canadian border; and 758 by other routes. (13–14)

In the mid-1970s, then, apprehension figures indicated that "illegal" immigration continued to be a rapidly growing phenomenon. They also showed that the illicit movement of Mexican bodies across the southern border remained the primary source of the mounting "problem."

Central as well to the problematization of illegal immigration as an event of some magnitude were numerous expert counts of the stock and flow of illicit bodies. As apprehension figures mounted during the 1970s, a number of entities – demographers, researchers, the INS, and so forth – became concerned with getting a better handle on the scale of the "illegal" immigration problem. Arrest statistics had served well in signaling that the number of illegal "aliens" entering the United States was increasing, but they could not really be taken as gauges of magnitude. The drawback with these statistics was that they did not actually measure the size or flow of illegal immigration. They simply tallied the number of arrests in violation of immigration law. Put otherwise, apprehension data documented not the number of aliens who successfully dodged detection but the number who were caught. It was the former figure that one needed in order to determine the extent of the "problem."[17]

Taking the lead in gauging the magnitude – that is, stock and flow – of "illegal" immigration was the Immigration and Naturalization Service. This agency put forward a series of essentially speculative estimates during the 1970s.[18] In terms of stock, the earliest calculation came in 1972. Speaking before a Congressional committee, INS Commissioner Raymond Farrell (1972) testified that the total "illegal" immigrant population surpassed 1 million. This number would be upped significantly a few years later. In 1975, Farrell's successor, Leonard Chapman (1975a), noted that the unauthorized population added up to between 4 and 12 million. Subsequent INS counts would put the number of illegal bodies variously at 8.2 million (Lesko Associates 1976), 8 million (Chapman 1976a), 6 million (Chapman 1976b; Guss 1977), and 3 to 6 million (Castillo 1978). Notably, a number of the INS's total stock calculations contained subtotals on the "illegal" population of Mexican origin. Estimates of the size of this population included 5.2 million (Lesko Associates 1976), 6 million (Chapman 1976a), and 3 to 3.5 million (Chapman 1976b). As for the flow of "illegal" immigration, the estimates put forward, which were not as many as those of stock, ranged from 500,000 total entries per year (Chapman 1976a) to 0.97 million annual entries for Mexicans alone (Lesko Associates 1976).

Of all the INS numbers, perhaps the most important were those proposed by Commissioner Chapman. It is not so much the actual numbers that were significant, although they did matter, as the way they were presented. What Chapman did, first of all, was put these numbers forward in very public ways: through magazine articles, mass media interviews, public talks, testimonies before Congress, and so forth. And second, he made it very clear that, numerically, "illegal" immigrants constituted a grave problem. Consider, for example, the following quotes:

While scant attention has been paid to it, the problem [of illegal aliens] has grown rapidly to the point where it is now completely out of control. From 70,000 apprehensions of illegal aliens which the Immigration Service made in 1960, our arrests in the current fiscal year have grown to over 800,000. And, we know that we are apprehending only a small percentage of those who are here. (Chapman 1975a: 15)

The number of illegal aliens in the United States is, quite simply, alarming. . . . When I became commissioner of the Immigration and Naturalization Service (INS) in 1973, we were outmanned, under-budgeted, and confronted by a growing, silent invasion of illegal aliens. Despite our best efforts, the problem – critical then – now threatens to become a national disaster. (Chapman 1976a: 188–9)

The image that Chapman and the INS fostered for a good portion of the 1970s was thus that unauthorized immigration was very much out of control. It was that "illegal" immigrants were overrunning the country.

Soon after the INS started counting "illegal" bodies, other entities – demographers, statisticians, academics, the Mexican government – joined the effort. A primary factor motivating these entities, or at least a good percentage of them, was the conviction that the INS's numbers were highly speculative – often little more than guesses – and generally inaccurate (Siegel, Passel, and Robinson 1981; Briggs 1984). The idea was thus to put the counting of "illegal" immigrants on more solid analytical footing.[19] The estimates produced using analytically based procedures, which numbered no more than a handful during the 1970s, were generally lower than those of the INS. For instance, Clarice Lancaster and Frederick Scheuren (1978) calculated that there were a total of about 3.9 million "illegal" immigrants residing in the United States in 1973. This number was derived from matching the Census Bureau's Current Population Survey records for March 1973 with Internal Revenue Service individual earnings data and Social Security Administration benefit and income figures.[20] In terms of immigration from Mexico, to use another example, the Mexican government assessed that only about 500,000 to 1.2 million of its nationals were living clandestinely in the United States at the beginning of 1977 (García y Griego 1980). This estimate was obtained through comparing INS apprehensions data with the migration histories of persons whom US authorities had caught and returned to the Mexican border. And with respect to the flow of "illegal" immigrants, to employ a final illustration, David Heer (1979) determined that the range of annual clandestine immigration from Mexico between 1970 and 1975 was in the order of 80,000 to 220,000. This range was derived from measuring the excess growth of the Mexican-origin population as registered in the Current Population Survey. What analytically based estimates showed, then, was that the number of "illegal" immigrants residing in the United States, Mexican or otherwise, was probably not as high as the INS had been suggesting. In the long run, the impact of such analytical estimates would be significant. To begin with, they would help set standards as to what constituted good counting practices. These are standards that even the INS would follow. And second, they would be instrumental in eventually lowering the range of what were considered acceptable counts of "illegal" immigration. In the short term, however, the impact of these estimates was minimal. During the 1970s, the numbers that were generally taken as speaking the truth about "illegal" immigration were those that the INS put forward.

The final, and perhaps most important, element in the problematization of illegal immigration as a phenomenon of great magnitude was the mass media. Essentially, they took the various enumerations of unauthorized bodies and used them to construct a public image of "illegal" immigration as out of control. US News & World Report will serve as our prime example here.[21] During the late 1970s, this magazine devoted a good amount of rather sensationalist attention to the subject of illegal immigration.

Consider, for instance, its April 25, 1977 issue. The cover story was titled "Border Crisis: Illegal Aliens Out of Control?" Presumably, if one were to judge by the title, the out of controlness of illegal immigrants is being raised as a question here. The article, however, makes it abundantly clear that illegal immigration is indeed "out of control." One need only read the first few lines of the text to discern this:

> The problem of illegal immigrants in the US has reached the point where a massive search is on for new and dramatic ways to stem the tide.
>   Already, millions of aliens are in the country – no one knows how many, only that the number is mushrooming. Each year, up to a million persons who have no legal right to be here arrive and spread throughout the country. (Kelly 1977: 33)

This sense that illegal immigration is "out of control" is then reinforced through various statements made later on in the text:

Despite disagreements over the nature and the seriousness of illegal immigration, there is general agreement that it is a problem – and that it is going to get worse. (38)

The flow of illegal aliens to this country is now so large that whole sections of cities have been taken over. (39)

Notably, the article signals out the flow of unauthorized immigrants across the US–Mexico border as the primary source of the problem. Indeed, statements pointing to the particularly troublesome nature of the border abound (e.g., "the US has lost control of its borders," "the problems are most severe along the Mexican border," and "the most visible evidence of the sieve-like quality of the border is the way thousands of Mexicans and others cluster just across the line at dusk each day and then slip into this country after dark"). Perhaps more significant than these statements, however, are the photographs that accompany the text. Practically all are of the US–Mexico border. One photograph, for example, depicts several Border Patrol agents apprehending about a dozen undocumented immigrants. The caption reads: "Where US and Mexico meet, it is a constant battle between authorities and those who would enter illegally." Another picture shows a lone patrolman on watch at the border. He is peering through a night-vision device. Finally, a third image, this one adorning the cover of the magazine, depicts two Border Patrol officers standing beside a vehicle – one on each side, both facing forward. On their left is a chain-link fence with barbed wire on top. It is the boundary line separating Mexico from the United States. These agents too are keeping watch over the border. A low-flying surveillance plane visible in the background is aiding the effort. What the cover story highlights, then, is not just that "illegal" aliens are "out of control." More specifically, it underscores that the crisis of immigrant illegality is largely connected to the porous nature of the US–Mexico border.

Subsequent to this initial cover story, US News & World Report would publish two others during the 1970s focused on "illegal" immigration. These too would train their attention on Mexican immigrants and the US–Mexico border. One was titled "Time Bomb in Mexico: Why There'll Be No End to the Invasion by 'Illegals'" (Migdail 1977). This story essentially focused on how the magnitude of the "illegal" immigrant problem in the United States was destined to get worse. At issue was Mexico's mushrooming population and slow economic development. Mexico was simply producing and, for the foreseeable future, would continue to produce too many people and not enough jobs. An ever-increasing number of Mexicans would thus be forced to turn to the United States in search of livelihoods. Accompanying the story is a cover picture. Not surprisingly, this picture is of the US–Mexico border. It is an apprehension scene. A group of "apparently" Mexican men are standing in the dark amid light shrubbery. A powerful light is making them visible. Most are holding their hands up high or behind their heads. Noticeable in the background is a Border Patrol agent. The second cover story was titled "Illegal Aliens: Invasion Out of Control?" Like the initial feature story we discussed, the title of this one poses the crisis of illegal immigration as a question. Once again, however, the article makes it clear from the outset that "illegal" immigrants are indeed out of control. Just consider the following opening lines:

> The guardians of America's borders, handcuffed by policy disputes at home and diplomatic hazards abroad, are falling steadily behind in their struggle to close the door to thousands of illegal aliens sneaking into the US every day.
> Federal officials frankly admit that they are running out of acceptable options to stem a mounting flow of unregistered immigrants estimated to have reached 800,000 a year. New arrivals add daily to an existing population of noncitizens so shadowy that its numbers are pegged anywhere from 3 million to 12 million persons. (Powell 1979: 38)

Aiding in the construction of illegal immigration as an overwhelming phenomenon are a couple of visual devices. One device, as in the other cover stories, is the photograph. The photographs accompanying this article deal in the main with Mexican immigration. The cover picture, for example, depicts yet another apprehension scene. Here a Border Patrol agent is shown arresting three Mexican immigrants. The second device is the INS apprehensions chart. Reproduced in the text is a graph documenting annual apprehension figures from the late 1960s through the late 1970s. It shows that alien arrests have climbed rather steeply: from a little over 200,000 in 1968 to over a million in 1978. The accompanying description reads: "Upsurge in Arrests . . . But – Hundreds of thousands of other aliens sneak in successfully each year, say authorities. As many as 12 million illegals may be in the US today." Reinforced in this article, as well as in the previous one, is thus the idea that "illegal" immigration is very much out of hand – particularly when it comes to illicit crossings of the US–Mexico border. What happens during the 1970s, then, particularly toward the end of the decade, is that "illegal" immigration becomes visibilized as a phenomenon of enormous magnitude. To be more precise, what we get, as an effect of various enumerative practices, is the creation and consolidation of a general image of "illegal" immigrants as invasive and out of control. Significantly, this image would remain popular through the mid-1980s. It would then fade away somewhat in the late 1980s, only to reappear with a vengeance in the early to mid-1990s.

Post-IRCA Enumerations

The second important moment in the visibilization of "illegal" immigration as a phenomenon of vast magnitude takes place during the early to mid-1990s. This period is noteworthy because it witnessed a particularly intense problematization of "illegal" immigration as spinning out of control.

Central again to this problematization were INS apprehension figures. In the mid-1980s, the United States Congress enacted a landmark immigration law: the Immigration Reform and Control Act of 1986 (IRCA). This law had two main provisions: one was the legalization of certain immigrants already living in the country, the other the imposition of penalties on employers who knowingly hired illegal aliens. IRCA's primary objective was to reduce the flow of illegal immigration into the United States (Cornelius 1989; Bean, Edmonston, and Passel 1990). Early on, the new law seemed to have an effect on the movement of illicit bodies. According to INS statistics, the number of alien apprehensions dropped rather dramatically following IRCA's passage, from an all-time high of 1,767,400 in 1986 to 1,190,488 in 1987 and then to 954,243 in 1989.[22] The downward trend would not continue into the 1990s, however. Instructive here are the 1990 and 1993 *Statistical Yearbooks*. The former, for instance, showed not only that apprehension figures had stopped going down but, more importantly, that they had actually increased rather sharply in 1990 – rising to 1,169,939, an increase of almost 23 percent from the previous year. Notably, though, INS Commissioner Gene McMary tried to minimize the significance of the upsurge in arrests. In a cover letter introducing this *Statistical Yearbook*, he noted: "Apprehensions of deportable aliens also increased in 1990. However, the 1,170,000 aliens apprehended in 1990 are still less than two-thirds the apprehensions in 1986, and considerably below the level that could be expected without better controls on illegal immigration" (US INS 1991: 3). There still seemed to be some optimism here that IRCA was doing its job. This optimism would soon dwindle, however. Subsequent *Statistical Yearbooks* indicated that the halt in the downward trend in apprehensions was more than temporary. It actually amounted to an all-out reversal. The 1993 *Statistical Yearbook* (US INS 1994), for instance, showed that, after their sharp initial increase in 1990, apprehension numbers continued to rise, reaching 1,327,259 in 1993. These numbers did not quite match the record levels of the mid-1980s. But they did indicate that the movement of illicit bodies was again solidly on the upswing.[23] What statistics on apprehensions showed, then, was that while IRCA might have had an effect on the flow of "illegal" immigrants, this effect was at best only temporary. In the 1990s, "illegal" immigration would go back to being a growing phenomenon (at least in terms of apprehensions). Significantly, Mexicans continued to be signaled out as the primary source of the "illegal" immigrant problem.[24]

Solidifying the impression that, despite IRCA, "illegal" immigration remained a significant and growing phenomenon were various estimates of stock and flow. These estimates, unlike those put forth during the 1970s, tended to be largely analytical. They also tended to be the products of more sophisticated quantitative methodologies.[25] A key player in the enumeration of illegal bodies was once again the INS. In a 1994 paper, it issued estimates showing how the unauthorized immigrant populace had fared since the passage of IRCA (Warren 1994). The INS estimated that in early 1987, just prior to IRCA's legalization program, the total "illegal" alien population residing in the United States numbered nearly 5 million. Following legalization, this population would then experience a rather substantial drop in size: With more than 2.7 million people granted legal status, its numbers were reduced to about 2.2 million in October 1988. The downward turn would not be sustained, however. The INS estimated that the illegal immigrant population had subsequently gone back up in size: to 2.6 million in 1990 and then to 3.4 million in 1992. The average annual growth rate (or net flow) from 1988 to 1992 was pegged at 300,000. In terms of the Mexican-origin clandestine population, it is estimated to have gone from 2.9 million in 1987 to 827,000 in 1988 and then back up to about 1.3 million in 1992. These numbers signify that Mexicans went from accounting for well over 50 percent of the unauthorized population right before IRCA to making up only about 39 percent five years afterward.[26] Nevertheless, they were estimated to have remained by far the largest undocumented group.[27] Appreciably, the INS also highlighted that California was the preferred state of residence for "illegal" immigrants both before and after IRCA. In 1992, for example, there were an estimated 1.4 million people residing illegally in the state. This number corresponds to about 43 percent of the total undocumented population. Other key players in the enumeration of unauthorized immigrants included the US General Accounting Office (US GAO) and the Census Bureau. Their estimates were not significantly different from those of the INS. The US GAO (1993), for example, put the total number of "illegal" bodies at no more than 3.4 million for April 1990, the number of Mexicans at a maximum of 2.7 million for the same date, and the sum total of illicit entries (or gross inflow) at between 1.3 and 3.9 million for 1988. As for the Census Bureau, it gauged the number of "illegal" immigrants at 3.3 million for April 1990 and the annual rate of growth at 200,000 (Woodrow 1991). By all accounts, then, even with the passage of IRCA, the "illegal" immigrant population in the United States remained rather sizable. Moreover, it was again clear that this population was a growing one.

With IRCA apparently unable to stop the flow of illicit bodies, and in the context of a rather severe economic recession, the image of "illegal" immigration as out of control came to enjoy particularly widespread popularity in the early to mid-1990s, especially in California. Central in popularizing this image (through the mass media) were a variety of politicians and leaders of immigration reform organizations. Of the politicians, perhaps the most important figure was California Governor Pete Wilson (1991–9). During his tenure, the governor consistently put the problem of "illegal" immigration at the top of his political agenda. A noteworthy strategy he employed to call attention to this "problem" entailed likening the flow of "illegal" immigrants to an invasion. On September 22, 1994, for example, Governor Wilson filed a lawsuit against the federal government seeking to have California reimbursed for its expenditures on educating undocumented children. The suit was based on Article IV, Section 4, of the Constitution, which states: "The United States shall guarantee to every state in this union a republican form of government, and shall protect each of them against invasion" (Weintraub 1994: A3). The basic argument was that the presence of illegal immigrants in California was so mammoth and harmful that it amounted to nothing less than an invasion: "The massive and unlawful migration of foreign nationals . . . constitutes an invasion of the state of California against which the United States is obligated to protect California" (A3). Notably, Governor Wilson also liked to dramatize the "problem" of "illegal" immigration using the US–Mexico border as a prop. As part of his 1994 gubernatorial primary campaign, for instance, he ran a widely circulated, immigration-focused television commercial that prominently featured this southern boundary line. The ad opens with black and white footage of about a dozen (presumably Mexican) "undocumented" immigrants running between cars at the California–Mexico border in San Ysidro. Simultaneously, a voice intones: "They keep coming. Two million illegal immigrants in California. The federal government won't stop them at the border, yet requires us to pay billions to take care of them." Inscribed on the lower left-hand corner of the screen are the words "Border Crossing, Interstate 5, San Diego County." The message here is thus that the US–Mexico border is chaotic and out of control. It is that the problem of "illegal" immigration is very much linked to the sieve-like quality of the southern border.

This imagining of "illegal" immigration as out of hand reached its high point in the second half of 1994. The precipitating factor was California's Proposition 187 – a grassroots voter initiative, also known as "Save Our State," that proposed to bar undocumented immigrants from receiving access to public services such as education, welfare, and health care.[28] The proposition generated a great deal of public discussion and mass media documentation. Crucial voices here were the leaders of various immigration reform organizations that backed Proposition 187. Much like Governor Wilson, these leaders tended to liken the flow of clandestine bodies to an invasion or conquest. Moreover, they made it plain that the "illegal" immigrant problem was principally due to the unauthorized movement of people from Mexico. For example, Glenn Spencer, the head of a group called the Voice of Citizens, described illegal immigration as "part of a reconquest of the American Southwest by foreign Hispanics." He then added: "Someone is going to be leaving the state. It will either be them or us" (Martinez and McDonnell 1994: A36). Similarly, Ruth Coffey, a grassroots activist who ran Stop Immigration Now, commented that she had "no intention of being the object of 'conquest,' peaceful or otherwise, by Latinos, Asians, blacks, Arabs or any other group of individuals who [had] claimed [her] country" (A36). And finally, Linda Hayes, the Southern California media director for Proposition 187, noted:

> Proposition 187 is . . . a logical step toward saving California from economic ruin. . . . By flooding the state with 2 million illegal aliens to date, and increasing that figure each of the following 10 years, Mexicans in California would number 15 million to 20 million by 2004. During those 10 years about 5 million to 8 million Californians would have emigrated to other states. If these trends continued, a Mexico-controlled California could vote to establish Spanish as the sole language of California, 10 million more English-speaking Californians could flee, and there could be a statewide vote to leave the Union and annex California to Mexico. (1994: 18)

So clearly, not only did the leaders of immigration reform organizations construct the "problem" of undocumented immigrants as being rather sizable. They also conceptualized it as being a largely Mexican affair.

What takes place during the early to mid-1990s, then, is the renewed visibilization of illegal immigration as an event of considerable scale. More to the point, what we witness is particularly forceful imaginings of undocumented immigrants as invasive and overwhelming. Such imaginings would eventually subside later in the 1990s. But they have never quite gone away. In fact, as we will see, they have resurfaced in the post-9/11 context: with a twist.

SURVEYING ROUTINES

Having focused on one kind of numerical knowledge – enumerative – used to make up undocumented immigrants, I now want to turn to another: what I have called surveying. This type of knowledge has been instrumental in specifying the problematic nature of there being "large" numbers of unauthorized people residing in the United States. To be more precise, surveying routines have produced a host of statistical data regarding the effects of mass "illegal" immigration on various domains of US social and economic life. Two domains have received particular attention: the labor market and public services. With respect to the former, the concern has been that "illegal" immigrants displace native workers and depress wages; while in terms of the latter, the worry has been that the undocumented produce a substantial drain on programs such as welfare, food stamps, hospital care, and public education. What various data sources have suggested (not unproblematically) is that, in some ways, "illegal" immigrants have had an adverse impact on the labor market and put a strain on public services.[29] During the 1970s, for example, the general tendency in the policy research community was to argue that "illegal" immigrants competed with and displaced low-wage native workers in the secondary labor market. And in the 1990s, the tendency was to suggest that the undocumented were generally a net cost to society, using more in public resources than they contributed in taxes. Perhaps more significant than the actual data, however, has been how actors at the popular level – politicians, INS officials, and immigration reform organizations – have taken it up and framed it. Their inclination has been to dramatize the figures and portray "illegal" immigrants as people who take jobs away from Americans and abuse precious social services. The popular image regularly constructed of "illegal" immigration has thus been as insecurities that threaten the well-being of the social body. Given the importance of surveying practices in the making up of "illegal" immigrants, what I would like to do in this section is delve into the specifics of their workings. We will begin with a look at how the effect of "illegal" immigration on the labor market has been problematized.

They Take Our Jobs

The labor market impact of "illegal" immigrants has been a constant governmental concern in the post-1965 period. However, its principal problematization took place during the mid-1970s to mid-1980s. Indeed, this time period was privy to a particularly keen focus on the relation between the undocumented and the labor market. Other "illegal" immigration impact issues, while important, were generally secondary concerns (e.g., public service use).[30] Crucial in producing knowledge about the effects of undocumented immigrants on the labor market were a variety of entities: independent researchers, the US General Accounting Office (US GAO), the public, and a host of government committees and commissions. The knowledge these entities produced was of at least three kinds. One kind was empirical research. Encompassed here are various empirical studies dealing, on some level, with the role of "illegal" immigrants in the labor market. The second type consisted of review and analysis. Covered here are numerous government reports assessing the general impact of undocumented immigration on the United States. This assessing was generally based on available empirical evidence. Finally, the third type consisted of public interpretation and dissemination. Included here are countless magazine articles, political speeches, pamphlets, and so forth that circulated popular understandings apropos the labor market effects of the undocumented. The conclusion these knowledges generally came to was that, in certain ways, undocumented immigrants had a harmful impact on the labor market. Let us first consider the empirically based knowledges.

During the mid-1970s through the middle of the 1980s, the undocumented immigration research industry was very much in its infancy stage. The empirical research produced at this time on the relationship between "illegal" immigrants and the labor market was thus on the whole rather scant. It also tended to be somewhat on the speculative side. Most studies focused on particular population samples – undocumented aliens in specific industries, persons at the border, INS apprehendees – and then made generalizations about the characteristics and impact of the undocumented community as a whole.[31] This empirical research was nevertheless often taken as speaking general truths about "illegal" immigration. The most influential study of the labor market impact of undocumented immigrants was published in 1976 under the auspices of the Department of Labor. It was titled *The Characteristics and Role of Illegal Aliens in the US Labor Market: An Exploratory Study*. Its authors were David North and Marion Houstoun, two independent researchers. Like most studies, this one did not actually measure or quantify the effect of "illegal" immigrants on the labor market. Rather, it gathered information on the work history of a small sample of undocumented persons and then made inferences about the labor market impact of the entire clandestine population.

The sample consisted of 793 apprehended "illegal" immigrants who had worked for at least two weeks in the United States before being seized by the INS. Of this total, 481 were from Mexico, 237 from other Western Hemisphere nations, and 75 from the Eastern Hemisphere. The study found that these "illegal" immigrants had generally been employed in the secondary labor market: that is, in low-wage, low-status jobs. Half, for example, had most recently worked in unskilled occupations, as services workers or as laborers (both farm and non-farm), while another 30 percent had done semi-skilled work, principally as operatives (North and Houstoun 1976: 109). The study further found that the immigrants in its sample earned considerably less than comparably employed US workers – while the latter earned an average of $4.47 an hour, the hourly wage of the former only averaged $2.66 (124) – and that their average hourly pay varied radically according to the area of US employment (the lowest being the Southwest at $1.98) and region of origin (the least remunerated group being Mexicans at $2.34) (115). Based on these and other figures, as well as on the data of other researchers, North and Houstoun concluded that illegal immigrants were probably clustered in the secondary labor market and appeared "to increase the supply of low-wage labor and compete with disadvantaged US workers" (153). The logic they used was the following:

If most illegal workers in the US are disadvantaged persons employed in low-level jobs, illegals are of course increasing, to an undetermined degree, the supply of low-wage workers in the nation. It follows, then, that the subgroups of the US labor force with which illegals are most likely to be competing are disadvantaged US workers: the young, the old, members of minority groups, women, immigrants, and the handicapped, who, in some instances, tend to be clustered in the same parts of the nation, e.g., the Spanish-speaking in the Southwest, and minority groups generally and immigrants in major urban centers. (153–4)

Other studies of the period by and large corroborated North and Houstoun's conclusions regarding the likelihood that "illegal" immigrants had some negative impact on the labor market. The US GAO, for example, calculated that the number of jobs the undocumented took away from legal workers in 1976 probably ranged from 0 to 3.9 million (1980: 63). And Walter Fogel (1979), a UCLA economist, determined that the low incomes of South Texas were primarily due to the availability of large supplies of Mexican unskilled (and often illegal) labor.[32]

Bolstering the idea that illegal immigrants presented a problem with respect to the US labor market were a number of government committee and commission reports. A major aim of these reports was to assess the impact of illicit immigration on the United States, including labor market impact. The most significant report was undoubtedly the US Select Commission on Immigration and Refugee Policy's *US Immigration Policy and the National Interest* (1981).[33] The analyses and recommendations found there formed the basis of the Immigration Reform and Control Act of 1986. The report's examination of the labor market impact of the undocumented focused on two issues: job displacement and wage depression. With respect to each issue, the examination entailed surveying the existing empirical research and the testimony of experts. The report showed that in both cases there was conflicting evidence about the impact of illegal immigration. Regarding job displacement, for example, it noted the following:

> On one end are those who believe that undocumented/illegal workers take jobs that would otherwise go to US workers. Some argue that competition from cheap labor tends to depress sectors of the economy and make some otherwise desirable jobs undesirable. It is also suggested that undocumented aliens, especially in border areas, compete for jobs

with economically disadvantaged minorities. On the other end of the continuum are those who believe that undocumented/illegal workers take jobs that US workers do not want and will not take. Some also suggest that undocumented aliens, by taking undesirable jobs, maintain industries that would otherwise move outside of this country for labor. (US Select Commission 1981: 39–40)

And concerning wage depression, the report stated:

According to some experts, the differential in wages between the home countries of most undocumented/illegal aliens and the United States make these aliens less concerned than citizens about the actual level of their US wages. The potential threat of apprehension and deportation, they argue, may also make undocumented/illegal workers more willing to work for lower wages. Other analysts question this theory. They argue that there is little evidence to indicate that undocumented/illegal aliens have any overall effect on US wages and salaries. Some economists even argue that the wages of skilled US workers will rise as a consequence of an increase in the relative number of unskilled, undocumented/illegal aliens who are working in this country. (40–1)

Despite the contradictory evidence, however, the report reached a definite conclusion about the impact of "illegal" immigrants on the labor market. It determined that "the continuing flow of undocumented workers across US borders has certainly contributed to the displacement of some US workers and the depression of some US wages" (41).[34] Significantly, other government reports generally concurred with the Select Commission's verdict. For example, a report prepared for the Committee on the Judiciary of the US House of Representatives noted: "The available evidence suggests that illegal aliens compete successfully with US workers in the secondary labor market and that they tend to adversely affect the wages and working conditions in occupations where they are present in considerable numbers, most notably in the Southwest" (Congressional Research Service 1977: 14). And a preliminary report from the Domestic Council Committee on Illegal Aliens, a group established to undertake a comprehensive review of undocumented immigration and its implications, concluded: "To the extent that illegal aliens are predominantly lower skilled workers, their presence tends to lower the wages and working conditions of US workers in low skilled jobs" (1976: 185).

A final element in the problematization of "illegal" immigrants as in certain ways harmful to the labor market was a host of public actors – politicians, INS officials, and so forth. Their tendency, as I noted above, was to sensationalize the whole matter. An important figure here was INS Commissioner Leonard Chapman. As with the case of magnitude, Chapman repeatedly drew public attention to the labor market effects of "illegal" immigration. In a 1976 *Reader's Digest* article, for example, he blamed the undocumented for massively displacing American workers:

> There was a time when our country could absorb these immigrants. No longer. Today, 40 percent of our black teen-agers are unable to find employment. Frustrated, hostile, many turn to crime. In border states such as Texas, California, Arizona and New Mexico, unemployment among unskilled field hands reaches as high as 25 percent.
> It is in these hard-pressed labor markets that illegal aliens make the greatest impact. Often they work for wages that are a third lower than those offered US citizens. Thus, of the 190,000 illegal aliens we found in our southwest region last year, 134,000 – 70 percent – were earning less than $2.50 an hour. And for every one of them, an American or legal resident remained out of work. In fact, if we could locate and deport the three to four million illegals who currently hold jobs in the United States, replacing them with citizens and legal residents, we could reduce our own unemployment dramatically – *as much as 50 percent*. (Chapman 1976a: 189–90)

What's more, in a 1975 *Immigration and Naturalization Reporter* piece, Chapman argued that the displacement of native workers severely hurt the economy: "Our largest city, New York, has one million people on welfare, and that will grow by another quarter of a million this year to some 15 percent of the city's population. One million dollars per hour is being doled out in the form of relief checks in that city. I believe it is imperative that we find and implement ways to halt the illegal flow of persons into the United States and the drain they cause upon our economy" (1975a: 17–18). The implication here is that, if it were not for illegal immigrants, there would not be so many people on welfare sapping the economy. Other important voices in the problematization of "illegal" immigrants as detriments to the labor market were Ray Marshall, Secretary of Labor under President Jimmy Carter (1977–81), and Richard Lamm, then governor of Colorado (1975–87). Much like

Chapman, these two figures repeatedly blamed illegal immigrants, at least in part, for America's unemployment problems. In a *US News & World Report* article, for instance, Marshall is noted as stating that more effective immigration controls could cut the jobless rate in half (Chaze 1982: 48). And, in an *Atlantic Monthly* piece, Lamm is quoted as saying: "the unemployed . . . will never get jobs as long as we continue to take in twice as many immigrants as the rest of the world combined" (Fallows 1983: 48).

All told, then, we find that during the mid-1970s to the mid-1980s "illegal" immigrants become perceived as having a generally negative impact on the labor market. To be more specific, what we get, as an effect of various survey practices, is the association of "illegal" immigration with job displacement and wage depression, particularly in relation to the secondary labor market. Moreover, we also witness the construction of undocumented immigrants as insecurities that threaten the economic welfare of the nation.

Sponging Off the American People

As with the case of labor market impact, the public service use of "illegal" immigrants has been an issue all through the post-1965 period. Its main problematization, though, occurred during the 1990s. Indeed, this was a period in which the impact of undocumented immigration on social benefits was of particular concern to researchers, politicians, and the public. In fact, it was their main preoccupation then. The entities involved in creating knowledge about this issue were several. The list includes independent researchers, policy research organizations, the GAO, the public, and various state and local governmental bodies. The knowledge forms these entities produced added up to at least three: empirical research, governmental reviews, and public interpretation. These were the very same forms created in the case of labor market impact. Significantly, these knowledges generally focused on two issues. One issue was the general cost of providing public services to "illegal" immigrants. The concern here was that the undocumented as a whole were adversely affecting the social and economic welfare of the United States. The second issue was the cost associated with providing public services just to "undocumented" women and their children ("illegal" or otherwise). The worry here was that the reproductive practices (both social and biological) of "illegal" immigrants were particularly taxing on US coffers. The conclusion these knowledges generally reached was that, in monetary terms, undocumented immigrants received more from society (in the form of public services) than they gave in return (in the form of taxes), and that their reproductive practices were indeed especially burdensome. Let us first consider how the empirical and review-type knowledges (with an emphasis on the former) constructed these issues.

Calculations of the general costs associated with "illegal" immigration occurred on three scales of analysis: the national, the state, and the local. With respect to the national scale, there were three important studies produced during the early to mid-1990s (see US GAO 1995a). First, there was Donald Huddle's *The Costs of Immigration* (1993). The Urban Institute – a non-partisan, non-profit, policy research organization – then followed with a reassessment of Huddle's work, *How Much Do Immigrants Really Cost? A Reappraisal of Huddle's "The Cost of Immigrants"* (Passel and Clark 1994). Finally, Huddle produced an updated study called *The Net National Cost of Immigration in 1993* (1994). These studies all concentrated on measuring the national net cost of "illegal" immigrants: that is, the costs they generated, minus the revenues they produced. In each case, the net cost estimate was obtained from measuring three principal components. First, there were the direct expenditures. These were the costs generated as a result of providing public benefits and services to the undocumented. Included here were such government programs as primary and secondary education, school lunches, Head Start, Medicaid, the Special Supplemental Food Program for Women, Infants, and Children (WIC), and housing assistance.[35] Second, there were the displacement outlays. These were the costs incurred from providing public assistance to US workers whom "illegal" immigrants had displaced. Finally, there were the public revenues that the undocumented generated. Included here were a variety of federal, state, and local taxes: income tax, Social Security tax, unemployment insurance tax, and gas, sales, and property taxes. The conclusion reached in the three studies was that undocumented immigrants were a net fiscal burden on the United States. Huddle's updated study, to begin with, calculated the net cost of "illegal" immigrants at $19.3 billion for 1993. This was the highest estimate. Next came the initial Huddle study with a 1992 estimate of $11.1 billion. And last was the Urban Institute's report with a net expenditure total of $1.9 billion for

1992. The discrepancy in the estimates, which was considerable, can be attributed in large part to differing assumptions as to what counts when measuring costs and revenues. Both Huddle studies, for example, calculated the costs of displacement at $4.3 billion. The Urban Institute report, in contrast, came up with a figure of $0. The difference here was that the latter took into account the positive economic effects of illegal immigration (e.g., the new jobs and extra spending the undocumented generated through consuming goods and services), determining that these sufficiently offset any job displacement expenditures. One further illustration: the updated Huddle study included monies ($4.6 billion) spent on educating the citizen children of illegal immigrants as a cost, while the other two did not. These expenditures were taken into consideration, according to Huddle, because they were part of the overall fiscal impact connected with undocumented immigration. To be sure, these children were not illegal. But they would not have been in the country using public resources if their parents had been prevented from crossing the border illegally. Regardless of the wide variation in estimates, though, the fact remained that all three studies calculated that "illegal" immigrants generated more in costs than they produced in revenues.[36] Indeed, despite quibbles over actual amounts, there was considerable agreement among researchers that, at the national level, the undocumented were generally a net cost.

With respect to the state and local scales, there were also a number of important studies produced during the 1990s. These studies, not surprisingly, focused primarily on California and some of its localities (e.g., Los Angeles and San Diego Counties). California was the site with the largest undocumented population in the country and thus where the fiscal impact of "illegal" immigration, if any, was likely to be the greatest. At the state level, the most influential study came from the California Governor's Office. It was titled *Shifting the Costs of a Failed Federal Policy: The Net Fiscal Impact of Illegal Immigrants in California* (Romero and Chang 1994). The study unequivocally concluded that illegal immigrants posed a tremendous burden on California taxpayers:

> Even after the taxes they pay are considered, illegal immigrants will cost State taxpayers at least $2.7 billion in FY 1994–95. The taxes raised by 800,000 jobs – one out of every fifteen in California – are needed to raise the taxes to offset the costs of federally mandated health care, education and incarceration for the 1.7 million illegal immigrant

residents. Moreover, these estimates specifically exclude significant costs associated with illegal immigration and definitively represent a low-bound cost estimate. The actual costs to California taxpayers are almost certainly higher – perhaps significantly higher. (Romero and Chang 1994: 19)

Put otherwise, the report reckoned that the net cost of "illegal" immigrants to the state was rather considerable. The undocumented might have made significant tax contributions. But these did not come close to covering the price tag of the public services they consumed.[37] At the local level, meanwhile, there were at least two significant studies, one focused on the Los Angeles area, the other on San Diego County. The former study, titled *Impact of Undocumented Persons and Other Immigrants on Costs, Revenues, and Services in Los Angeles County* (LA County Internal Services Department 1992), was prepared for the LA County Board of Supervisors.[38] Its main goal was to determine the immigration-related costs borne by the County of Los Angeles.[39] A major conclusion reached in the report was that "illegal" immigrants generally took more from the county than they gave in return. For FY 1991–92, as a case in point, it was calculated that LA County spent an estimated $308 million in public services for the undocumented but received approximately only $36 million in taxes from them. The net county cost of illegal immigrants that fiscal year was thus $272 million. Most of the money was spent on health care and criminal justice services. As for the San Diego study, titled *Illegal Immigration in San Diego County: An Analysis of Costs and Revenues* (1993), it was prepared for the California State Senate Special Committee on Border Issues. Its main goal was "to estimate the net annual fiscal impact upon State and local governments in San Diego County of providing public services to undocumented immigrants who are present in the County either permanently or temporarily" (Parker and Rea 1993: ii). Like the LA study, this one concluded that "illegal" immigrants were unquestionably a fiscal burden: the net state and local government cost of providing them with public services in the San Diego area was estimated to be $244 million for FY 1992–93. The main services that the undocumented made use of were criminal justice, public health, education, and welfare. As with the case of national studies, then, local- and state-scale investigations generally calculated that "illegal" immigrants were net costs. Indeed, the general conclusion was that the undocumented were economic burdens not just on a national scale but also on more localized levels.

Besides being preoccupied with measuring the general costs of "illegal" immigration, researchers and policy analysts were concerned about calculating the more specific expense of providing public services to undocumented women and their children, whether legal or illegal. The general belief seemed to be that the costs associated with the biological and social reproduction of the immigrant family were particularly burdensome on US taxpayers. Biological reproduction here refers simply to the process of bearing children. Public costs incurred in relation to this process were principally for health care (e.g., childbirth services and prenatal care). Social reproduction, on the other hand, refers to the practice of raising, educating, and caring for children. Expenses contracted as a result of this practice were largely for public education, health care (e.g., Medicaid), and social services (e.g., Temporary Assistance for Needy Families [TANF], formerly Aid to Families with Dependent Children [AFDC]). That measuring the price tag of reproduction was a concern is already somewhat clear from the general cost studies discussed above. They all, on some level, dealt with reproduction-related expenditures. For example, the LA County Board of Supervisors' report measured the cost of providing public education to undocumented children; the two Huddle national studies estimated the expense of making AFDC available to "illegal" immigrant families; and the report to the State Senate Special Committee on Border Issues calculated the cost of delivering health services to undocumented women and their children. This concern over reproduction becomes clearer still if we look at more narrowly focused cost studies. Indeed, there were a number that concentrated specifically on reproductive issues. Take, for instance, a 1997 US GAO report titled *Illegal Aliens: Extent of Welfare Benefits Received on Behalf of US Citizen Children*. Its main purpose, as the title indicates, was to determine the cost of providing public benefits – such as AFDC and Food Stamps – to illegal immigrant parents for the care of their citizen children.[40] The report summarized its results as follows:

In fiscal year 1995, about $1.1 billion in AFDC and Food Stamp benefits were provided to households with an illegal alien parent for the use of his or her citizen child. This amount accounted for about 3 percent of AFDC and 2 percent of food stamp benefit costs. A vast majority of the households receiving these benefits resided in a few states – 85 percent of the AFDC households were in California, New

York, Texas, and Arizona; 81 percent of food stamp households were in California Texas, and Arizona. California households alone accounted for $720 million of the combined AFDC and Food Stamp benefit costs, with such households representing about 10 percent of the state's AFDC and Food Stamp caseloads. (US GAO 1997a: 3)

Now take another 1997 US GAO report, this one titled *Undocumented Aliens: Medicaid-Funded Births in California and Texas* (1997b).[41] The concern of this report was not actually to measure costs. Rather, it was simply to determine the number of publicly funded births to "illegal" immigrant mothers. The implication, though, was that the outlay might be substantial. For 1995, to give an illustration, the number of Medicaid-financed births to undocumented women was estimated to be close to 25,000 in Texas and over 78,000 in California. In the latter state, these births represented 14 percent of all deliveries and 34 percent of Medicaid-funded ones. As far as these last two reports go, then, the expenses associated with the provision of public services to undocumented women and their children were quite considerable, especially in California. The overall indication of cost studies was thus that the reproductive practices of the undocumented were on the face of it taxing.

Significantly, the research and policy concern over the costs of providing public services to "illegal" immigrants, both generally and with respect to women and children, translated with a bang into the public arena. The popular mood during most of the 1990s was such, in fact, that the undocumented were widely blamed for abusing public resources and bankrupting local and state governments. Nowhere was this atmosphere more in evidence than in the state of California. And in no phenomenon was it better instantiated than in Proposition 187. This Proposition, as I noted earlier, was a grassroots voter initiative that sought to prohibit "illegal" immigrants from accessing public services. Its basic premise, as stated in a voter pamphlet, was that "the people of California [had] suffered for too long from the impact of illegal immigration, specifically in the areas of crime and from the costs of health, education, and welfare for illegal aliens" (Save Our State 1994a). The general idea here was that, as a result of having to spend large quantities of money (calculated at $5 billion) on the undocumented, California did not have enough funds to adequately care for its own population (i.e., citizens and legal residents). With respect to social services, for example, another pamphlet noted the following:

Every time an illegal alien takes something out of the system, through whatever program, it means there is less money available for a citizen who is legally entitled to that service. As a result, allocations for the elderly and needy are being cut back. For example, food stamp allocations are being reduced. How can it be explained to American citizens that there isn't enough money to help feed their families because it has gone to people who are here illegally? (Save Our State 1994b)

And as regards publicly funded health care, it stated:

Public health care in California is in crisis. The costs are spiraling out of control. Too much of it is due to free health care given to illegal aliens. They have learned how to take advantage of our system. For example, in the year 1988–89, 23,000 illegals received free health care at a cost of almost $5 Million. By the year 1992–93, these figures exploded to 322,000 illegals receiving care at a cost of nearly $900,000 Million (increases of 1,200% and 1,800% respectively). The consequences of this are cut-backs in services for everyone else. (1994b)

Notably, the many Californians who supported the Proposition – politicians, immigration reform activists, and lay people – would avidly echo and bolster these claims. For instance, Dennis Walker, a resident of Orange County, made the following statement in a local paper opinion piece: "Squandering our scarce tax dollars to fund illegal aliens and their offspring has brought our state and country to the verge of bankruptcy" (1994: Metro 9). And Anthony Coulson, another Orange County resident, expressed his outlook as follows: "The argument that [illegal immigrants] are a problem is based on the fact that federal laws, state laws, and judicial decisions have forced our welfare, education, and health-care system into crisis for the last seven to 10 years in order to pay their bills" (1994: Commentary 5). The public image that Proposition 187 and its supporters thus created of "illegal" immigrants was as a mass bent on exploiting California's public services; it was of the undocumented as tremendous burdens on the state.

Importantly, while this public image covered all "illegal" immigrants, it was also clear that the primary burdens were perceived to be undocumented women and their children. Indeed, it was they, rather than immigrant men, who were imagined as the principal abusers of California's health care, education, and welfare services. Consider, for instance, the statements of the Federation for American Immigration

Reform (FAIR), one of the most influential immigration reform groups in the country. With respect to health care, for instance, it had the following to say about the undocumented:

Health care costs in California have continued to soar as people flood the state to take advantage of Medi-Cal. It is estimated that the state paid $1 billion in emergency and pregnancy-related services for undocumented aliens in 1993. This figure is up almost 43 percent from the $700 million paid in 1992. (FAIR 2001)

In 1994, California paid for 74,987 deliveries to illegal alien mothers, at a total cost of $215.2 million (an average of $2,842 per delivery). Illegal alien mothers accounted for 36 percent of all Medi-Cal funded births in California that year. (FAIR 1997)

The focus here is obviously on undocumented women and their children (both legal and illegal). FAIR unmistakably considered the expense of providing them with public services to be rather exorbitant. Now consider the following newspaper titles: "Births to Illegal Immigrants on the Rise: California Taxpayers Finance Soaring Number of Foreigners' Babies" (Dalton 1994); "Medi-Cal Fraud Cases Soaring Here: State Probers Blame Mexicans Seeking Free Care" (Duerksen 1990); and "Blockade at Border Hasn't Cut Births" (Cleeland 1994). The spotlight here was again on undocumented women and their children. They were singled out as being particularly burdensome on the United States. Besides creating a general public image of "illegal" immigrants as exploitative, then, popular knowledges also fashioned a specific picture of undocumented women as welfare mothers. Indeed, they, as reproducers, were seen as specially prone to being public charges.

During the 1990s, then, particularly toward the middle part of the decade, "illegal" immigrants come to be largely perceived as having a negative impact on public services and, more generally, on the well-being of the nation. The general image that thus gets produced of the undocumented is as drains on the economy. Indeed, they are imagined as rather parasitic, with undocumented women and their children deemed particularly so.

ETHICAL TERRITORIES
OF EXCLUSION

So far we have explored how, through numerical technologies, "illegal" immigration has been constituted as a problematic dimension of experience. To be more specific, we have noted how, on the one hand, enumerative practices have made "illegal" immigration visible both categorically and as a phenomenon of vast magnitude; and, on the other, how survey procedures have constructed the undocumented as having a negative impact on the labor market, public services, and just generally on the social and economic well-being of the nation. Now I would like to suggest that this post-1965 problematization of "illegal" immigration has largely taken place in ethical terms – that the "problem" of "illegal" immigration, that is, has on the whole been rendered understandable as an ethical one. Ethical here, of course, refers to how persons comport themselves and comprehend their existence. The basic argument I will make is that "illegal" immigrants have by and large been cast into an ethical territory of exclusion, viewed as having failed to comport themselves ethically. It is that they have generally been constructed as imprudent subjects, as anti-citizens incapable of exercising responsible self-management, unable or unwilling to enterprise their lives or manage their own risks.

The clearest indication that "illegal" immigrants have been constructed as unethical comes from the widespread tendency to cast them as lawbreakers. Indeed, the propensity has been to characterize them as criminals. Their criminality is generally attributed to the simple fact that they have no legal right to be in the United States. Telling signs that "illegal" immigrants have been marked as delinquents are the various definitions and labels that have been attached to them. These have generally highlighted their illegality: the fact that they exist in the shadow of the law. A basic government definition of unauthorized persons, for example, generally goes something like this: "An illegal alien is a person who is in the United States in violation of US immigration laws" (US GAO 1995a: 1). As for the labels used to refer to them, while these have been many, the most commonly used in the post-1965 period contain the adjective "illegal" (e.g., illegal alien and illegal immigrant) (Nevins 2002).[42] The choice of adjective, of course, is rather purposeful. We can see this purposefulness in statements such as the following from UCLA economist Walter Fogel: "I shall use the term 'illegal alien' rather than 'undocumented workers,' the designation preferred by some. . . . The former term . . . more accurately conveys the fact that these aliens are violating US immigration laws" (1977: 243). Other telling, and possibly more forceful, signs that the undocumented have been cast as lawbreakers are scores of policy and mass media statements that have explicitly dubbed illegal immigration a criminal phenomenon. Here are some cases in point:

Illegal aliens are of concern to law enforcement officials, urban planners, and policymakers, first, because they are lawbreakers. (US GAO 1993: 10)

The effect illegal immigration has on the economy is irrelevant. Whether illegal immigration stimulates or burdens economic growth is of no importance to the residual fact that the law is being broken. Illegal immigration is illegal. Period. (Olson 1994: Commentary 5)

One of the most common and devastating crimes committed in America is committed by people who are not even American citizens. To many, it is not even considered a crime, even though its name, illegal immigration, makes it clear that it is. . . . People who enter or stay in this country illegally are criminals by definition. (Coleman 1994: B11)

From the perspective of numerous commentators, then, as well as definitionally, "illegal" immigrants are always already in violation of the law. They lack respect for order and authority. They are inherently criminals. To be "illegal" is thus to be fundamentally an improper subject. It is to have failed to conduct oneself ethically. It is to exist outside the circuits of civility and responsible self-management.

The criminality of the "illegal" immigrant is seen to represent a problem for at least two reasons. The first problem, of course, is that to the extent that the undocumented are by definition criminals, they can never live up to the obligations of responsible citizenship. They cannot possibly meet the ethical duties required to be respectable subjects. "Illegal" immigrants are thus in essence anti-citizens. They constitute an undeserving class: a community of anti-civility that contravenes the post-social norms of proper conduct. The second problem has to do with the insidious effect that the undocumented are believed to have on the rule of law. The conviction is that "illegal" immigration generally erodes respect for authority – that the toleration of lawlessness undermines consideration for law and order (Nevins 2002: 141). This conviction was perhaps best articulated in the US Select Commission on Immigration and Refugee Policy final report. The report stated:

> There is evidence that shows that the toleration of large-scale undocumented/illegal immigration can have pernicious effects on US society. . . . Most serious is the fact that illegality breeds illegality. The presence of a substantial number of undocumented/illegal aliens in the United States has resulted not only in a disregard for immigration law but in the breaking of minimum wage and occupational safety laws, and statutes against smuggling as well. As long as undocumented migration flouts US immigration law, its most devastating impact may be the disregard it breeds for other US laws. (1981: 41–2)

There have also been similar articulations on the popular level. For example, Richard D. Lamm and Gary Imhoff, in their popular book *The Immigration Time Bomb: The Fragmenting of America* (1985), noted that "illegal" immigration encourages other crimes:

> Illegal immigration is surrounded by many other crimes, which it encourages by the very nature of its secretiveness. The border gangs that prey upon illegal border crossers, that rob, rape, terrorize, beat, and even kill them, are paralleled by the pimps and thieves who prey upon prostitutes. In both cases, the reluctance of those who are outside the law to call upon law enforcement agencies makes them easy game for more vicious criminals. (1985: 54–5)

Not only do the undocumented conduct themselves unethically, then, they also compel others to follow suit. As such, they are seen to represent a danger to the social body. Their disregard for the rule of law, indeed, is understood to pose a threat to the general welfare of the population.

A second clear indication that the undocumented have been constructed as unethical comes from the penchant for identifying them as job takers. Indeed, "illegal" immigrants have often been portrayed as taking jobs away from Americans. Just consider the following citations:

> On one end are those who believe that undocumented/illegal workers *take jobs* that would otherwise go to US workers. (US Select Commission 1981: 39, emphasis added)

> In better times, the alien wave probably wouldn't be considered much more than a nuisance. But with 8 million or more Americans out of work and the nation recovering from its worst recession in 40 years, the strain illegal aliens place on the economy is becoming increasingly noticeable. Illegal workers not only *take jobs away from Americans* but their participation in government programs including food stamps, welfare and Medicaid . . . costs taxpayers at least $13 billion a year. (Mayer 1976: 56, emphasis added)

> Yet there is evidence that illegal aliens are *taking at least some jobs away from Americans* because of their willingness to work for less money. . . . The INS figures that in 1975, 1 million jobs that were held by illegals could have been switched to Americans. . . . That would be enough today to reduce the unemployment rate from 7.3 percent to 6.3 percent. (*Time* 1977: 30, emphasis added)

Such problematization, I would suggest, is absolutely an ethical one. Any number of ways could have been used to talk about the insertion of undocumented immigrants in the US labor market. But the preference has been to use the language of displacement: job taking, job stealing, and so forth. And this is very much an ethical language. Undocumented immigrants have essentially been viewed as taking jobs that do not rightly belong to them and in the process hurting American workers. They are thus not seen as proper ethical subjects. A proper ethical subject is one who adheres to core values of honesty and integrity and does not seize things that belong to others. For many, then, undocumented immigrants are plainly anti-citizens who have failed to conduct themselves ethically and manage their lives responsibly.

A final indication that undocumented immigrants have been constructed as unethical comes from the general tendency to characterize them as public burdens. Indeed, the undocumented have by and large been labeled as drains on society. They have been seen as bent on sponging off the American people. The issue here, as with the public service use of the "American" poor, is one of dependency. The term "dependency," as I noted in Part One, has two important (and inter-related) registers, one economic, the other ethical. From an economic standpoint, "dependency" merely points to how the undocumented have putatively come to rely on the state for their well-being: Whether it is health care, social services, or education, "illegal" immigrants are said to take advantage of public resources. The cost of this abuse is seen to be borne, of course, by tax-paying citizens. From an ethical stand-point, "dependency" refers to how, in relying on the state for their well-being, the undocumented have demonstrated that they lack self-discipline and the competence to function as responsible subjects. A responsible subject is one whose security is guaranteed not through the procurement of public largesse but via active self-promotion. She is one who adopts a calculative and prudent disposition toward risk and takes upon herself primary responsibility for managing her welfare and that of her family. As public burdens, then, the undocumented have been perceived as constituting a class of economically and ethically suspect persons. They have been identified as making up an underclass of dependent subjects who lack moral character and are unwilling or unable to be self-sufficient and take responsibility for their own care. The archetype of this underclass has, of course, been the poor immig-rant woman, imagined as a mother prone to bearing children she cannot support. Indeed, it is the undocumented woman who has first and foremost been marked as a public charge and thus as an ethical failure.

What has taken place during the post-1965 period, then, is that "illegal" immigrants have essentially been anathematized as unethical subjects. Indeed, they have been deemed as uncommitted to personal responsibility and the rule of law. They have been viewed as unable or unwilling to take proper care of their selves. They have, in short, been signaled out as condensing in their bodies all that is anti-prudent: disorderliness, economic dependency, and crime. The putative con-sequence of such irresponsibility has, of course, been social and eco-nomic wounding of the social body. Significantly, this anathematization of the undocumented has not come without its consequences. As we will see in the next part, the fact that they have been cast as insecurities that endanger the social body has rendered them suspect and thus vulnerable to authoritarian interventions. It has located them in a realm of abjection where they could be subjected to all kinds of punitive measures in the name of protecting the welfare of the population.

AFTER 9/11

Before turning to the next part, though, I just want to make a few remarks about the post-9/11 problematization of "illegal" immigration. On one level, the tragic events of September 11, 2001 – when "foreigners" hijacked four airplanes and deliberately crashed them into several sites around the United States, including the Twin Towers in New York and the Pentagon in Washington, DC, killing thousands of people – have not altered the basic landscape of immigration politics. For one, "illegal" immigration continues to be made visible as a phenomenon of "vast" and/or increasing magnitude. Take apprehension figures, for example. These show that in FY 2000 apprehensions reached an all-time high of 1,643,679 along the Southwest border. Then for three consecutive years afterward there was a marked decline in arrests: In 2001, the number of apprehensions along the southern boundary line was 1,235,718; in 2002, it was 929,809; and in 2003, it was 905,065 (US DHS 2004a: 155). This downward trend appears to be over, however. Since October 2003, apprehension figures have risen sharply. Through August of FY 2004, the number was already back up to 1,059,265 (US DHS 2004b). It thus appears that, after a short period of decline, "illegal" immigration is today once again on the upswing, at least in terms of apprehensions. Now take the calculations of stock and flow. These show that the undocumented population grew robustly throughout the 1990s and continues to expand in the new millennium. The INS, for example, estimated that 7 million unauthorized immigrants were living in the United States in January 2000 and that on average this populace grew by about 350,000 per year from 1990 to 1999 (US INS 2003b: 1). And researchers from the Urban Institute calculated that in March 2002 there were 9.3 million "illegal" immigrants in the country (Passel, Capps, and Fix 2004: 1). These estimates suggest that the undocumented population these days is more than twice as large as it was in the early 1990s when the INS pegged their number at 3.4 million for October 1992 (Warren 1994: 19). Finally, consider the popular construction of "illegal" immigration. While anti-immigrant sentiment is not as fervent today as it was in the early to mid-1990s, there is still a high degree of animosity toward the undocumented and a marked tendency to associate them with terms such as "invasion," "flood," and "out of control." For example, newspaper headlines such as the following are not uncommon: "America Is Changing and Not Necessarily for the Better. Immigration is Out of Control" (Mallette 2004); "Trash Dumping Endemic in State with Flood of Illegal Immigration" (Rotstein 2004); "US Faces Silent Invasion" (Rouse 2004); and "What is Occurring in California is a Takeover Invasion of Lawbreakers" (Silver 2004).

Second, there also continues to be a strong concern with the impact of undocumented immigrants on social services. Consider, for example, the two following GAO reports: *Undocumented Aliens: Questions Persist about Their Impact on Hospitals' Uncompensated Care Costs* (US GAO 2004a) and *Illegal Alien Schoolchildren: Issues in Estimating State-by-State Costs* (US GAO 2004b). The former report determined that, since hospitals generally do not gather data on patients' immigration status, it could not calculate the impact of undocumented aliens on hospitals' uncompensated care costs (costs not paid by patient or insurances). However, the reason the report was commissioned in the first place was because: "Concern [had] been raised that uncompensated care costs due to treating undocumented aliens [placed] financial strain on hospitals in many areas of the United States, including along the US–Mexican border" (US GAO 2004a: 1). As for the latter report, it too was unable to determine the price tag of "illegal" immigration: in this case, that associated with educating undocumented children. But it did suggest that "concern about the costs of illegal alien schoolchildren may be heightened because education costs are high and the illegal immigrant population is thought to be large" (US GAO 2004b: 4). Or take these next two reports: *Medical Emergency: Costs of Uncompensated Care in Southwest Border Counties* (MGT 2002), a study conducted by MGT of America on behalf of the United States/Mexico Border Counties Coalition,[43] and *Breaking the Piggy Bank: How Illegal Immigration is*

Sending Schools Into the Red (FAIR 2003), an analysis from the Federation for American Immigration Reform (FAIR). The Border Coalition study concluded the following:

> The problem of uncompensated emergency services has far reaching implications beyond loss of hospital revenues. . . . High liability costs and low levels of compensation are threatening the viability of emergency rooms and emergency transportation providers along the border. Some counties with high rates of uncompensated care can no longer afford to provide "charity" care for local needy residents. In some instances, high levels of unpaid medical bills related to undocumented immigrants have forced local healthcare providers to reduce staffing, increase rates, and cut back services. (MGT 2002: iv–v)

As for the FAIR report, it noted that:

> With states straining under gaping budget shortfalls, public schools throughout the country are facing some of the most significant decreases in state education funding in decades. . . .
> While these massive budget deficits cannot be attributed to any single source, the enormous impact of large-scale illegal immigration cannot be ignored. *The total K-12 school expenditure for illegal immigrants costs the states $7.4 billion annually – enough to buy a computer for every junior high student nationwide.* (FAIR 2003: 1)

Unlike the GAO reports, then, these last two reached more clear-cut conclusions: that the undocumented are on some level a drain on public and social services. Whatever the case may be, though, it is evident that the costs associated with "illegal" immigration remain an issue.

Finally, in the post-9/11 context, there continues to be a strong link between immigrant illegality and Mexicans and the US–Mexico border. We can see this concern, for example, in the stock enumerations of "illegal" immigrants. Counting the Mexican component of this population remains a big priority. Both the INS and the Urban Institute have calculated that Mexicans make up over half of the undocumented population: the INS put their number at 4.8 million for January 2000 (US INS 2003b: 1), while the Urban Institute estimated that 5.3 million resided in the United States in March 2002 (Passel, Capps, and Fix 2004: 1). Furthermore, if we look at apprehension figures, we find that DHS is continuing the practice established by the INS of highlighting arrests along the Southwest border. Case in point, the "Enforcement" section of the *Yearbook of Immigration Statistics*, like that of the *Statistical Yearbook* before it, contains a segment titled "Southwest Border Apprehensions." This segment details the movement of illicit bodies across the southern boundary line. The majority of those apprehended, in the order of 90 percent, are of Mexican origin. Perhaps more important than the above enumerations, though, is the ongoing public tendency to signal out the flow of people across the US–Mexico border as the primary source of the "illegal" immigration "problem." For instance, in the fall of 2004, *Time*, continuing a tradition *US News & World Report* began in the 1970s, ran a cover story underscoring the porous nature of the US–Mexico border (Barlett and Steele 2004). The words on the cover read: "America's Border: Even After 9/11, It's Outrageously Easy to Sneak In." The accompanying image is of two hands tearing apart a red and white striped fabric, presumably the American flag. Inside, the main story is titled "Who Left the Door Open?" It begins like this:

> The next time you pass through an airport and have to produce a photo ID to establish who you are and then must remove your shoes, take off your belt, empty your pockets, prove your laptop is not an explosive device and send your briefcase or purse through a machine to determine whether it holds weapons, think about this: In a single day, more than 4,000 illegal aliens will walk across the busiest unlawful gateway into the US, the 375-mile border between Arizona and Mexico. No searches for weapons. No shoe removal. No photo-ID checks. Before long, many will obtain phony identification papers, including bogus Social Security numbers, to conceal their true identities and mask their unlawful presence. . . .
>
> The US's borders, rather than becoming more secure since 9/11, have grown even more porous. And the trend has accelerated in the past year. It's fair to estimate, based on a TIME investigation, that the number of illegal aliens flooding into the US this year will total 3 million – enough to fill 22,000 Boeing 737-700 airliners, or 60 flights every day for a year. It will be the largest wave since 2001 and roughly triple the number of immigrants who will come to the US by legal means. (No one knows how many illegals are living in the US, but estimates run as high as 15 million.) (Barlett and Steele 2004)

So from stock enumerations and apprehension figures to mass media documentation, there is today still a marked tendency to associate "illegal" immigration with Mexicans surreptitiously crossing the US–Mexico border.

On another level, the tragic events of 9/11 have unquestionably altered the terrain of immigration politics. Perhaps the most significant change involves how the issue of immigration, undocumented or otherwise, has generally come to be viewed through the prism of homeland security. "Homeland security" is a way of thinking and acting that developed in the wake of the September 11, 2001 "terrorist" attacks. It has been defined as "a concerted national effort to prevent terrorist attacks within the United States, reduce America's vulnerability to terrorism, and minimize the damage and recover from attacks that do occur" (OHS 2002: 2). Basically, what has happened is that, subsequent to the 9/11 attacks, terrorism has generally come to be regarded as the greatest threat facing the nation. And since all the 9/11 hijackers were foreigners who somehow managed to get into the United States, the movement of people in and out of the country has become indissociable from this threat. This linking of immigration and terrorism is perhaps best articulated in a *Providence Journal* piece by Mark Krikorian, executive director of the Center for Immigration Studies, a policy think-tank in Washington, DC. Krikorian articulates the link as follows:

Of the DHS's many responsibilities, immigration control is central. The reason is elementary: No matter the weapon or delivery system – hijacked airliners, shipping containers, suitcase nukes, anthrax spores – terrorists are needed to carry out the attacks. And those terrorists have to enter and operate in the United States. In a very real sense, the primary weapons of our enemies are not the inanimate objects at all but, rather, the terrorists themselves, especially in the case of suicide attackers. (Krikorian 2004)

Also instructive is the Office of Homeland Security's *National Strategy for Homeland Security* (OHS 2002), a document that has provided the basic framework for mobilizing and organizing government, the private sector, and individual citizens to safeguard the US homeland from terrorist attacks.[44] Consider the following quote, for example:

For more than six decades, America has sought to protect its own sovereignty and independence through a strategy of global presence and engagement. In so doing, America has helped many other countries and peoples advance along the path of democracy, open markets, individual liberty, and peace with their neighbors. Yet there are those who oppose America's role in the world, and who are willing to use violence against us and our friends. Our great power leaves these enemies with few conventional options for doing us harm. One such option is to take advantage of our freedom and openness by secretly *inserting terrorists into our country* to attack our homeland. Homeland security seeks to deny this avenue of attack to our enemies and thus to provide a secure foundation for America's ongoing global engagement. (OHS 2002: 5, emphasis added)

Clearly expressed here is the idea that there is an ever-present possibility that foreigners might seek to enter the United States in order to commit acts of terrorism. Moreover, there is an articulation of the need to protect against this threat and safeguard the homeland.[45]

A related change in post-9/11 immigration politics involves the increased problematization of non-Mexican immigrant illegality. Without a doubt, Mexicans continue to be the main group associated with "illegal" immigration. However, now there is also a concern that others, particularly from populations not friendly to the United States, are attempting to sneak into the country. This problematization has been explicit at both the popular and policy level. At the popular level, a good example is the *Time* article discussed earlier (Barlett and Steele 2004). Following the brief discussion of numbers (that is, of the size of the undocumented population) quoted above, the authors ask: "Who are these new arrivals?" The answer:

While the vast majority are Mexicans, a small but sharply growing number come from other countries, including those with large populations hostile to the US. From Oct. 1 of last year until Aug. 25, along the southwest border, the border patrol estimates that it apprehended 55,890 people who fall into the category described officially as other than Mexicans, or OTMs. . . . [L]ocal law officers, ranchers and others who confront the issue daily tell TIME they have encountered not only a wide variety of Latin Americans (from Guatemala, El Salvador, Brazil, Nicaragua and Venezuela) but also intruders from Afghanistan, Bulgaria, Russia and China as well as Egypt, Iran and Iraq. Law-enforcement authorities believe the mass movement of illegals, wherever they are from, offers the perfect cover for terrorists seeking to enter the US, especially since tighter controls have been imposed at airports. (Barlett and Steele 2004)

Clearly, there is a strong concern here with other than Mexicans crossing the US–Mexico border clandestinely. But not all OTMs are equally worrisome. The mention of Egypt, Iran, and Iraq in the context of terrorism makes it patent that the OTMs of particular concern are those from Muslim countries. These are the places deemed to breed terrorists. With respect to the policy level, we can turn to a February 12, 2004 House of Representatives hearing on "Preventing the Entry of Terrorists into the United States." The anxiety about other than Mexicans entering the United States surreptitiously is best expressed by Bill West, a consultant for the Investigative Project, a counterterrorism research institute based in Washington, DC, and former INS employee in the Investigations Division. Speaking before the Subcommittee on International Terrorism, Nonproliferation, and Human Rights, West notes:

> Border security and especially preventing the entry of foreign terrorists into the United States are clearly issues critical to our national security. Unfortunately, our border security is more illusion than reality. America's border defenses are penetrated thousands of times a day by unsophisticated, unskilled and uneducated foreign laborers. It would be foolish to assume foreign terrorists, with access to sophisticated support networks, substantial illicit funds, smuggling organizations and routes and a myriad of false identity documents would find it difficult to enter the United States. In fact, such terrorists find our borders to be barely an inconvenience. (West 2004: 45)

In this case, the troublesome OTMs are not explicitly linked to Muslim countries. However, it has become obvious that, in the post-9/11 context, to speak of foreign terrorists is to speak of Muslims. It was Muslim "extremists" who carried out the 9/11 attacks. And it is they who are seen as continuing to wish America harm.

A final adjustment in the post-9/11 politics of immigration is the increased problematization of the US–Canada border and official ports of entry (POEs). Unquestionably, the Southwest border, particularly between ports of entry, continues to be seen as the primary doorway for unauthorized entry into the United States. Now, though, there is more attention being placed on other avenues of illicit access. One avenue is the US–Canada border. This border has historically been largely unguarded and the flow of people between the two countries relatively unfettered. But given the "threat" of terrorism today, the fear is that the unregulated nature of this dividing line is being exploited by those who seek to commit violent acts against the United States. The US–Canada border has thus come to be constructed as a potential source of danger. Such a construction can be seen, for example, in the testimony of witnesses who appeared at the hearing mentioned above. One such witness, Peter Nunez, a faculty member of the Department of Political Science and International Relations at the University of San Diego, articulated the danger of the northern border as follows:

> As long as our land borders with Mexico and Canada remain as open as they now are, terrorists can enter the US as easily as any of the hundreds of thousands of illegal aliens who regularly shred our land border security.
>
> Canadian security officials have long-admitted that there are approximately 50 terrorist groups operating in Canada. The border between Canada and the "Lower 48" states is 4,000 miles long, and was patrolled by 300 Border Patrol agents on 9/11 (now increased to 1,000 agents). Throw in the additional 1,000 mile border between Canada and Alaska and you have a huge hole in the dike. (Nunez 2004: 43)

Another avenue that has been problematized is ports of entry. POEs are the officially designated spaces through which people may legally enter the United States. There are approximately 300 of these in the United States: land, sea, and air (US DHS 2004a: 145). POEs have become an issue because every one of the 9/11 hijackers came to the United States through an official entryway: all nineteen had visas, some fraudulently obtained (West 2004: 46). The fear is that "terrorists" are continuing to exploit weaknesses in the inspections process at ports of entry in order to make their way into the United States. This fear is best expressed in a GAO report titled *Land Border Ports of Entry: Vulnerabilities and Inefficiencies in the Inspections Process* (US GAO 2003). The purpose of this report was to evaluate "immigration-related inspections at land border POEs" (US GAO 2003: 1). Among the problems it found were the following: inspectors sometimes experienced problems authenticating the identity of travelers; inspections were not consistently carried out according to policy; lack of technology and equipment hampered access to data systems; and inspectors lacked the time and training to collect, analyze, and use intelligence information. The report concluded that persons wishing to enter the United States illegally could take advantage of any of these weaknesses. Moreover, it noted: "given the threat of terrorism against the country, it is particularly important that inspectors at land border POEs have the support they need to collect, analyze, and use intelligence information" (US GAO 2003: 4).

All things considered, there have been some significant changes in the post-9/11 problematization of "illegal" immigration. The concern now is not just with the prototypical "job-stealing," "welfare-depending" unauthorized immigrant but also with those who would sneak into the country to commit acts of terrorism. Whichever figure we are dealing with, though, the "problem" of immigrant illegality is still basically understood as an ethical one. Both types of unauthorized persons are deemed to be irresponsible non-citizens tied to communities of anti-civility and uncommitted to the rule of law. One would do the United States harm through abusing social services, the other through mass destruction. The anathematization of unauthorized migrants as unethical had already rendered this group susceptible to various kinds of authoritarian interventions prior to September 11, 2002. Now, with every illegal entrant potentially a terrorist, they have been cast even more deeply into a realm of abjection where punitive measures carried out in the name of protecting the well-being of the social body are deemed all the more legitimate.

PART THREE

Anti-Citizenship Technologies and the Regulation of the Border

GOVERNING THROUGH CRIME

In the last part, I noted that the problematization of "illegal" immigrants in the post-1965 period has largely taken place in ethical terms – that is, that the "problem" of "illegal" immigration has on the whole been rendered understandable as an ethical problem. To be more precise, I explored how a variety of immigration "experts" – social scientists, INS/DHS bureaucrats, policy analysts, immigration reform organizations, and the popular press – have constructed "illegal" immigrants – typically imagined as Mexican – as imprudent subjects who have failed to comport themselves ethically: as anti-citizens incapable of exercising responsible self-management, unable or unwilling to enterprise their lives or manage their own risks. Significantly, to the extent that the undocumented have been anathematized as criminal and undeserving, as insecurities that imperil the well-being of the nation, the efforts to govern them and thus solve the problem of "illegal" immigration have generally fallen on the repressive side of ethopolitics. Indeed, the tactics, techniques, and programs that have been deployed to deal with them have tended to be rather exclusionary, restrictive, and punitive, focusing principally on control and containment.

The most significant ethopolitical way of managing "illegal" immigrants has undoubtedly been through crime. To govern through crime, as I previously noted, is to make crime and punishment the institutional context under which the efforts to guide the conduct of others take place. Today, of course, crime and punishment are a primary means through which political and other authorities generally seek to govern. This crucial facet of post-social rule is clearly visible in the widespread popularity of tough on crime sentencing regimes of just desserts, deterrence, and retribution. These regimes include such measures as: quality of life campaigns and zero tolerance policing; harsher penalties and the extensive utilization of imprisonment; "three strikes" and compulsory minimum sentencing policies; redress in juvenile court and the incarceration of minors; and more extensive parole restrictions. This facet is further noticeable in the common practice of securitizing private spaces as a way of dealing with crime risks and insecurities. The most visible manifestations of this practice are undoubtedly fortified enclaves. These enclaves are segregated spatial enclosures designed to provide a safe, orderly, and secure environment for those who dwell within them. The rationale for governing through crime and punishment seems to be twofold. On the one hand, the thinking is that irresponsible individuals must be held accountable for their misdeeds: that they must be made to shoulder the burden of their lifestyle decisions. And on the other, it is that normal people must protect themselves and be protected from the hordes of anti-citizens – the criminal, the underclass, the homeless, the vagrants, the truly disadvantaged – who threaten their security and quality of life.

With respect to "illegal" immigrants, governing through crime has most notably taken the form of intensified law enforcement and border management. The US federal government has essentially determined that the best way to deal with the problem of illegal immigration is through expanding the operations of border policing agencies, particularly the US Border Patrol. Until March 1, 2003, this agency was the main law enforcement arm of the Immigration and Naturalization Service (INS). Now it is part of US Customs and Border Protection (CBP) in the Department of Homeland Security. Its primary mission has historically been "to detect and prevent the illegal entry of aliens into the United States," chiefly between official ports of entry. The expansion of the Border Patrol as a way of governing "illegal" immigration has been most conspicuous, not surprisingly, along the US–Mexico border. I say not surprisingly, of course, because Mexico has historically been seen as the primary source of the "illegal" immigrant problem. This expansion began more or less in the late 1970s. Then it really burgeoned in the early 1990s. That is when the INS put into effect a broad plan to "gain control" of the Southwest border and reduce the flow of illicit immigration. As articulated in the *Border Patrol Strategic Plan: 1994 and Beyond, National Strategy*, this comprehensive border control scheme was based on a strategy of "prevention through deterrence." The objective was to increase fencing, lighting, personnel, and surveillance equipment along the main gates (or hot spots) of illegal entry – such as San Diego, California and El Paso, Texas – in order to raise the probability of apprehension to such a high level that unauthorized aliens would be deterred from crossing the border. The thinking here was that such localized practices of governmental intervention would disrupt traditional illegal crossing patterns, forcing migrants to consider passage through more arduous, remote locations. Potential border crossers would thus either be dissuaded from ever attempting to cross, or those who did try would eventually give up after repeated failures (Andreas 2000). The main solution to the illegal immigration problem, then, has been to turn the United States into a fortified enclave of sorts. It has been to cast a wide net of control and surveillance over the border in order to discourage illegal incursions and thus keep troublesome individuals out of the body politic. As with the government of crime more generally, the rationale for managing illegal immigrants through police measures is that the public must be protected from the would-be criminals who threaten their well-being and contentment.

What I would like to do in this part is explore this intensification of border policing as a way of governing "illegal" immigration. I will focus specifically on the technical dimensions of this process – that is, on border policing as a technology. Not just as any technology, however, but as an anti-citizenship technology. Generally speaking, technologies, drawing on Nikolas Rose (1999a), are assemblages of practical knowledge, architectural arrangements, mechanical devices, types of authorities, and so forth oriented toward the calculated transformation of human conduct in order to bring about particular outcomes and prevent certain unwanted events. An anti-citizenship technology is one that seeks to shape human conduct and achieve specific ends not through the empowerment of individuals but through their incapacitation and containment. Put otherwise, it is a technology bent on disempowerment: on the abjection (that is, casting out) and exclusion of particularly troublesome individuals and populations. Border policing is an anti-citizenship technology in the sense that it brings together an array of practical and intellectual mechanisms in an effort to affect the conduct of illegal immigrants: to affect it in such a way as to forestall illicit border crossings and keep these unwanted elements out of the United States. The goal here is social prophylaxis. It is to prevent undocumented immigrants from becoming "problems" in the social body through preventing their entry into the country.[1] The instruments that comprise the technology of border policing include: reform proposals (the US Select Commission on Immigration and Refugee Policy's *US Immigration Policy and the National Interest*) and the Sandia National Laboratories' *Systematic Analysis of the Southwest Border*); plans of action (the *Border Patrol Strategic Plan: 1994 and Beyond, National Strategy*); police personnel (INS/CBP Border Patrol agents); material structures (metal fences and stadium-type lights); and surveillance devices (helicopters, ground sensors, TV cameras, and infrared night-vision scopes). The focus on border policing as an anti-citizenship technology, then, points our analysis to the complex technical forms that have been deployed to direct and contain the conduct of "illegal" immigrants. It calls attention to how practices of government fundamentally work through technical means "to structure the possible field of action of others" (Foucault 2000: 341).

INTERLUDE²

HARLINGEN, TEXAS. June 1, 1996. Maria Elena Gonzalez was planning to join her husband in New Jersey. After crossing the Rio Grande, the 30-year-old illegal immigrant from Mexico was taken by smugglers north from the border and dropped off along the highway near the Falfurias checkpoint. To avoid detection by the US Border Patrol, Gonzalez and her brother took the long way around, setting off on foot through the parched South Texas ranchlands. But Gonzalez never made it to her destination. She died of heat exhaustion.

On Thursday, her husband and two brothers claimed her body at the Brooks County Sheriff's Department and made arrangements to transport it back for burial in Guanajuato in central Mexico. Gonzalez – and two other women who died last week as they hiked across the rugged brushlands – were among a flood of undocumented Mexican immigrants so desperate to cross the border that they risk dying in the heat.

Each year, illegal immigrants by the hundreds are preyed upon by bandits, drown as they swim the Rio Grande, suffocate in sealed freight cars or are maimed or killed after falling from moving trains. Add to the list the new – and often lethal – passage north on foot. While the most dangerous routes into the country are usually taken only by young, healthy men, Border Patrol agents say more women and children are making the back-country treks to evade immigration checkpoints on the major highways leading north from the Texas–Mexico border.

"The groups we're catching now, they're walking 15 to 20 miles, which is a long trek," said Chuck Roberson, Border Patrol agent-in-charge of the Falfurias station. "It takes one and a half, two or three days, and we're finding more women in these groups." The brushwalkers, as the Border Patrol calls them, spend days walking across private ranches without food, sufficient water, proper shoes or protective clothing. They are guided by – and often abandoned by – smugglers whose cruel tactics have earned them the nickname "coyotes."

"What usually happens is, if somebody gets sick, they leave them behind," said Roy Vasquez, assistant agent-in-charge of the Kingsville station. "Last year we had a rash of aliens who died in our area. I think within two months we had about four bodies we found out in the brush," Vasquez recalled. Next week, McAllen Border Patrol Sector Chief Joe Garza plans to run public service announcements on Mexican television and in newspapers to warn immigrants of the hazards of walking across South Texas. "I don't know what else to do," said Garza, who is in charge of 520 agents who patrol the Rio Grande from Falcon Dam to the Gulf of Mexico. "These people want to get to the interior (of the United States), they're desperate, and they take chances," he said. "We're trying to spread the word about the dangers they face when they take these kinds of risks." (Pinkerton 1996)

ASSEMBLING AN ANTI-CITIZENSHIP TECHNOLOGY

As I noted above, the expansion of border policing as a way to deal with the "illegal" immigrant "problem" has been taking place since at least the late 1970s.[3] The 1970s, of course, was a period that witnessed the visibilization of "illegal" immigration as a phenomenon of immense magnitude. To be more specific, it was a decade that beheld the creation and consolidation of a general image of unauthorized immigration as "out of control." Notably, the out of controlness of illicit immigration was largely linked to movement of bodies across the US–Mexico border. An important entity making this link was the INS. As pointed out in Part Two, a key aspect of the INS's enforcement activities entailed keeping statistics about the number of aliens apprehended for violating US immigration laws. These statistics indicated that the vast majority of apprehensions occurred along the Southwest border and that these were generally of people who had attempted to enter the United States clandestinely (as opposed to being of individuals who had entered the United States legally and subsequently lost their lawful status). INS officials, quite significantly, generally interpreted their apprehension figures as signaling that the border was being overrun. Also important in linking the out of control character of undocumented immigration to the movement of people across the US–Mexico border were the mass media. These often dramatized the "illegal" immigrant problem precisely through shining the spotlight on the United States' southern boundary and the traffic of bodies across it. During the 1970s, then, it was not just "illegal" immigration that was deemed out of control. It was also the US–Mexico border. Indeed, this boundary line was generally judged to be rather unruly.

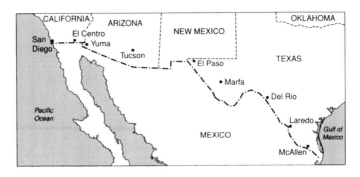

FIGURE 3.1   Map of the US–Mexico border.
Source: US GAO 2001.

A principal reason commonly offered to account for the out of control nature of the Southwest border was that the INS simply lacked the necessary resources to cope with the ever-increasing flow of illicit bodies. The perception was, indeed, that law enforcement just did not have enough weapons to adequately secure a boundary that ran for close to 2,000 miles: from the Pacific Ocean in the west, across deserts, canyons, plains, and mountains, and all the way to the Gulf of Mexico in the east (see Figure 3.1). Perhaps the loudest voice calling attention to the lack of enforcement resources at the border was the INS itself. Through mass media articles, INS publications, and so forth, this agency routinely highlighted how it was underfunded, outmanned, and just generally lacked the proper means to adequately enforce the nation's immigration laws. In the cover letter to the 1974 *INS Annual Report*, for example, Commissioner Leonard Chapman underscored the issue as follows:

> The most serious problem facing the Immigration Service, and one of the Nation's most pressing problems, is the continuing surge of illegal aliens into the United States. Persons are illegally entering the country across our borders and through ports of entry by the millions, *far outstripping INS capability to enforce adequately the laws pertaining to entry and residence.* (Chapman 1975b: iii, emphasis added)

Chapman then reaffirmed his convictions in a 1976 *Reader's Digest* article:

> The Immigration and Naturalization Service . . . is charged with overseeing our immigration policies and enforcing the laws. One of our

primary missions is to protect the American worker by detecting and deporting illegal aliens employed here. But the *task is overwhelming*. The Service has fewer than 2,000 Border Patrol officers to guard 6,000 miles of land border with Canada and Mexico. (Chapman 1976a: 190–1, emphasis added)

Other important voices signaling that law enforcement lacked the necessary resources to properly police the border included immigration reform organizations, the mass media, the public, and a variety of Congressional committees. A case in point is the House Committee on Government Operations. During the 93rd Congress (1973–4), one of its units, the Legal and Monetary Affairs Subcommittee, held a series of hearings on the INS and its operations regarding "illegal" immigration. Based on these hearings, the Government Operations Committee determined that "the ever-increasing number of illegal aliens in this country appears to be due in great part to the inability of the Service to control and enforce immigration laws in every section of the country" (Congressional Research Service 1977: 32). In turn, the INS's failings were found to be due principally to underfunding and inadequate staffing: "Fiscal policies and budget requests have consistently failed to provide INS with necessary levels of support to maintain effective levels of enforcement activity" (32).

Given the perception that the US–Mexico boundary was poorly policed and wildly overrun, and that as a consequence illegal immigration was out of control, the 1970s and early 1980s bore witness to myriad calls for stepped-up boundary enforcement. During this period, indeed, numerous entities began agitating for the securitization of the border as a way to manage the "illegal" immigrant problem. One key agitating entity, not surprisingly, was the INS. This agency repeatedly noted that, with enhanced resources, it could better police the border and consequently help to curtail the flow of undocumented immigrants into the United States. The main resource the INS felt it needed was manpower. In a 1977 *US News & World Report* article, for example, Commissioner Chapman noted that "the Service should expand its force from the present 3,300 to 6,100, with two thirds of the additional 2,800 officers assigned to the borders or airports" (Kelly 1977: 39). Other resources deemed important included: spotlight-equipped helicopters for better aerial surveillance, more ground sensors to detect the movement of people and vehicles, and funds to build a 10-foot-high chainlink fence in heavily traversed sections of the border (39). Joining the INS's call for enhanced boundary enforcement were numerous public officials, government commissions, and immigration reform organizations. Their proposals for gaining control of the border ranged from the mild, relatively speaking, to the severe. On the "mild" side, there was the US Select Commission on Immigration and Refugee Policy. This Commission, like the INS, principally called for more funds in order to augment border personnel and surveillance technologies: "The Select Commission recommends that border patrol funding levels be raised to provide a substantial increase in the numbers and training of personnel, replacement sensor systems, additional light planes and helicopters and other needed equipment" (US Select Commission 1981: 47). The feeling was that, in the context of ever-increasing "illegal" immigrant flows, augmenting the INS's resources was necessary for effective border interdiction.[4] On the severe side, there were public officials such as California Senate minority leader George Deukmeijian and immigration reform organizations such as the Federation for American Immigration Reform (FAIR). For Deukmeijian, the solution to the "illegal" immigration problem, at least in the case of California, was to establish a military reservation along the fourteen westernmost miles of the US–Mexico border (Nevins 2002: 71). For FAIR (1989), on the other hand, the key to arresting the flow of illicit bodies – or at least one of them – was to wall off the United States from Mexico. It was to erect imposing physical barriers – ranging from concrete walls to fourteen-mile-wide trenches – on key spots along the border.

The impact of the myriad calls for dealing with "illegal" immigration through enhanced border enforcement would be tremendous. Beginning in the late 1970s and continuing through the 1980s, we see a rather marked intensification of border policing.[5] The indicators of this intensification were several. One indicator was the increase in the INS's financial resources. Between 1978 and 1988, Congressional support for this agency grew considerably from $283.1 million to $807.8 million – that's an increase of 185 percent. A key beneficiary of this augmentation was the Border Patrol, the INS's primary enforcement unit. Its funding shot up from $78.1 million to $205.3 million. A second sign was the growth in INS staffing levels. From 10,071 in 1978, the number of overall INS positions authorized by Congress jumped to 15,453 in 1988.[6] The Border Patrol accounted for a good portion of this growth. Its authorized staffing levels went from 2,580 to

5,530. A third indicator was the upgrading of border architecture. Case in point, the INS constructed a 10-foot-high chainlink fence in certain spots along the border – namely, portions of the El Paso, San Diego, Yuma, and Tucson Border Patrol sectors[7] – with high rates of illicit crossings. The chainlink fences were basically improved and expanded versions of previous fences. Their general purpose was to visibly demarcate the boundary line separating the US from Mexico and to deter would-be immigrants from entering the country illegally. A final sign of intensified border policing was the dramatic enhancement of surveillance technologies. The most notable enhancement undoubtedly occurred in the area of aerial surveillance. Between 1978 and 1988, the INS not only added significantly to its fleet of fixed-wing aircraft, which grew from a little over twenty planes to close to fifty, but also introduced high-tech helicopters – twenty-two of them – into operations. Five of the helicopters were of the A-Star 350-B variety. Equipped with heat-sensing capabilities, these aircraft enabled nocturnal surveillance and detection. The rest of the helicopter fleet was composed principally of OH-6A spotter-observation aircraft. These helicopters lacked the nocturnal capabilities of the A-Star 350-B sort but were still powerful tools of observation and detection. Other kinds of surveillance equipment were also introduced, improved, or expanded during the period in question. For instance, the INS replaced and upgraded the electronic ground sensor systems it initially installed in the early 1970s to detect movement in isolated areas of the Southwest border. Furthermore, the agency added noticeably to its stock of night-vision scopes, raising the total from 59 to 344, as well as introduced a variety of vision-enhancing devices: night-vision goggles, vehicle-mounted infrared telescopes capable of remote-imaging, and large tripod-mounted "starlite" and infrared scopes. Finally, the INS set up low-light TV cameras in key segments of the border in order to detect nocturnal illicit crossings.

Thanks to the unrelenting calls for fortifying the border, then, boundary enforcement became, in the course of just over ten years, a rather formidable anti-citizenship technology for governing illegal immigration. It was a technology that brought together bodies, material structures, and technical devices in order to shape the conduct of illegal immigrants in such a manner as to obviate unwanted border incursions. The way this policing technology generally worked to discourage illegal entry was to focus on apprehending aliens once they had crossed over into the United States (US GAO 1994b: 12). Put otherwise, the Border Patrol's principal tactic was not necessarily to block people from entering the country (although border fences did serve this purpose to some extent) but to forcefully pursue them once they had transgressed its boundaries. The thought seemed to be that it was not possible to adequately seal the border and thus that an aggressive strategy of pursuit and apprehension was the most feasible way to dissuade would-be immigrants from trespassing.[8] Involved in the implementation of this strategy were a wide array of practices (Domestic Council Committee 1976: 78–84). The main one was what the INS called line watching. Line watching simply refers to the routine of keeping watch over the border so as to prevent illegal entry and/or detect and intercept illegal entrants. Activities associated with this routine included the physical patrolling of the border (on foot or using vehicles, aircraft, bicycles, all-terrain motorcycles, and horses), sign cutting (the process of detecting the passage or presence of vehicles, people, or animals through interpreting disturbances in natural terrain conditions), video and night-vision scope surveillance, tower watching, and electronic sensor monitoring. The import given to line watching had to do with the belief that interdiction and seizure were most effectively realized at the immediate border. Other policing practices included traffic checks, city patrols, and transportation inspections. These were all considered supplementary to line watching. Traffic checks targeted illegal entrants who had evaded detection at the border and were making their way to an inland destination. These checks occurred on major highways leading to the interior and at selected roads running from and through the border area. City patrols were aimed at locating the illegal entrant who had managed to make it to one of the metropolitan areas adjacent to the border. These entailed the inspection of such locales as factories, hotels, jails, and businesses. Finally, transportation inspections focused on the successful entrant who was trying to abscond from the immediate border on mass transportation. Involved here was the checking of buses, marine craft, passenger and freight trains, and commercial aircraft.[9] Notably, aliens who were caught as a result of the INS's policing practices were generally taken to detention facilities for processing. A few – typically repeat offenders or criminal violators – were kept in custody pending prosecution and/or deportation proceedings. The majority, however, were detained only briefly and then allowed to depart the country "voluntarily."[10]

INTERLUDE

IMPERIAL VALLEY, CALIFORNIA. August 19, 1998. Florina Zacarias Salguero begged her husband not to leave their small Mexican village to find work in the United States, but he was determined. Fernando Salguero Lachino, a 48-year-old peasant from Charo and veteran of many border crossings, said goodbye to his wife and six young children on June 26 and took a bus 1,200 miles north to Tijuana.

"He said he wouldn't take long," his wife said. "He said he would send money soon to buy shoes for one of the boys who didn't have any." She never heard from her husband again. Lachino's badly decomposed body was one of eight found last week in the Imperial Valley near the Salton Sea.

Authorities believe he was part of a group of 22 people that crossed the border June 30. From the group, federal officials have found nine bodies, including one discovered July 3, but do not know what happened to the 13 others. Authorities believe the nine deaths are the largest group of undocumented immigrants to die while crossing the desert since the 1970s, when 14 Central Americans died in Arizona. The 13 not accounted for either died in the parched desert or eluded Border Patrol agents, said Thomas L. Wacker, the patrol's chief agent in El Centro.

Border Patrol agents in the air and on the ground searched a 50-square-mile area of the desert Tuesday south of Highway 78 and east of Highway 86 but found nothing, he said. They planned to resume their search at dawn today. The dead included seven Mexican immigrants and two smuggler guides. Authorities said they believe the group's vehicle broke down or the members were dropped off and died waiting for another van that never arrived.

On Tuesday, the Border Patrol eliminated its most hopeful scenario – that agents had caught the 13 migrants and sent them back to Mexico in early July. A review of agency records showed that did not happen, he said. Rita Vargas, head of the Mexican consulate in Calexico, said immigrants risk dangerous border crossings over irrigation canals and the desert because they are desperate for work.

Jobs are hard to find in Charo, a village of about 1,000 people in the state of Michoacan west of Mexico City, said Antonio Gil, a 36-year-old store clerk who helps oversee the town's three public telephone booths. Hundreds of people like Lachino leave the village every year to find work in the United States, Gil said. So many go, it's hard to find people to work the fields in Charo, he said. Once they reach the United States, villagers contact family by calling one of the public phones, and messengers pass the word to loved ones that they have a call, he said.

Salguero, 42, said villagers had all heard stories about the dangers of desert border crossings. She said her husband "never told me that they went through the desert." Each of the last four years, her husband left home to find jobs picking apples, cherries, pears and other crops in California, Oregon and Washington, she said. Lachino would stay six to eight months, sending $300 every other month, before returning home.

Lachino told his wife of getting caught by the Border Patrol in earlier crossings. When that happened, he would borrow money and try again, Salguero said. He usually left in the cooler winter months and complained to his family about the dangers, she said. "They had to walk a lot when he crossed," she said. "He said the cold temperatures were very intense and they didn't take anything to cover themselves." But he took the risk because he felt he needed the job.

Mexican officials called last week to tell her of his death. The family plans to have his body returned to Charo for an all-night vigil and Catholic burial Mass, she said. (Portillo and Henry 1998)

SECURITIZING THE
BORDER

While the expansion of border policing that took place during the 1970s and 1980s was undoubtedly significant, it was rather inconsequential in comparison to that which has occurred since then. Indeed, since the 1990s, boundary enforcement has become an exponentially more intense and sophisticated anti-citizenship technology. What generally happened is the following. As I noted in Part Two, INS apprehension figures declined rather dramatically at the end of the 1980s following the implementation of the Immigration Reform and Control Act of 1986 (IRCA). The general feeling initially was that IRCA, along with enhanced border enforcement practices, was having a deterrent effect on "illegal" entry. When apprehension figures rose in 1990, however, and then continued climbing in subsequent years, it became clear that the measures the US government had taken to stem the flow of undocumented immigrants had not really worked. Given this apparent failure, and in the context of a rather harsh early 1990s economic downturn, the image of "illegal" immigration as out of control became more widespread and popular than ever, especially in California. Demonstrably, as was the case in the 1970s and 1980s, the unruly nature of undocumented immigration was largely associated, at least at the popular level, with the traffic of people across the US–Mexico divide.[11] Indeed, from immigration reform leaders and the mass media to politicians and the public at large, they were all fond of dramatizing the problem of illegal immigration using the US–Mexico border as a stage. For example, a quick flip through the pages of early 1990s southern California newspapers reveals a strong preoccupation with depicting the illicit movement of people across the border. Commonly pictured in these pages, for instance, were would-be immigrants amassed around dilapidated border fencing just waiting for the cover of darkness in order to dart into the United States. Typically figured as well were groups of people making their way clandestinely across the border and Border Patrol agents searching and arresting suspected aliens. In the early 1990s, then, just as in the 1970s and 1980s, it was not just undocumented immigration that was judged out of control. It was also the Southwest border. Indeed, this boundary was generally constructed as chaotic and wildly overrun.

There were two major reasons generally offered to account for the out of control character of the Southwest border. The first had to do with resources. The feeling was (still) that the INS simply did not have the necessary wherewithal to handle the flow of undocumented immigrants. Instructive here is a 1991 GAO report titled *Border Patrol: Southwest Border Enforcement Affected by Mission Expansion and Budget*. The report showed that even though the Border Patrol's funding increased 61 percent between fiscal years 1986 and 1990 (from $164 million to $263 million), the agency still had significant resource deficiencies (US GAO 1991: 3). Two important areas in which it was deemed lacking were personnel and field equipment. With respect to the former, the number of Border Patrol agents working in the nine Southwest border sectors actually increased between 1986 and 1990, going from 3,222 to 3,669 (1991: 9). However, this increase did not translate into significantly enhanced boundary enforcement. In fact, the number of yearly hours spent on boundary control duty went up only marginally – 2 percent – during this period (1991: 2). The primary reason for the negligible increase was that, as a result of IRCA, the Border Patrol was assigned additional responsibilities, the main one being to help enforce employer sanctions.[12] More responsibilities meant, of course, that agents had less time to devote to boundary enforcement activities. INS officials interviewed for the report noted that this adjustment in tasks left the Border Patrol without sufficient personnel to adequately secure the border. As for field equipment, the GAO report found that Border Patrol vehicles and electronic detection devices were by and large old and in poor condition. For example, it was determined that over 60 percent of the vehicles potentially needed to be replaced. Most simply had too many miles on them and were thus not very dependable. In terms of sensors, the finding was that many were older models that were unreliable or just did not work. This poor state of the Border Patrol's field equipment was largely attributed to budget constraints. There simply was not enough money to fund replacement vehicles and sensors. Predictably, the report concluded that the dearth of suitable equipment had a negative impact on the Border Patrol's ability to carry out its enforcement mission.

The second reason generally given to explain the unruly quality of the US–Mexico border had to do with tactics. As I noted earlier, the Border Patrol's traditional strategy for dealing with illegal entry concentrated not so much on preventing aliens from crossing the border as on tracking them down and apprehending them once they had trespassed. The general feeling – in policy, academic, and popular circles alike – was that this tactic did not work. For example, the chief agent of the El Paso Border Patrol sector noted that under the INS's strategy of apprehension the border area was in "complete chaos" (US GAO 1995b: 11), and a study commissioned by the Office of National Drug Control Policy (ONDCP) to pinpoint ways to enhance border security called the tactic inefficient (Sandia National Laboratories 1993). The basic problem seemed to be that fear of apprehension did not function all that well as a deterrent. There were just too many "holes" in the border to make being seized a high probability.[13] Besides, even if a person were caught, s/he faced no substantial penalties. Chances were that s/he would just be sent "voluntarily" back to Mexico. And once back, there was really nothing stopping him/her from making another crossing attempt.[14]

Given the continuing assessment that inadequate policing was the principal reason for the out of control character of the border, and hence of undocumented immigration, the early 1990s became witness to renewed and forceful public calls for enhanced boundary enforcement. These calls for dealing with the "illegal immigrant problem" through securitizing the border came from numerous sources. Especially key fonts were politicians. Regardless of party affiliation, they tended to adopt a rather tough posture toward boundary policing. This was particularly the case in California. On the Democratic side, for example, gubernatorial candidate Kathleen Brown appealed for the imposition of a $1 border-crossing toll in order to finance an expansion of the Border Patrol (Berstein 1994: Metro 7), while Senator Barbara Boxer advocated using the National Guard to aid in monitoring the Southwest boundary line (Nevins 2002: 89). And on the Republican side, Governor Pete Wilson insisted on major funding increases for the "grossly understaffed Border Patrol" (Wilson 1994: A25), while a couple of San Diego-area Congressmen, Randy Cunningham and Duncan Hunter, pushed for expanding the power of the federal government to compel private citizens to allow the construction of access roads and security fences on land they owned along the border (Nevins 2002: 85–6). Other key sources were ordinary citizens and the leaders of various immigration reform organizations. Their letters and statements proclaiming support for beefed-up border enforcement littered the pages of newspapers across the country. For example, Marion O'Toole, a resident of Costa Mesa, CA, wrote in an *Orange County Register* opinion piece that a "long-overdue strengthening of the border patrol [would] . . . stem the tide of the current daily invasion which is draining the state of its fast-dwindling resources" (1994: Metro 9). Ruth Coffey, head of Stop Immigration Now, penned a column in the *Nationalist Times* (PA) asking that "our border fences" be electrified and for the military to "patrol all ports of entry" (Coffey 1994). And Harold W. Ezell, chairman of Americans Against Illegal Immigration, published a piece in the *Orange County Register* suggesting that the way to stop the flow of illegal immigrants was to close interior checkpoints and move all agents to the border (Ezell 1994: Metro 7).

Significantly, the public calls for enhanced boundary enforcement were echoed in a number of important government reports. Two in particular are worth mentioning. One is the Sandia National Laboratories' *Systematic Analysis of the Southwest Border* (1993). This report was commissioned by the ONDCP through the INS. Its purpose was to recommend measures for securing the US–Mexico border against the traffic of people and drugs. The report made one central recommendation: that the Border Patrol change its border control strategy from apprehending illegal immigrants once they had crossed over into the United States to precluding their entry. The feeling was that the Border Patrol's traditional strategy was too inefficient and that in truth the only good approach to managing the border was one that prevented people from crossing at all. The way to carry out this strategy of prevention, the report concluded, was to impose "effective barriers on the free flow of traffic." Proposed were two specific barriers. One was multi-tiered fencing or comparable physical obstructions in urban border areas, the standard practice having been to use single barrier systems. It was reasoned that such fencing would give the Border Patrol a greater capacity to "(1) discourage a significant number of illegal border crossers,

(2) detect intruders early and delay them as long as possible, and (3) channel a significantly reduced level of traffic to places where border patrol agents [could] adequately deal with it" (US GAO 1994b: 13). The second proposed barrier was enhanced checkpoint operations. Specific suggestions were that more checkpoints be created and that all operate around the clock (rather than part time as was the common practice). The purpose of augmenting checkpoint operations would be to better contain those aliens who had succeeded in crossing the border.

The other significant report calling for enhanced boundary enforcement was the US Commission on Immigration Reform's *US Immigration Policy: Restoring Credibility*. Congress created this Commission in 1990 "to assess US immigration policy and make recommendations regarding its implementation and effects" (US Commission on Immigration Reform 1994: i). *Restoring Credibility* was the Commission's interim report. This report, like the one from the Sandia Laboratories, took the position that the underlying principle of border control should be prevention rather than apprehension and removal. Its reasons for adopting this posture were three: first of all, prevention would be more cost-effective than apprehension following illicit entry; second, it would eliminate the "cycle of voluntary return and reentry" that epitomized unauthorized boundary crossings; and third, it would curtail "potentially violent confrontations on the border" (vi). Bearing in mind this strategy of prevention, the report made a number of recommendations for dealing with the border. One was that resources for prevention be boosted. Specific areas that required boosting included personnel, technology (e.g., infrared scopes, sensors, and data systems to rapidly identify repeat offenders), and equipment (e.g., vehicles and radios). Another recommendation was that Border Patrol agents be trained to carry out preventative strategies. And a third was that fences be given greater import: these were believed to facilitate enforcement and cut down on border violence.

From politicians and private citizens to government reports, then, all and sundry were asking that the difficulty of crossing the border clandestinely be substantially increased. And this is precisely what they got. Since the early 1990s, thanks to a major boundary control offensive, the Southwest border has become progressively tougher to traverse. The beginnings of this offensive can be traced to the Texas–Mexico boundary line. On September 19, 1993, the Chief of the El Paso Border Patrol sector, Silvestre Reyes, in an effort to curtail illegal immigration from Mexico into El Paso, launched a two-week border control drive dubbed Operation Blockade (Bean et al. 1994; US GAO 1994b; US INS 1996a).[15] The operation, which targeted a 20-mile stretch of border between El Paso and Juarez,[16] represented at base an attempt to deal with the cross-border traffic of "illicit" bodies through a change in strategy. This change, notably, was very much in line with the Sandia recommendations: it involved shifting the El Paso Border Patrol's enforcement focus from apprehension and removal to stopping immigrants at the border. Concretely, this shift in strategy entailed a drastic enhancement of line-watch operations. The thinking was that the border could be brought under control with more aggressive and high-profile monitoring. The El Paso line-watch operations were augmented in three basic ways (Bean et al. 1994: 7–8). First of all, the number of agents assigned to line-watch duty was substantially increased: from around 200 to more than 400.[17] These 400+ agents were deployed in shifts along the border 24 hours a day, 7 days per week. They were deployed in such a manner as to produce a saturation effect. That is to say, the way the agents were positioned down the border created a highly visible line of force. Bean et al. describe the deployment in the following fashion:

> Parked in their distinctive, signature-green Chevrolet Suburbans on the levee roads along the Rio Grande from border monument number one in the west to the Ysleta headgates in the east, the agents, through the sheer force of numbers, were intended to deter potential illegal border crossers. Agents were stationed close enough together to have visual contact with other agents on either side of them. Some were as close as fifty yards and others as far apart as one-quarter mile, depending on the terrain. Agents were instructed to apprehend and detain illegal border crossers and to call for assistance and reinforcements as required. Concentrations of agents were particularly heavy at the most common border penetration locations, such as railroad bridges and shallow points in the river. (1994: 7–8)

Second, line-watch operations were augmented through the increased use of helicopters. Four of them were utilized to patrol the border throughout the time-span of the operation. These airborne units coordinated with agents on the ground to carry out prevention efforts. And third, the enhancement of line-watch operations involved the mending and remending of a 9-mile expanse of fence running along the border in the downtown area of El Paso. At the start of the operation, the fence had some 125 apertures. These were all repaired. And as migrants attempting to enter the United States clandestinely opened new holes in the barrier, these were patched up as well. Significantly, the shift in strategy for dealing with illegal immigration seems to have had the desired effect. According to Border Patrol officials, the two-week operation sharply curtailed the flow of undocumented immigrants into El Paso (Martin 1993).[18] The evidence of this curtailment was found in INS apprehension figures: the number of average daily arrests went down from about 800 prior to the operation to approximately 150 afterward (Nevins 2002: 90). Encouraged by this apparent success, instead of terminating the operation after its two weeks were up, Chief Reyes decided to continue it indefinitely. The effort, however, was renamed Operation Hold the Line in order to avoid the negative implications of the word "blockade."

Subsequent to the ostensibly triumphant implementation of Operation Blockade, the drive to enhance control of the US–Mexico border gained considerable momentum. For starters, in February 1994, Attorney General Janet Reno and INS Commissioner Doris Meissner unveiled a comprehensive scheme to strengthen enforcement of the United States' immigration laws. The scheme consisted of five initiatives: (1) augmenting border control; (2) expelling criminal aliens; (3) reorganizing the asylum process; (4) putting in force workplace immigration laws; and (5) encouraging citizenship for eligible legal immigrants (US GAO 1997c: 64). While all of these initiatives were important, the scheme's number one priority was to strengthen control of the border. Better boundary enforcement was seen as the main key to solving the "illegal" immigrant problem. The way that the border was to be brought under control was through a strategy called "prevention through deterrence." The idea was to make it "so difficult and so costly to enter this country illegally that fewer individuals [would] even try" (US INS 1996a: 3). Carrying out this strategy of prevention – of stopping immigrants at the border, in other words – was to involve concentrating technology and personnel resources in a phased approach along the main corridors of illegal entry (urban areas, generally), increasing the amount of time that Border Patrol officers devoted to boundary enforcement activities, and maximizing the utilization of physical barriers (US GAO 1999a: 3). Put otherwise, the strategy was to entail the thorough fortification of the principal illegal entry routes. With these popular routes closed off, the hope was that potential immigrants would either be deterred from crossing the border or be forced to attempt entry through locations – remote deserts and mountains, for example – where the Border Patrol had a tactical advantage (US GAO 1997c: 64).[19] Importantly, soon after the Attorney General and the INS Commissioner announced their strategy of prevention through deterrence, the Border Patrol developed a strategic plan to implement it (US Border Patrol 1994). This strategic plan called for a four-phased approach to fortifying and gaining control of the border. Phase one would involve buttressing the two main illicit entryways into the United States: the San Diego and El Paso areas. These two areas had traditionally accounted for a large percentage (65) of all arrests along the US–Mexico border (US GAO 1997c: 65). Phase two would then focus on Tucson, Arizona and South Texas (Del Rio, Laredo, and McAllen), the next most important passageways; phase three would deal with the rest of the Southwest border; and finally, phase four would see to the coastal waterways and the US boundary with Canada. Beginning with the areas of greatest illegal activity, then, the idea was to gradually and systematically concentrate resources – personnel, technology, and physical barriers – along the border until all of it was secured. Each Border Patrol sector was given the responsibility for determining how the plan was to be carried out in its area.

With a plan in hand, the Border Patrol officially set to work on October 1, 1994. The targeted areas at this initial point were El Paso and San Diego. In the former area, the Border Patrol simply continued to execute Operation Hold the Line. The only major change to the operation was the addition of fifty new agents (US INS 1996a: 3). In San Diego, meanwhile, the Border Patrol launched Operation Gatekeeper. The initial goal of this operation was to gain control of a 5.5-mile stretch of border between the Pacific Ocean and the San Ysidro port of entry known as Imperial Beach. This stretch was the busiest illicit crossing point along the Southwest border, accounting for almost 25 percent of all apprehensions (US INS 1996a: 4). Its location close to US residential neighborhoods and transportation routes inland made it the ideal entryway. For once an immigrant got across the border, s/he could just blend in with the urban population and easily make his/her way north. The principal feature of Gatekeeper was enhanced line-watch operations. As in the case of Operation Hold the Line, the thinking was that if enough resources were located along the border, it could be brought under control. Line-watch operations were most notably enhanced in terms of personnel (Sanchez 1994; US DOJ 1998). The implementation of Gatekeeper resulted in the immediate doubling – to over 150 – of the number of agents positioned in the vicinity of the Imperial Beach border. These agents were strategically deployed in three tiers or lines of defense. The first line was placed adjacent to the boundary. This line was very much a fixed one. Agents positioned along it were directed to stay put in designated spaces and not to move beyond them in pursuit of illicit traffic (US DOJ 1998). The hope was that the installation of a highly visible and stable contingent of agents at the immediate border would have a deterrent effect. The second and third tiers of defense were positioned at intervals of more or less half a mile behind the front line. The agents assigned to these tiers were highly mobile. Their job was to intercept any aliens who were not scared off by the first line of defense and managed to get past it. Also enhancing line-watch operations was the upgrading of equipment and infrastructure. With respect to equipment, the Border Patrol was provided with additional ground sensors, video cameras, portable radios (to facilitate communication and the coordination of operations), night scopes, and all-terrain vehicles (Rotella 1994; Suro 1994; US DOJ 1998). And as regards infrastructure, the most notable developments were the installations of stadium-style lights and of a 10-foot-high steel-matting fence along key sections of the boundary line (Parrish 1994; US GAO 1994b: 15).[20] The floodlights covered approximately 4.5 miles of border, including 3.5 in the Imperial Beach area. With their powerful illuminating capacity, these lights made it easier for Border Patrol agents to spot nighttime border traffic. As for the steel-matted fence, it covered approximately 14 miles of border, including most of Imperial Beach. This fence, while not impenetrable, was substantially stronger and harder to breach than the chainlink barrier it replaced. Notably, Gatekeeper, with its hyper-emphasis on line watching, seems to have had the desired outcome. According to INS officials, the flow of people attempting to cross the border clandestinely through Imperial Beach was curtailed dramatically. Reduced apprehension figures were given as proof of this curtailment. For example, the number of aliens arrested during October 1994 – the first month of the operation – totaled 4,261. In contrast, the number of apprehensions during the same period the previous year was 8,593 (Press Enterprise 1994). This change represents an arrest reduction of more than 50 percent. Commenting on this reduction, one Border Patrol agent noted: "What we have is proof that if you give us the manpower and equipment, we can go a long way toward solving the problem of illegal aliens" (Ayres 1994).

Given the apparent initial success of the Border Patrol's strategic plan for gaining control of the border, the Attorney General and the INS Commissioner decided to keep going forward with it. With great resolve, the plan continued to be implemented through the 1990s and into the new millennium. The Border Patrol's initial targets, as I noted above, were the San Diego and El Paso areas. These two areas, which comprised phase one of the strategic plan, continued to be the primary focus of Border Patrol operations through FY 1997.[21] Then in FY 1998, after the Border Patrol determined that the San Diego and El Paso corridors were sufficiently under control, the emphasis shifted to phase two sectors (South Texas and Tucson, Arizona), with some attention also placed on areas scheduled to be targeted in phases three (El Centro, CA, Yuma, AZ, and Marfa, TX) and four (the US–Canada border and the coastal waterways). This implementation of the Border Patrol's strategic plan principally entailed the amassing of policing resources at the border.[22] The signs of this amassing were several. One sign was the tremendous growth of the INS's budget. Between 1993 and 2001, Congressional monetary backing for this agency grew from $1.52 billion to $5 billion (US DOJ 2002). That is a remarkable increase of 228 percent. A major beneficiary of this budget windfall was the Border Patrol. Its funding skyrocketed from $354 million to $1.2 billion (Andreas 2000: 89; US GAO 2001: 5). A second indicator was the expansion of INS staffing levels. From 17,876 in 1993, the total number of INS positions soared to 31,971 in 2001 (TRAC-DHS 2002). Also significant in terms of staffing was the fact that the proportion of time Border Patrol agents in the Southwest spent on boundary enforcement activities (as opposed to training, supervision, and program support duties) increased. Between 1994 and 2000, the proportion went up about 8 percent, from 61 percent to 69 percent (US GAO 1997c: 22; US GAO 2001: 8). A third sign was the upgrading of border architecture. Prior to 1994, there existed very little in the way of substantial physical barriers between ports of entry, only about 14 miles of reinforced steel fencing in San Diego and largely ineffective chainlink fences in other areas (US GAO 1997c: 19). But over the course of the 1990s and early 2000s, the INS added quite a few barriers. In May 2001, there were about 76 miles of fencing along the Southwest border (US GAO 2001: 8). The general purpose of this fencing was to deter illegal entry. A final sign of the amassing of policing resources at the border was the dramatic enhancement of surveillance technologies. The most notable enhancements undoubtedly occurred in the area of computerized identification and tracking systems. The INS developed three of these (US INS 1996b). One is known as IDENT. This system records the fingerprints and photographs of every person apprehended, the goal being to keep track of criminal aliens and repeat border crossers. The other two systems are ENFORCE and ICAD (Intelligent Computer-Assisted Detection). ENFORCE is an automated form-processing system used to document and track the identification, apprehension, detention, and/or removal of persons in violation of US immigration law. It supplanted the labor-intensive manual typing of forms when booking an alien. And ICAD is a computerized system that alerts agents to unlawful incursions with the help of underground sensors. This system increased the efficacy of electronic surveillance along the US–Mexico border. Other kinds of surveillance technologies that were enhanced include night scopes, remote video surveillance systems, and helicopters.

What happened, then, during the 1990s and early 2000s, is that boundary enforcement became an even more formidable anti-citizenship technology for managing illegal immigration. It is a technology that brought together an impressive and ever-increasing number of police personnel (Border Patrol agents), material structures (fences and lights), and surveillance devices (helicopters, ground sensors, TV cameras, and infrared night-vision scopes) in order to shape the conduct of illegal immigrants in such a way as to prevent illicit border crossings. Put otherwise, what occurred is that a continually densening web of control and surveillance was cast over the US–Mexico border. Indeed, as vast amounts of resources were poured into boundary enforcement, this southern border became super-enveloped in a police and criminal dragnet. The goal: keeping unwanted elements out of the United States.

INTERLUDE

TIJUANA, MEXICO. August 2, 2000. Guadalupe Martinez was a newlywed, aiming to cross the border to meet her husband in central California. Juan Manuel Vargas Dimas was an unemployed engineer, heading with his son to Los Angeles. Both migrants died before reaching their destinations, abandoned by smugglers, the latest victims of scorching desert temperatures along Mexico's northern border.

Their cremated remains are being sent home this week to the Pacific Coast state of Michoacan; hers to the town of Chavinda, his to the capital, Morelia. "We are devastated," said the dead woman's older sister, Ramona Martinez, reached by telephone in Chavinda. "She left very happy because she was going to be reunited with her husband."

The US Border Patrol reports that 58 people have died since October while trying to cross illegally in the El Centro sector, with 13 of those deaths attributed to the heat. Mexican officials say seven other migrants, including Martinez and Vargas, have died in the Tecate–Mexicali region since Jan. 1.

Martinez's remains were found Thursday about a mile south of the border, in rocky desert terrain east of the mountain town of La Rumorosa. The 36-year-old woman had been dead for about two months, said Francisco Acuna, chief medical examiner for Baja California.

Vargas' body was found by agents from Mexico's migrant protection unit, Grupo Beta, in the same area on Saturday following a massive search for him on both sides of the border. He had been missing since July 26, when his 17-year-old son left him by a small tree as he searched for help. Vargas was 55 years old, married, and the father of two, said his son-in-law, Marcelo Canavad. An engineer, Vargas had been unemployed for 18 months when he decided to head to Los Angeles. It was his first trip across the border, the son-in-law said.

Father and son were among a group of 30 migrants who began their journey into the desert east of La Rumorosa at 5:30 p.m. July 25, said Hector Orozco, legal adviser for Grupo Beta in Mexicali. The son told Orozco that their leader was a man they only knew as Pedro. "He told them they would be walking for two to three hours," Orozco said. But six hours later, they were still walking. By midnight, the father could no longer keep up, due to a previous foot injury, and the group continued without him, Orozco said. The son stayed with his father, then left the next morning to seek help. Sixteen hours later the son found a road, and flagged down a truck that brought him to the Red Cross unit in La Rumorosa.

Agencies on both sides of the border began searching for the elder Vargas. Using a description of Vargas' shoe print, US Border Patrol agents spotted his tracks Friday afternoon south of Skull Valley, said Kerry Anderson, assistant chief in El Centro. The tracks led back to Mexico, where two Grupo Beta agents found the body at 1:40 p.m. Saturday. "He was lying on his side, by two brown knapsacks," said Jesus Cesar Aguila Rodriguez, one of the agents. When the son, who had joined the rescue effort, saw his father's body, "He lowered his head, and shook it, as if to say, 'No,'" the agent said.

Less is known about the final hours of Guadalupe Martinez. She had been married in December, and was eager to join her husband, Salvador Garcia, a farm worker in Madera in central California. "It was love that prompted her to go to her husband, just as many people here leave to join their family members," said her sister in Michoacan. The husband is a legal US resident, the sister said. But the process of petitioning for Martinez to join him legally would have taken months or years, depending on whether he was a US citizen or a permanent resident, according to the US Immigration and Naturalization Service. In either case, the couple was too impatient to wait, the sister said, so the husband hired a smuggler to take her across. "He wanted to have her with him as soon as possible," the sister said.

Martinez and a companion flew to Tijuana on May 25, believing she wouldn't have to hike across the border but would be smuggled across at San Ysidro. On May 26, she called her husband to tell him she would be crossing on foot, but the smuggler snatched the phone away from her, the sister said. "The smuggler told her husband, 'We won't walk a lot, just two or three hours,'" she said. When they didn't hear from her again, Martinez's relatives began to suspect the worst. Three weeks ago, the body of her companion, Alejandro Alvarado Gomez, turned up in the same area. "They left her out there without protection," the sister said. "We don't know why." (Dibble 2000)

THE AFTERMATH OF "TERROR"

Now that we are in a post-9/11 context, what has happened to border policing as a way of governing "illegal" immigration? The answer to this question is in many ways rather straightforward. Border policing has only intensified in the aftermath of the September 11 "terrorist" attacks. However, the goal is no longer just to keep out the classic unauthorized immigrant who comes to the United States in search of work (and putatively to get on welfare), but also the "terrorist" who seeks to commit acts of violence against "Americans." And while the main enforcement target continues to be the US–Mexico border, there is now also more attention placed on the boundary with Canada and official ports of entry (POEs).

That "terrorists," and not just prototypical "illegal" immigrants, are nowadays a main concern of boundary enforcement officials is perhaps most clearly visible in the fact that the Immigration and Naturalization Service (INS) has been abolished and its functions and units transferred to the Department of Homeland Security (DHS). DHS was created in January 2003 as a response to the events of 9/11, its primary mission being to "prevent and deter terrorist attacks and protect against and respond to threats and hazards to the Nation" (US DHS 2004c: 4). Immigration-related duties were transferred to this new Cabinet department on March 1, 2003. These duties include providing services and benefits such as naturalization and work authorization, now the purview of US Citizenship and Immigration Services (USCIS); investigating breaches of and enforcing federal immigration, customs, and air security laws, now the task of US Immigration and Customs Enforcement (ICE); and border security, now the domain of US Customs and

Border Protection (CBP). For our purposes, the key DHS entity is CBP. It has responsibility for the overall protection of the nation's borders: land, air, and sea. It is also the new parent body of the Border Patrol. The centrality of terrorism to CBP is clearly indicated in its mission statements. The priority mission of this DHS unit, as articulated in its *Performance and Annual Report: Fiscal Year 2003*, is homeland security. This means:

> preventing terrorists and terrorist weapons from entering the US. This important mission calls for improved security at America's borders and POEs. . . . The terrorist threat is a very real, continuing danger that will be with us for years to come, and our nation must continue to act accordingly to combat that threat and defend the American people against it. CBP's plan for the FY 2004–FY 2009 time period reflects a continued focus on the priority homeland security mission. (US CBP 2003: 6)

Supplementary CBP missions include "apprehending individuals attempting to enter the U.S. illegally" and "stemming the flow of illegal drugs and other contraband" (US CBP 2003: 7).

With DHS's assumption of responsibility for immigration-related matters, then, the figure of the terrorist has come to occupy a central place in border enforcement policy. In fact, it is principally the threat of terrorism and the need to protect against it that, in the post-9/11 context, is propelling the drive toward enhanced boundary policing. There are at least two important elements to the current border enhancement drive. One element is the ongoing implementation of the Border Patrol's strategic plan. This plan, however, has been modified somewhat. It now involves only three phases instead of four (US CBP 2003: 42). Phase one, which is considered complete, concentrated on the San Diego and El Paso areas; phase two, the current focus, now encompasses South Texas, Arizona, and the northern border (formerly in phase four); and phase three will target coastal areas (formerly in phase four) and the remainder of the Southwest border. Overall, the current implementation of the strategic plan has entailed the continued pouring of resources – personnel, technology, aircraft, and tactical infrastructure – into policing the United States' borders between ports of entry, particularly in the Southwest. The goal: "to prevent the illegal entry of terrorists, terrorist weapons, contraband, and illegal aliens into the US"

(US CBP 2003: 41). Specific actions taken since 9/11 include: the boosting of Border Patrol personnel from 9,651 in FY 2001 to about 11,200 in FY 2004; the augmentation of the Integrated Surveillance Intelligence System (ISIS), a program that employs remotely monitored night–day camera and sensing systems to better identify, observe, and react to illicit crossing; the erection of additional Remote Video Surveillance Systems (RVSS), which are cameras mounted on various structures (poles, for example) that provide 24 hours a day/7 days a week coverage of isolated border locations; the establishment of more Border Patrol checkpoints in strategically located zones leading away from border areas; and the implementation (in July 2004) of the Interior Repatriation Program, an experimental initiative that repatriates apprehended Mexican nationals not to the closest port of entry into Mexico, as has traditionally been the case, but to their regions of origin, the goal being to prevent apprehendees from immediately trying to reenter the United States and hopefully to derail their reentry efforts altogether (US CBP 2004a).

In addition to this buildup of resources, CBP has developed a specific strategy to police the northern border (NB). Historically, this border has been largely unguarded and the flow of people between the United States and Canada relatively unregulated. This has changed somewhat since 9/11. As one CBP report put it: "In the wake of September 11, 2001, deficiencies in personnel and resources along the NB have received increased attention. Concerns over our Nation's vulnerability to the illegal entry of terrorists and their weapons of mass destruction across our relatively unprotected NB has caused the CBP to significantly increase our enforcement presence in this area" (US CBP 2003: 44). The strategy developed to police the US–Canada border has three phases (US CBP 2003: 45). The first phase focuses on expanding intelligence sharing and cooperation between CBP and other law enforcement agencies, both in the United States and Canada. The second phase involves installing enforcement-related technology, such as cameras and sensors, along the border. The idea behind these technologies is to expand the area that can effectively be policed given limited manpower. And the third phase entails the deployment of extra Border Patrol personnel in the northern border sectors. Since 9/11, the number of agents assigned to these sectors has tripled to about 1,000 (US CBP 2004a). Significantly, this northern border strategy is fundamentally different from the one employed in the

Southwest. It relies less on manpower and fences and more on technology, aircraft, and tactical infrastructure. The rationale for the different strategies "is based upon historical volume in illegal cross-border activity, level of economic parity, and cooperation with foreign law enforcement" (US CBP 2003: 45). Essentially, the feeling is that because there have historically been low levels of illegal traffic across the northern boundary, traditionally strong economic (as well as cultural) ties between the United States and Canada, and long-standing co-operation between law enforcement agencies of the two nations, the policing of the northern border, while important, does not warrant the same kind of resource investment as that of the southern boundary line.

The second important element of the current border enhancement drive is the more rigorous policing of ports of entry. Traditionally, the job of safeguarding the nation's POEs – land, air, and sea – has fallen on three separate federal agencies: the US Customs Service, the INS, and the US Department of Agriculture (USDA). Customs has had responsibility for monitoring the entry of goods into the United States, the INS for regulating the movement of people, and the USDA for inspecting agricultural and related products. In the post-9/11 context, oversight of the nation's POEs has become the responsibility of just one entity: CBP. In essence, CBP at ports of entry represents a merger of the operations and workforce of the US Customs Service, the INS, and the USDA. The logic behind this merger was that one integrated, cohesive unit would be better able to enforce and uphold the nation's laws and secure its borders (US CBP 2003: 39). A notable feature of this new POE enforcement regime has been the elimination of Customs, Immigration, and Agriculture inspectors and the creation of a new frontline officer position: the CBP officer. This new officer performs:

> the critical, priority mission of preventing terrorists and terrorist weapons from entering the US, while facilitating the flow of legitimate trade and travel. In addition, building on the knowledge and skills of the consolidated workforce, the CBP Officer . . . continue[s] to carry out the important traditional missions that were joined together at the ports, including the interdiction of illegal drugs and other contraband, enforcing trade and immigration laws, apprehension of those attempting to enter the US illegally, and protection of US agricultural and economic interests from harmful pests and diseases. (39–40)

In effect, what has been achieved with the formation of CBP is the institution of a first line of defense against terrorism. Moreover, we have also witnessed the creation of "one-stop processing," a development that is supposed to make the routine of entering and exiting the United States more efficient (39).

With respect to immigration, the critical function of CBP and the CBP officer is to inspect individuals seeking entry into the United States and determine their admissibility. According to CBP guidelines, an officer:

> is responsible for determining the nationality and identity of each applicant for admission and for preventing the entry of ineligible aliens, including criminals, terrorists, and drug traffickers, among others. US citizens are automatically admitted upon verification of citizenship; aliens are questioned and their documents are examined to determine admissibility based on the requirements of the US immigration law. (US CBP 2004b)

In this inspections process, the CBP officer is aided by a host of new technologies and programs. One program is the Secure Electronic Network for Travelers' Rapid Inspection (SENTRI) (US CBP 2003: 22). SENTRI is a project that allows low-risk travelers to enter the United States through special lanes at Southwest land border crossings (specifically, El Paso in Texas and San Ysidro and Otay Mesa in California) in an expedited manner with little or no delay. Such a project is deemed important because it allows CBP to concentrate its resources and efforts on high-risk individuals, while making certain those travelers who are legally admissible into the country and pose no risk of terrorism are not held up at the border. A second, and perhaps more important, program is the United States Visitor and Immigrant Status Indicator Technology (US-VISIT). US-VISIT is a continuum of security measures that uses biometric technology to verify an alien's identity and authenticate his or her travel papers (US DHS 2004d, 2004e, 2004f). The program currently affects all visitors (mainly non-Europeans) who need a visa to travel to the United States. Typically, US-VISIT begins at the Department of State's visa-issuing posts overseas, where US consular officials collect a visitor's biometric identifiers (digital fingerscans and photographs) and check them against watch lists of suspected "terrorists" and known criminals. This biometric information is used in making visa determinations. Then, when a visitor arrives at a US port of entry, CBP officers collect the same biometric information and examine it to ensure that the person seeking entry is the same one to whom the visa was issued. As of December 31, 2004, US-VISIT entry procedures were in operation at 115 airports, 14 seaports, and the 50 busiest land POEs. Eventually, all visitors will also have to undergo biometric exit procedures. The basic purpose of US-VISIT is to enhance the security of the United States through reducing "fraud, identity theft, and the risk that terrorists and criminals will enter the US undetected or by using stolen or fraudulent documents" (US DHS 2004e).

All told, then, in the post-9/11 world, the policing of the nation's borders as a way to govern "illegal" immigration has continued to be enhanced. The focus now, though, is on policing not just the US–Mexico boundary, although it certainly continues to be central, but also the northern border and ports of entry. And the concern is not just with keeping out Mexican unauthorized immigrants but, perhaps more importantly, also "terrorist" threats. Significantly, this drive toward enhanced border enforcement shows no signs of abating. The FY 2005 Homeland Security Appropriations Act, which President George W. Bush signed on October 18, 2004, includes $419.2 million in new funding to enhance border and port security efforts (US DHS 2004g). This includes monies for improving the detection of individuals attempting to enter the United States clandestinely.

INTERLUDE

EL EQUIMITE, MEXICO. June 1, 2001. Even as Raymundo Barreda and his 15-year-old son were lowered into their graves on Friday, relatives still agonized over the economic pressures that drove the would-be immigrants from their lush homeland into the unforgiving Arizona desert.

Barreda and his son, Raymundo Jr., were among the 11 people buried Friday who came from these tranquil villages in the mountains of Veracruz state. "Their journey is over, their walking is done," Father Isaias Huerta Campo said at the Barredas' funeral. Father and son were buried side by side in a brick tomb dug by their neighbors from their own red earth and covered by boards cut from their native forests. Family and friends wept and tossed flowers into the grave.

Huerta said he had officiated at 15 funerals so far this year in his parish in nearby San Pedro for migrants who died in the United States in accidents or in border violence. As the Barredas were laid to rest, nearly simultaneous funerals were held in neighboring villages for men who died in the same journey. "There are so many funerals, everywhere you look," said Huerta. To the living, many of whom get by on a dollar a day and some of whom think of going north, he had other words: "I tell my parishioners don't go. But if you have to, I understand."

The migrants' deaths represent a strange paradox in this verdant territory, where exotic purple, yellow and white flowers sprout by the rocky roadsides – but making a living is a daily struggle. "Oh there's plenty of work here, but there's no money," said Vicente Hernandez, of San Pedro, about a half-mile from El Equimite. His 34-year-old son Lorenzo was among those who died in the desert in Arizona on May 24.

Other parts of Mexico have a long tradition of young men traveling north to work part of the year in the United States, but most families here have stayed put, depending on their coffee, citrus and banana crops. But with the recent collapse of prices for those products – and US work opportunities – an increasing number each year now make the dangerous odyssey. "There are a lot of us who are just giving up on farming," Andres Hernandez said Thursday as chickens, pigs and horses wandered through the yard where his younger brother, Lorenzo, lay in a coffin.

Lorenzo was one of 26 immigrants who crossed the border into the Cabeza Prieta National Wildlife Refuge in southwest Arizona on May 19. US Border Patrol agents started finding them four days later. Of the 14 found dead, all but three came from Veracruz state.

Lorenzo's 30-year-old widow, Juana, said she did not know how she would support her family: She gets about 7 cents a pound for her green coffee. "He always loved his children very much and his greatest dream was to see them go to college," she said Friday of her late husband. Her son, 12-year-old Lorenzo, had just told her that he was going to quit school and go to work to support the family. "No," she said, "that's not what your father would have wanted."

In a way it was almost logical that the men would go, with tens of thousands of Central Americans streaming through Veracruz each year on their way to the United States. And then there was the siren song of immigrant traffickers from other states offering to smuggle them across the border. The lure to migrate even comes in the form of frequent radio announcements offering work in border assembly plants. Some see those jobs as a jumping-off point into the United States.

Filadelfo Landa, the brother-in-law of Raymundo Barreda Sr., noted a sad irony of the North American Free Trade Agreement, which slashed at limits on movement of goods and capital between Mexico and the United States while leaving restrictions on labor intact. "We have a free trade agreement with the United States, but that's just a cruel joke for farmers here," he said. "Products can cross the borders, but they (workers) can't." (Stevenson 2001)

THE SURFEIT OF
DEAD BODIES

Now let me focus on the effects of border policing as a way of governing illegal immigration, particularly in relation to the US–Mexico border. I noted earlier that, in its early stages, the Border Patrol's effort to gain control of the border was very much regarded as a success. This general assessment has continued to hold true as the implementation of the strategic plan has unfolded.[23] Indeed, the process of building up the border has generally just kept on getting great reviews. Take, for example, the following quote from Alan Bersin, United States Attorney for the Southern District of California:

> As a result of neglect for almost all of American history, [the San Diego] border was completely porous. Just under 600,000 people were being apprehended each year in a 14-mile corridor inland east from the Pacific Ocean. . . . Then Ms. Reno set to work. The Attorney General and INS Commissioner Doris Meissner made a commitment to the Border Patrol that sufficient resources would be provided for agents to do their job. With the support of the President and the consent of Congress, resources have flowed into San Diego in a significant way. . . . The situation now represents a dramatic improvement from the one that existed in August 1993. Gone are the days and nights when hundreds of undocumented persons would rush across the border, with Border Patrol agents attempting to grab one person in each hand. The plan was to create an identifiable border, light it, and provide the Border Patrol with resources to patrol it professionally. Those basic changes have taken place in one of federal law enforcement's most positive stories of progress. (Bersin 1996)

Or consider this related citation from a 1998 *San Diego Union-Tribune* editorial:

> Think back less than 10 years ago. The Tijuana River Valley was like a war zone, with ill-equipped, outnumbered Border Patrol agents chasing wave after wave of illegal immigrants.
>
> Otay Mesa was also overwhelmed. And the San Ysidro crossing was even worse. Illegal immigrants would simply run through the checkpoints in packs.
>
> Today, all that chaos is history. And Operation Gatekeeper is the reason for the success. (Quoted in Nevins 2002: 127)

And finally look at this quote from a recent CBP report:

> Where implemented with the appropriate balance of resources, the national strategy has succeeded as is demonstrated by the results of the operations listed below. . . .
>
> In McAllen Sector, alien apprehensions had risen to the high of 243,793 in FY 1997. Since its inception in FY 1997, Operation Rio Grande has reduced successfully alien apprehensions down to 89,927 (a 63 percent decline). In support of this operation, the McAllen Sector has received over 1,000 agents, permanent lighting, all-weather roads, 31 RVS cameras, and 2 aircraft. (US CBP 2003: 43)

This general evaluation of the Border Patrol's strategic plan as successful, I would suggest, is not without merit. If we look at the San Diego–Tijuana border, for example, there is no doubt that it has been significantly "pacified" in the course of the past decade. Indeed, all indications are that a semblance of peace and order has come to reign over the area. To begin with, large crowds of unauthorized migrants no longer assemble along the boundary waiting for the cover of darkness in order to scuttle into the United States. Second, the "banzai run" – that is, the practice of immigrants rushing through ports of entry en masse – has become a thing of the past. And third, the number of annual apprehensions in San Diego has dropped rather precipitously, from 531,689 in FY 1993 to 111,515 in FY 2003 (US GAO 2001: 31; US DHS 2004a: 155). This drop appears to be a sure sign that the flow of clandestine traffic through the area has slowed down considerably. A similar story can be told of the El Paso–Juarez border. This area too has become relatively quiet in terms of illegal immigrant activity. Case in point, the number of yearly arrests there dropped from 285,781 in FY 1993 to 88,816 in FY 2003 (US GAO 2001: 31; US DHS 2004a: 155). To all intents and purposes, then, the Border Patrol's strategy of prevention through deterrence has had the desired effect in San Diego and El Paso. It has generally stopped unauthorized immigrants at the border.

While the positive assessment of the Border Patrol's strategic plan may not be without merit, I would also suggest, though, that it is not entirely correct. To be sure, the implementation of the plan has produced "encouraging" results in San Diego and El Paso. However, indications are that it has not had an impact in reducing the overall number of unauthorized boundary crossings. Indeed, all signs suggest that tighter controls have on the whole not put off would-be border crossers. Take INS apprehension figures, for example.[24] Total arrests along the Southwest border rose sharply from 1,212,886 in FY 1993 to 1,643,679 in FY 2000 (US GAO 2001: 31). They then fell for the next three years to a low of 905,065 in FY 2003 (US DHS 2004a: 155). Now arrests appear to be back on the rise: in FY 2004, the total was 1,130,282 (US DHS 2004h). So for all the resources that have been poured into boundary enforcement, there does not appear to have been much of a dent made in lowering apprehensions: the total number is basically the same now as it was in 1993. Or consider the statistical efforts to measure the size of the undocumented immigrant population. These generally show that this populace has continued to grow despite the massive buildup at the border. For example, researchers from the Urban Institute calculate that in March 2002 there were 9.3 million "illegal" immigrants in the country (Passel, Capps, and Fix 2004: 1). And the INS estimates that 7 million unauthorized immigrants were living in the United States in January 2000 and that on average this populace grew by about 350,000 per year from 1990 to 1999 (US INS 2003b: 1). These calculations suggest that the undocumented population nowadays is more than twice as large as it was in the early 1990s when the INS put its number at 3.4 million for October 1992 (Warren 1994: 19). Or finally, consider the social scientific stabs at calculating the labor market effects of intensified border enforcement. These generally reveal that undocumented workers are not in short supply. For instance, a 1996–7 study of street-corner labor markets in San Diego determined that Operation Gatekeeper had not appreciably curbed the number of illicit job seekers arriving in the area (Cornelius 1998:

130).[25] The story behind this lack of drop-off in the overall number of illicit border incursions is relatively simple. What has happened is that as the Border Patrol has closed off urban routes to illicit traffic, would-be crossers, instead of being deterred, have simply sought to cross through less policed remote locations (Andreas 2000; US GAO 2001; Nevins 2002).[26] Put otherwise, what has occurred is that rather than stopping the flow of unauthorized immigrants, the strategy of prevention through deterrence has merely displaced it. The evidence of this displacement can be found in INS apprehensions statistics. These clearly show that as arrests plummeted in San Diego and El Paso in the late 1990s, they concomitantly went up elsewhere along the Southwest border. The most dramatic upsurge was registered in the El Centro, California area. The number of arrests here went from 30,058 in FY 1993 to 238,126 in FY 2000 (US GAO 2001: 31). That is a growth of 692 percent. Other areas that experienced considerable increases in apprehensions during the late 1990s include Yuma and Tucson, Arizona. The number of arrests in the former rose from 23,548 in FY 1993 to 108,747 in FY 2000; in the latter it went from 92,639 to 616,346 (US GAO 2001: 31). When all is said and done, then, while Border Patrol operations may have disrupted the flow of illicit bodies, they have certainly not brought it to a halt.

There is more to the analysis of the Border Patrol's strategy, though, than simply determining whether or not official goals (i.e., deterring illegal immigration and bringing order to the Southwest boundary) have been met. Just as significant to consider, I would suggest, are the ramifications of the strategy for undocumented border crossers themselves. These, unfortunately, have tended to be somewhat on the injurious side. What enhanced boundary enforcement has meant for many migrants is pain, suffering, and even death. As I noted above, a main effect of the Border Patrol's operations has been to shift the traffic of undocumented immigrants away from urban areas to less policed remote locations. This shifting, quite significantly, has transformed the act of crossing the border from a relatively simple endeavor into a complex and dangerous venture. When undocumented immigrants were entering the United States primarily through urban routes, for instance, they generally did not have to travel very far to reach populated areas and transportation routes north. Moreover, the terrains they had to traverse were generally hospitable. And even if they were not, the fact that travel distances were short meant that the natural environment did not as a rule present a significant obstacle. All these factors combined to make unauthorized border entry a more or less straightforward affair. It was sufficiently straightforward in fact that self-smuggling was a common practice (Andreas 2000: 95). That crossing the border was relatively easy should not be taken to suggest, though, that un-documented immigrants did not face any dangers. They certainly did. Obstacles confronting them included such natural and man-made hazards as the weather, fast-moving waterways, snakes, and gangs oper-ating along the border (Nevins 2002: 144–5). On the whole, however, border crossers were out of harm's way. With the recent enhancement of border policing, the process of crossing the boundary has changed considerably. The out-of-the-way places through which most undocu-mented immigrants are currently entering the United States are less than ideal crossing points. There are two basic problems with them. One is their remoteness. The fact that they are apt to be far removed from urban centers means that the undocumented have to traverse long distances before reaching populated areas and transportation routes. The second problem is the ruggedness of their terrains. These places tend to be barren deserts and/or mountains. Anyone crossing through them consequently has to contend with freezing temperatures at night and torrid weather during the day. What these two problems amount to – or rather, what having to walk long distances though hostile landscape means – is a more difficult and dangerous border-crossing experience. So great is the difficulty of crossing that immigrants now generally turn to smugglers to sneak them through (Andreas 2000: 95). And, more importantly, so great is the danger that border-related deaths have become routine events. Indeed, the US–Mexico border has become a landscape of death (Eschbach et al. 1999; Cornelius 2001; Nevins 2002).

That death on the border has become commonplace on account of stepped-up boundary policing is ascertainable in at least two ways. First and foremost, there are the statistics on the number of border fatalities. These show that incidences of death have increased significantly since the Border Patrol implemented its strategy of prevention through de-terrence. According to the Mexican Ministry of Foreign Relations, for example, the number of migrants who died trying to cross the California–Mexico border was twenty-three in 1994 (Cornelius 2001: 669); since then the number of yearly deaths has averaged over 100 (California Rural Legal Assistance Foundation 2004a). The figures tell a similar story for Arizona and Texas. In the former, the migrant death total came to seven in 1996; since then it has averaged about ninety per year.[27] In the latter the number of deaths was twenty-one in 1996; the yearly average since then has been about 140. Taking the Southwest border as a whole, the number of migrants who have died trying to cross it has averaged more than 300 per year since 1997.[28] The second way to ascertain the link between border-related fatalities and aug-mented boundary enforcement involves looking at the data on the spatial distribution of migrant deaths. Figures 3.2 and 3.3 will serve as our primary materials here. These figures document the geographic distribution of migrant fatalities in California for calendar years 1995 and 2001. A quick glance at the two figures plainly reveals that there has been a revolution in the number and location of migrant fatalities. Indeed, the change from 1995 to 2001 is quite dramatic. In 1995, for example, there were only about sixty border-related deaths in Califor-nia. Moreover, these casualties were localized in the urbanized areas of San Diego.[29] In 2001, by contrast, there were more than 130 migrant fatalities in the state – with the majority taking place not in urban San Diego but in the rural areas of Eastern San Diego County and the Imperial Valley.[30] This change in the landscape of death clearly indi-cates that the upsurge in migrant fatalities stems from the rerouting of illicit traffic through remote mountain and desert locations. The basic problem, as I noted above, is that the new crossing terrains are just too rugged. As Wayne Cornelius notes:

If migrants attempt to cross such terrain, they expose themselves to life-threatening environmental conditions. For example, a hike over the Tecate Mountains in East San Diego County can take two days. If migrants traverse this mountainous region between mid-October and mid-April, there is at least a 50 percent probability that they will encounter sub-freezing temperatures if not snow, conditions for which they are totally unprepared. Migrants entering through the Imperial Valley desert must walk a minimum of 20–30 miles before reaching a major roadway. During the summer, temperatures in this desert average 112°F and frequently reach 120°F in daytime. It is physically impossible for migrants to carry enough water to prevent dehydration during the two-day trek through the Imperial desert; indeed, many are dehydrated by the time

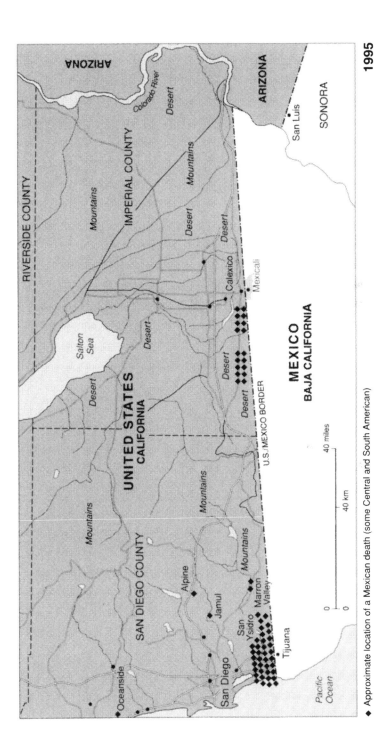

1995

◆ Approximate location of a Mexican death (some Central and South American)

FIGURE 3.2 Spatial distribution of migrant deaths along the US–Mexico border, 1995.
Source: California Rural Legal Assistance Foundation 2004b.

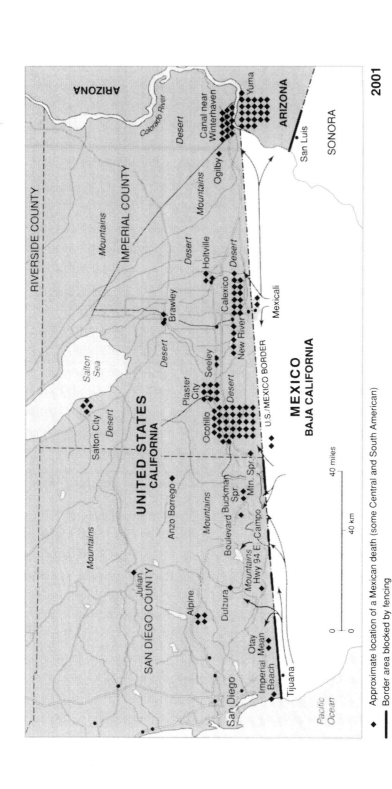

FIGURE 3.3 Spatial distribution of migrant deaths along the US–Mexico border, 2001.

Source: California Rural Legal Assistance Foundation 2004b.

◆ Approximate location of a Mexican death (some Central and South American)

▬ Border area blocked by fencing

➔ Diverted migration route due to fencing, lighting, and other tactics

2001

Year to date total as of December 31, 2001

they reach the Mexico–US border, having hiked for a day and a half from a bus stop in the Mexican interior. (Cornelius 2001: 674–5)

All indications, then, are that enhanced boundary policing has made illicit border crossings much more perilous. Indeed, there is little doubt that, as the traffic of illicit bodies has moved from urban areas to rural locations, the risk of migrant death has become greater.

Significantly, the fact that large numbers of border crossers are dying has not escaped the Border Patrol's attention. The agency actually seems quite concerned about this development. In 1998, for example, it launched an operation designed to curtail the number of border-related injuries and deaths (US GAO 2001: 24–8). This operation, called the Border Safety Initiative (BSI), has two main components. One focuses on education. The objective here is to inform would-be undocumented immigrants about the dangers of crossing the border. This educational component has principally entailed posting warning signs at high-risk areas along the border and running public service announcements on Mexican radio, television, and in newspapers. The dangers that immigrants are alerted to include extreme temperatures, snakes, and border bandits. The second component of the BSI involves search-and-rescue. The Border Patrol has established special units to search for and give assistance to border crossers who may have become distressed. The El Centro sector, for example, has a desert rescue team. This team is trained in first aid and emergency medical procedures. Moreover, it has the use of an ambulance equipped with extra water, electrolyte drinks, and lifesaving equipment. This component of the BSI appears to be paying off. In FY 2000, for instance, the Border Patrol undertook approximately 500 rescue missions and helped out close to 2,500 migrants in trouble (US GAO 2001: 27).

I should note though that while the Border Patrol may have noticed that immigrants are dying and taken some steps to remedy the situation, it has not acknowledged that its operations brought about the problem in the first place. Indeed, the agency has failed to take any responsibility for the rise in migrant deaths. As one Border Patrol officer put it: "Death on the border is unfortunate, but it's nothing new. It's not caused by the Border Patrol. It's not caused by Gatekeeper" (Ellingwood 1999: A28). The logic behind this refusal to accept any blame is rather straightforward. The Border Patrol contends that it is simply doing its duty of safeguarding the nation's border when it closes off busy urban crossing points. If immigrants consequently choose to cross through rural terrains, the responsibility for any unfortunate incidents that may occur is deemed to lie not with the Border Patrol but with the immigrants themselves and the smugglers who guide them. The reality is, however, that as long as urban crossing points stay virtually closed and immigrants are forced to seek passage through risky mountain and desert locations, the death toll will continue to climb. So while the Border Patrol may not strictly speaking be liable for the fatalities at the border, it does bear a certain amount of responsibility for them in so far as these deaths are an effect of the strict policing of the border. Indeed, immigrants are dying. And they are dying as a consequence of a stringent policy that propels them to cross the border through dangerous terrain.

All things considered, then, the results of the Border Patrol's strategy of prevention through deterrence have been rather mixed. On the one hand, there is no doubt that border areas such as San Diego and El Paso have largely been "pacified." Indeed, the flow of illicit bodies through these localities has been reduced considerably. On the other hand, however, the strategy has not proved to be effective overall. As a matter of fact, the traffic of undocumented migrants does not appear to have slowed down since the Border Patrol stepped up its operations. So while the strategy of prevention through deterrence might not be a resounding success, it is not a categorical failure either. Any success it has had, though, has not come without a rather high price: that of immigrant life.

INTERLUDE

TIJUANA, MEXICO. October 2, 2004. A group of Mexicans marched solemnly for miles along a road lined with white crosses to mark the 10 years since the United States launched a border crackdown they say has contributed to the deaths of thousands of migrants.

The US Border Patrol began Operation Gatekeeper on Oct. 1, 1994, to stop the flood of crossings from Tijuana to San Diego. The agency doubled the number of agents in San Diego, erected fences and installed brighter lights. Ten years later, supporters note that the crackdown has dramatically cut illegal border crossings into urban San Diego. But critics say the effort has simply forced migrants inland to remote and more treacherous areas where they risk dying of hypothermia, dehydration and drowning.

By the Border Patrol's count, 1,954 people have died crossing the border since October 1998. The preliminary death toll was 325 for the fiscal year that ended Thursday, down from 340 a year earlier. Human rights activists say more than 3,100 people have died along the border since Gatekeeper began.

The group of about a dozen protesters gathered Friday on the beach, near a painting of a skeleton holding two empty water jugs. The plywood board hung on a steel fence that separates Mexico from the United States. "For us, this is a day of mourning," said Oscar Escalada, who runs a YMCA migrant shelter in Tijuana. The migrants walked past a lighthouse and bullring that overlooks the ocean and onto the shoulder of a four-lane road to the San Ysidro Port of Entry, the world's busiest border crossing. The hilly, five-mile stretch was the focus of Gatekeeper.

They continued another three miles to the entrance of General Abelardo L. Rodriguez International Airport, where they hung the empty casket on the border fence. The casket, painted purple with orange flowers, hung next to nine others, each one marking a year since Gatekeeper's inception. The road to the airport is lined with hundreds of white crosses that activists have put up to honor the dead. "Gatekeeper has been a huge political success because it pushed things out of public view," Claudia Smith, border project director of the California Rural Legal Assistance Foundation, said as she walked up a hill. "It's the classic squeeze and bulge. You squeeze, and it just bulges elsewhere."

Mario Villarreal, a spokesman for the US Bureau of Customs and Border Protection, said Gatekeeper has restored a sense of normalcy to San Diego but conceded that too many people are dying along the border. "One death is one too many," he said. In an effort to prevent repeat crossings and save lives, the US government implemented a temporary voluntary program during which 14,000 undocumented Mexican migrants accepted free flights to Mexico City and Guadalajara instead of being deported to Mexican towns on the border. Officials in both countries say the program, which expired Thursday, has reduced the number of migrant deaths and they are studying the possibility of renewing it.

Ricardo Martinez of Veracruz city said Gatekeeper won't deter him. The 37-year-old, who joined Friday's protest march, plans to pay a smuggler $2,000 to drive him across the border, hidden in a compartment under a car's back seat. Martinez said he would go to Victorville, Calif., north of Los Angeles, for construction work. He wants to regain his old job working seven days a week for $2,000 a month.

Felix Cruz, 41, plans to hike through the mountains east of San Diego carrying two gallons of water, five cans of tuna fish and a bag of cookies. It will take him one night to walk 35 miles from Tecate, Mexico, to El Cajon, a San Diego suburb. He once earned about $700 a week working 14-hour days at two jobs in Orange County, Calif. – one hanging drywall and another selling ice cream. He returned to Mexico's central Puebla state to visit family. Cruz said he would cross the border with a friend, rather than trust a smuggler who might rob or abandon him. The California mountains are much safer than the Arizona desert, he said. "The desert has a lot of cactus spines and snakes," he said. "There's no water and the water that's there is dirty." (Spagat 2004)

DYING IN
ABANDONMENT

In this part, we have explored how, to the extent that undocumented immigrants have been constructed as criminal and undeserving, the efforts to govern them have generally fallen on the repressive side of ethopolitics. To be more specific, we delved into one of the more important ethopolitical means of managing this population: that being through crime. To govern through crime is to make crime and punishment the institutional context under which the efforts to guide the conduct of others takes place. With respect to "illegal" immigrants, governing through crime has principally meant the intensification of border policing. Essentially, the US federal government has determined that the best way to deal with the "problem" of undocumented immigration is through expanding the operations of the Border Patrol, particularly along the US–Mexico border. This expansion began in the late 1970s, intensified in the 1990s, and is continuing in the present. The main solution to the illegal immigration problem, then, has been to turn the United States into a fortified enclave of sorts. It has been to cast a wide net of control and surveillance over the border in order to discourage illegal incursions and thus keep troublesome individuals out of the body politic. As with the government of crime more generally, the rationale for managing illegal immigrants through police measures is that the public must be protected from the would-be criminals who threaten their well-being and contentment.

One important thing that has become apparent in exploring the government of immigration through crime is that the anti-citizenship technology of border policing has not exactly functioned as planned. This technology brought together an impressive array of practical and intellectual mechanisms (i.e., reform proposals, plans of action, police personnel, architectural structures, and surveillance devices) in order to affect the conduct of would-be undocumented immigrants in such a way as to forestall illicit border crossings. To be sure, the conduct of would-be immigrants has been dramatically affected. However, it has not been affected in such a way as to deter unauthorized boundary incursions. In fact, the size of the "undocumented" population has continued to grow in the era of enhanced border enforcement. What has happened instead is that the comportment of would-be immigrants has been shaped in such a way as to forestall urban border incursions and compel rural crossings. Indeed, as the border patrol has closed off familiar urban gateways, would-be immigrants, rather than desisting from entering the United States, have simply sought access through back country routes. The repercussions of this forced change in conduct have of course been tremendous. Border crossings have at once become more difficult and dangerous. So difficult and dangerous have they become that the number of border-related deaths has jumped dramatically. The INS/CBP and the Border Patrol are quite aware of this situation. Yet, they have refused to change their policy. They insist it is not their fault that immigrants are dying. The fact is, though, that immigrants are dying. And they are dying as a consequence of an anti-citizenship technology that has propelled them to cross through dangerous terrain. When all is said and done, then, the border has turned into a zone of abandonment. It is a place where immigrants are being channeled into danger. It is a place where their lives are being forsaken: where their death is being disavowed.

CONCLUSION: ITERATIONS

The purpose of *Targeting Immigrants* has been to examine the coinci-dence of knowledge and practice in the post-1965 government of "illegal" immigration. The book has had three general objectives. First of all, it has sought to analyze how "illegal" immigration has been constituted as a target of government and made thinkable, calculable, and manageable. Part of this exploration has entailed delving into the particular ways in which "illegal" immigrants have been problematized as unethical subjects: most notably as criminals, job stealers, and welfare dependents. Another part has entailed examining the specific regimes of truth and the various authorities – social scientists, politicians, INS/DHS bureaucrats, policy analysts, and the public at large – that have claimed to set forth facts about illicit border crossers. The concern here, then, has been to explore the constitution of "illegal" immigra-tion as a problem object, as well as the variable forms of truth, know-ledge, and expertise that have rendered it intelligible and governable. The second objective of this book has been to explore the program-matic aspects of governing "illegal" immigration. More precisely, it has endeavored to study a number of more or less explicit knowledgeable and calculated measures for reforming the conduct of "illegal" immi-grants, these measures being Operation Gatekeeper, Operation Hold the Line, and related boundary enforcement efforts. The goal here has been to detail how such governmental programs have sought to resolve the problem of "illegal" immigration in light of specific goals. The third general aim of this study has been to attend to the technological dimensions of managing "illegal" immigration. It has focused, that is, on the actual mechanisms or technical devices – such as border architecture, military know-how, pamphlets, policy reports, and statistical charts – through which governmental authorities have actualized particular programs. The objective here has been to draw attention to the material tools that make governing "illegal" immigration possible.

A more specific aim of *Targeting Immigrants* has been to situate the government of "illegal" immigration within what Nikolas Rose and other scholars have called advanced liberal or post-social modes of rule. They note that, over the last thirty years or so, there has been a gradual reconfiguration of the territory of government in Anglophone societies. The ideal of the social-welfare state, dominant for much of the twentieth century, has generally yielded to that of the post-social state. This new ideal is such that the political apparatus no longer appears obligated to safeguard the well-being of the population through maintaining a sphere of collective security. Social insurance – as an ensemble of state mechanisms that sought to insure individuals against the insecurities of social life – has thus largely given way to the privatized and individualized government of risk. Individuals are now asked to take upon themselves the primary responsibility for managing their own security and that of their families. They are expected to adopt an entrepreneurial disposition toward life and insure themselves (using market mechanisms) against the vicissitudes of ill health, accidental loss, unemployment, and anything else that could potentially threaten their contentment. The principal model of the political subject promoted these days is thus that of the prudential citizen: a rational (calculating) and responsible (ethical) individual whose needs are met not through the procurement of public largesse but through diligent self-management and the exercise of personal choice in the marketplace.

Targeting Immigrants has noted that while scholars have done a nice job of analyzing how advanced liberal forms of government generally work through promoting the self-managing capacities of individuals, they have paid scant attention to how such regimes also operate through technologies of exclusion. The way to understand these technologies, I suggested, was to think about them in relation to the responsibilization of the subject. For the obverse of the responsibilizing moral imperatives of contemporary government has been the construction and exclusion of populations seen as impervious to the demands of prudentialism. Said otherwise, post-social governments have produced a highly naturalized – and often racialized – division between those who can and do secure their own well-being through judicious self-promotion and those who are deemed incapable of managing their own risks: the criminal, the underclass, the homeless, the vagrants, the truly disadvantaged. Significantly, while the government of the former has largely taken place through the mechanisms of market and outside the formal political apparatus, the regulation of the latter has increasingly occurred through the widening reach of the repressive arms of the state. Indeed, law and order measures – "zero tolerance," "three strikes," and so forth – have become the preferred institutional contexts through which the government of marginal subjects is effected. The logic here is that responsible individuals must be protected from all those who threaten their security and quality of life. It is within this exclusionary and generally neglected side of post-social government – what I have called the repressive underbelly of ethopolitics – that the book has sought to situate the contemporary problematization of "illegal" immigration. The book has argued that "illegal" immigrants – typically imagined as criminals, job takers, and welfare dependents – have essentially been constructed as imprudent, unethical subjects incapable of exercising responsible self-government and thus as threats to the overall well-being of the social body. Moreover, it has noted that the programs and technologies that have been formulated to govern them and contain their threat – Operation Gatekeeper, for example – have been rather restrictive, exclusionary, and punitive. So much like the government of marginal citizens more generally, the preferred method of dealing with "illegal" immigrants has been through law and order measures. And this way of governing immigration has not been inconsequential. The maturation of border policing as an anti-citizenship technology has meant not so much the curtailment of illegal immigration – although, to be sure, areas such as San Diego and El Paso have been brought somewhat under control – but the putting of immigrants in harm's way. Indeed, as migrants have responded to the blockading of familiar urban crossing points by attempting to cross through desolate terrains, the trip north has become much more dangerous. The effect: a significant increase in the number of immigrant deaths. The message this sends is that governmental authorities are willing to tolerate casualties in their quest to gain control over the US–Mexico border. It is that the lives of immigrants are in some ways expendable.

Overall, then, *Targeting Immigrants* has been concerned with how assorted forms of knowledge, governing authorities, programs, and technical means have come together to construct "illegal" immigrants as targets of political intervention. The book can thus be seen as an effort to analyze the art of governing "illegal" immigration. Such an analysis has consisted, on the one hand, of empirical representation: it has described how certain knowledges, particularly numerical ones, have produced truths about "illegal" immigrants, and consequentially how various authorities – from the INS to DHS – have sought to regulate them. And on the other, the examination has entailed critical diagnosis: it has been diagnostic in the sense that it has sought to establish a critical connection to practices of government, attending to their exclusions, presuppositions, oversights, and costs. This analysis, then, has consisted of describing and diagnosing the assemblage of mechanisms and devices for creating knowledge about and intervening upon the problem of "illegal" immigration. The book can thus also be seen as an exploration of how the practice of government is intimately linked to the activity of thought. It has been intimately concerned with the connection between thinking and acting, representing and intervening, knowing and doing: in short, with power/knowledge.

NOTES

Introduction

1 On March 1, 2003, the Immigration and Naturalization Service, the federal agency traditionally responsible for enforcing the nation's immigration laws, was officially abolished and its duties – including border management – transferred to various agencies within the newly created Department of Homeland Security. This transfer of duties will be discussed more thoroughly later in the book.

2 We should note here that, for scholars of governmentality, governmental objects do not simply preexist the activity of governing. These objects are not just passively sitting there waiting to be discovered. Rather, according to Rose, "acts of governing actually constitute or make up the zones on which they act and the entities upon which they act" (Rose 2000a: 145).

3 This is not to suggest that, in the post-1965 period, border enforcement has been the only significant way of managing undocumented immigration. Other important programs include, to name only a few of the better known, the Immigration Reform and Control Act of 1986 (IRCA), California's Proposition 187, and the Illegal Immigration Reform and Immigrant Responsibility Act of 1996. For an examination of these other programs see Bean, Edmonston, and Passel 1990; Perea 1997; and Welch 2003.

4 I should note here that this project does not set out to speak or set right the truth about "illegal" immigration. It does not, for example, engage in debates about whether or not illegal immigrants are good for the economy, or seek to give a more accurate picture of their use of social services. Rather, it is concerned with how various forms of knowledge and expertise produce their own truths about illegal immigrants, and the part that such truths play in their management. That is to say, the book is interested in exploring the ways in which the problem of illegal immigration has been conceptualized and regulated. For the issue of unemployment, see Walters 2000.

5   This book essentially offers a Foucault-inspired take on "undocumented" immigration and immigration politics. For other recent takes see Perea 1997, Reimers 1998, Andreas 2000, Chavez 2001, Martínez 2001, Luibhéid 2002, Ono and Sloop 2002, Nevins 2002, Welch 2002, Hing 2004, and Romero 2005.

6   For a more thorough discussion of this critique of the social state, see Rose 1996a.

7   It is called "the new prudentialism" so as to distinguish it from older forms. According to Mitchell Dean:

> The new prudentialism differs from older, nineteenth-century forms of prudentialism in a number of ways. It first of all multiplies the domains to be monitored and prudently managed. Early nineteenth-century Malthusianism added procreative prudence and independence from poor relief to earlier injunctions to industry, frugality in domestic economy, and sobriety. Today the active citizen must add the monitoring of their risks of physical and mental ill-health, of sexually acquired disease, of dependency (on drugs, alcohol, nicotine, welfare or in personal relationships), of being a victim of crime, of a lack of adequate resources in retirement, of their own and their children's education, of low self-esteem and so on. Further, what is calculated is not the dangerousness of certain activities (e.g. gambling, drinking, poor hygiene), places (the alehouse, ghettos) and populations (the dangerous classes) but the risks that traverse each and every member of the population and which it is their individual and collective duty to control. (1999: 166)

8   This is not to suggest racial minorities are the only ones subject to exclusionary processes. Indeed not. Practices of exclusion also disproportionately affect women, gays, and working-class populations, regardless of their color (see Kinsman 1996; Weir 1996). All I mean to suggest, then, is that racial minorities are the ones most heavily affected by exclusionary practices.

9   My understanding of "ethnographic" is influenced by Paul Rabinow. Discussing "society," he notes the following: "An ethnographic approach to society as the product of historical practices combining truth and power consists of identifying society as a cultural object, specifying those authorized to make truth claims about it and those practices and symbols which localized, regulated, and represented that new reality spatially (form is equally a cultural object)" (1989: 11).

Part One: Ethopolitics and the Management of In/security

1   The term ethics is used here in a Foucauldian sense. It does not refer so much to moral practices as to the duty of individuals to take care of themselves. An ethical being is one who takes care of her or his self (see Foucault 1990).

2 This does not mean, however, that individuals are simply told how to conduct themselves. Rather, subjects are furnished with expert knowledges that they can use to determine their own particular health needs and thus to fashion a risk-minimizing mode of existence. The idea is to persuade individuals to conform voluntarily to the imperatives of good health. It is to convince them that observing a healthy lifestyle is in their best interest.

3 Of course, not everybody has the economic and social means to accept this duty, even if they want to do so.

4 The reasons for this rise in illegalities are numerous. Among them we can include: increased criminal opportunities ("the consumer boom of the post-war decades put into circulation a mass of portable, high-value goods that presented attractive new targets for theft"); diminished situational controls (during these same post-war decades "there was a reduction in situational controls as shops increasingly became 'self-service,' densely populated neighborhoods were replaced by sprawling suburban tracts or anonymous tower blocks, downtown areas became entertainment centers with no residents, and more and more well-stocked houses were left empty during the day while both wives and husbands went out to work"); a growth in the "at risk" population (the 1960s witnessed "the arrival of a large cohort of teenage males – the age group most prone to criminal behavior"); and a decline in the effectiveness of social controls (this period saw "a questioning of traditional authorities, a relaxation of the norms governing conduct in the realm of sexuality and drug-use, and the spread of a more 'permissive,' 'expressive' style of child-rearing") (Garland 2001: 90–1).

5 To be sure, the poor remain the main casualties of crime.

6 Of course, the state alone has not brought about this state of affairs. It has had significant help from both the commercial security industry, "whose sale of security devices fuelled the public's fears and insecurities at the very moment that it claimed to allay them" (Garland 2001: 161), and the private insurance sector, which has sought to educate the public about secure living, emphasizing the importance of insurance to any security plan (O'Malley 1991).

7 See Rose 1996c for a more detailed discussion of the post-social emphasis of government through community.

8 Community, of course, need not be an identifiable space on a map. It could also be virtual: "associated in neither 'real' space nor 'real' time but through a network of relays of communication, symbols, images, styles of dress and other devices of identification" (Rose 1996c: 333).

9 I should note here that the post-social activation of community does not in any way conflict with the ethos of individual responsibility. Indeed not. For the community is imagined as a voluntary association of active citizens – as a collectivity brought together in self-interested pursuit of mutual benefits. Put otherwise, the individual is addressed as both self-responsible and beholden to other individuals within a specific locale.

10   Self-governance in the gated community does not stop at the private control of crime. These communities are also more generally characterized by a kind of "private" government: the homeowners' association. Since normally public spaces are privatized here, these associations take upon themselves the responsibility not only for policing but also for the maintenance of parks, streets, recreation facilities, and so forth.

11   The question of dependency became so central that Congress passed an Act (the Welfare Indicators Act of 1994) that required the Department of Health and Human Services to produce an annual report on predictors and indicators of welfare dependency. The declared purpose of the Act is "to provide the public with generally accepted measures of welfare receipt so that it can track such receipt over time and determine whether progress is being made in reducing the rate at which and, to the extent feasible, the degree to which, families depend on income from welfare programs and the duration of welfare receipt" (quoted in Schram 2000: 63).

12   The root meaning of the verb *to depend* points to a physical relation in which one object or thing hangs from another.

13   Older schemes of welfare administration were more concerned with the allocation of income and the disbursement of benefits than with the monitoring of welfare subjects. See Schram 2000: 59–88.

14   Another case in point are the many women who have procured employment yet are unable to adequately take care of their families. The problem here is that, since these women often have low levels of education and few marketable skills, the only jobs they can get are low-wage, dead-end ones – retail sales, clerical work, cleaning, food service, child care, and so forth – that fall short of delivering self-supporting incomes (King 1999: 282). Numerous women have thus left the welfare rolls only to join the ranks of the working poor. What welfare reform has done, then, is actually produced "a sector of the laboring population that is casualized, underprotected against risk, insecure and desocialized" (Rose 1999a: 267).

15   The thinking here too is that today's beggars, loiterers, and so forth may very well be tomorrow's murderers, rapists, and robbers. So dealing with them now will forestall more serious problems later on.

Part Two: Producing "the Illegal," or Making Up Subjects

1   These restrictions were imposed on all immigrants, not just those from Mexico.

2   The first undesirable classes were barred in 1875. These included prostitutes and persons convicted of crimes involving moral turpitude. Other classes were barred in subsequent years. As Mae Ngai points outs, "the litany of excludable classes articulated concern over the admission of real and potential

public charges as well as late-nineteenth-century beliefs, derived from Social Darwinism and criminal anthropology, that the national body had to be protected from the contaminants of social degeneracy" (n.d.).

3   The law applied to people entering the United States after July 1, 1924.

4   There would have been no Mexican "illegal" aliens other than those who fell into one of the excludable classes.

5   The category of the deported is made up of two classes: those expelled formally under warrant and those allowed to depart voluntarily. As Ngai notes: "In order to make expulsion more efficient, in 1927 the Border Patrol allowed illegal aliens without criminal records to depart voluntarily, thereby avoiding the time and expense of instituting formal deportation proceedings" (n.d.).

6   The immigrants targeted for repatriation included those without proper documentation, as well as those who had become deportable or "illegal" as a result of turning into public charges. The latter was probably the more significant group. Like other workers, many Mexican immigrants lost their jobs during the Great Depression. Consequently, they were forced to seek relief from local welfare organizations. This made them public charges in the eyes of government officials.

7   To compensate growers for the loss of "illegal" immigrant labor, the US government significantly increased the number of braceros permitted into the United States (Carrasco 1997: 203).

8   Others, and not just braceros, would migrate illegally as well.

9   In 1976, a fixed national quota of 20,000 legal immigrants per year was imposed for every single country in the Western Hemisphere (De Genova 2002).

10   The Border Patrol still exists. It is now housed in the Department of Homeland Security. The Investigations Division has been disbanded and its duties generally transferred to Immigration and Customs Enforcement (ICE), an entity also housed in the DHS.

11   The years here refer to fiscal years. Currently, a fiscal year refers to the twelve-month period beginning October 1 and ending September 30. Historically, from 1868 through 1976, the fiscal year went from July 1 to June 30. Then there is a transition quarter for 1976 that covers July through September.

12   When the INS was disbanded on March 1, 2003, its statistics division was reorganized as the Office of Immigration Statistics, under the control of the DHS Under Secretary for Management, and the *Statistical Yearbook of the Immigration and Naturalization Service* was retitled *Yearbook of Immigration Statistics*. The *Yearbook* looks very much like the *Statistical Yearbook*.

13   This table has had various names including "Aliens Apprehended, Aliens Deported, and Aliens Required to Depart," "Aliens Apprehended, Deported, and Required to Depart," and "Deportable Aliens Located." The tables have also changed some. The more current tables do not contain information on the deported and required to depart. The change occurred in the 1997

Statistical Yearbook. Historically, this chart has also given information as to how many aliens have been expelled.

14 The practice of reporting estimates has continued under the DHS.

15 There are problems in using apprehension figures as indicators of the magnitude of illegal immigration. Nevertheless, they can still be used in a general way to infer that illegal immigration is increasing. Vernon Briggs articulates this as follows:

> There are severe problems associated with using the number of illegal immigrants apprehended as an indicator of the magnitude of illegal immigration. To begin with, the data reflect multiple counting. Some persons – especially in the Southwest – are caught more than once in a given year. About 95 percent of the persons who are apprehended each year are given the choice of departing voluntarily or being subjected to lengthy and costly deportation proceedings, and most choose the former. As a result, there is virtually no legal deterrent to keep them from again trying to enter the United States. Presumably, however, the problem of repeat captures has always been reflected in the data on apprehensions. There is no reason to believe that this problem is proportionately more severe now than it has been in the past. Hence, the increase in the number of apprehensions can be used in a general way to infer an increase in the number of illegal immigrants entering the United States, but it cannot be used as a precise indicator of the number of individuals involved. (Briggs 1984: 132–3)

16 The apprehensions table in the report shows that the number of apprehended bodies went from 110,371 to 345,353 (INS 1971: 85).

17 This is not to say that apprehension numbers could not be useful in measuring magnitude. What one would have to do, to put it simply, is somehow calculate the ratio of those who got through to those who got caught.

18 For a review of INS estimates as speculative see Keely 1977.

19 This is not to say that there were no problems with the more analytical methods. For a review of the problems associated with these early estimates of illegal immigration see Siegel, Passel, and Robinson 1981.

20 It is beyond the scope of this book to provide fine details of the procedures used to measure "illegal" immigration. What I do instead is just give a brief indication of where these numbers come from.

21 For a great analysis of media representations of immigration see Chavez 2001.

22 Some researchers suggest that this drop in apprehensions may have been due less to the deterrent effect of the policy and more to the legalization of close to 3 million people, many of whom habitually crossed the border illegally. So with less people needing to cross illegally, there was bound to be a drop in apprehensions (Donato, Durand, and Massey 1992: 155).

23 Eventually, apprehension figures would reach the levels recorded in the mid-1980s. In 2000, apprehensions topped 1.8 million (US INS 2003a: 239).

24 This signaling out of Mexicans was less blatant than during the 1970s. In 1987, the INS stopped the practice of dividing arrest figures into Mexicans and Other Nationalities – the latter constituting a homogeneous mass – and began collecting and reporting the nationality of each apprehended alien.

25 For a discussion of various methodologies see US GAO 1993, Van Hook and Bean 1998, and Passel 1999.

26 Two things happened here. First, a "disproportionate share of the unauthorized immigrant population from Mexico was legalized" (Warren 1994: 21). And second, the undocumented population was believed to have become more diverse in the 1980s and 1990s (US GAO 1993: 10).

27 The next closest group was Salvadorans at about 10 percent.

28 The voters of California approved the initiative (59 percent to 41 percent) on November 8, 1994. The measure never went into effect, however. Its main provisions were declared unconstitutional.

29 The argument here will concentrate on the general tendencies in the making up of "illegal" immigrants. The inclination has been to argue that the undocumented have an adverse impact on the labor market and put a strain on public services. We will not explore the problems with such assertions. Nor will we deal with the counter-tendencies: those suggesting that immigrants have a positive impact on the labor market and the general economic well-being of the country. For alternative assessments of the labor market and public service impact of the undocumented see Cornelius, Chavez, and Castro 1982; Simon 1999.

30 The likely reason for the focus on the labor market was that the 1970s and early 1980s were plagued by chronic unemployment.

31 As with efforts to enumerate illegal immigrants, the efforts to calculate their impact proved rather difficult. The general problem is the clandestine nature of this population. They are difficult to find and track down.

32 To be sure, there were some studies that disputed these claims. For a review of some of this literature see Cornelius, Chavez, and Castro 1982.

33 The Select Commission was established in 1978 "to study and evaluate . . . existing laws, policies, and procedures governing the admission of immigrants and refugees to the United States and to make such administrative and legislative recommendations to the President and to the Congress as are appropriate" (US Select Commission 1981: xi).

34 The report also noted that: "Since most undocumented/illegal migrants tend to be young and unskilled, it is likely that young, less-skilled natives will be the most adversely affected by their presence" (US Select Commission 1981: 41).

35 These are some of the public benefits for which the undocumented are eligible. They are actually not eligible for most federal programs: Supplemental Security Income, unemployment compensation, financial assistance, the Job Training Partnership Act (JTPA), and so forth.

36   This is not to suggest that there were no problems with these studies. They were all in fact deeply problematic. A GAO review of these studies put the problem in the following terms:

> National data on illegal aliens' use of public services and level of tax payments generally are not available. . . . Because of such data limitations, the national studies relied on indirect approaches to estimate the costs and revenues attributable to illegal aliens. In using these approaches, the studies made assumptions whose reasonableness is often unknown. To estimate direct program costs, for example, the studies multiplied their estimates of the average numbers of illegal aliens who received a benefit or service times the average annual program cost per illegal alien. However, data generally are not available to assess whether the assumptions used in estimating illegal aliens' receipt rates and average costs were reasonable. (US GAO 1995a: 9–10)

37   Other studies focused on California generally corroborated the Governor's Office's findings. A Donald Huddle (1993) study, for example, concluded that the net fiscal impact of the undocumented was $5 billion in 1992.

38   This study was prepared by a team of researchers from the LA County Internal Services Department.

39   Local, state, and federal government costs are omitted.

40   It is the child and not the parent who is eligible for benefits. But the parent receives the benefits on behalf of his or her US citizen child. As the report indicates: "A child born in the United States to an illegal alien obtains US citizenship at birth regardless of the parent's immigration status and, as any other citizen in need, may receive welfare and other benefits" (US GAO 1997a: 1).

41   Undocumented immigrants are eligible to receive certain medical services through an Act of Congress: "To provide for certain medical services, the Congress in 1986 revised the Social Security Act to stipulate that illegal aliens are eligible for emergency services, including childbirth, under the Medicaid program. . . . In California and New York, illegal aliens are also eligible to receive Medicaid prenatal services" (US GAO 1994a: 4).

42   Nevins' (2002) analysis of the mass media shows that the terms most popularly used to refer to undocumented immigrants contain the word "illegal."

43   The US/Mexico Border Counties Coalition is a non-partisan policy and technical forum established to tackle the challenges confronting county governments situated on the United States–Mexico border.

44   The Office of Homeland Security was established by President George W. Bush on October 8, 2001. It was the early incarnation of the Department of Homeland Security.

45   The linking of immigration and terrorism can, of course, also be seen in the *Time* article discussed earlier (Barlett and Steele 2004). The reference to how thousands of people a day are crossing the Arizona/Mexico border without

being checked for explosive devices and weapons is meant to evoke the possibility that terrorists are sneaking into the United States in order to commit violent acts.

Part Three: Anti-Citizenship Technologies and the Regulation of the Border

1　Border policing as an anti-citizenship technology is also prophylactic in the sense that preventing illegal immigrants from entering the United States also prevents them from reproducing and giving birth to children who, as a result of using public services, are putatively a burden on the economy. For technologies that specifically target the social and biological reproduction of immigrants see Inda 2002.

2　The "Interlude" sections of Part Three are verbatim news stories culled from newspapers in the southwest United States. They speak to the detrimental effects of enhanced border policing on undocumented immigrants and their families. Quotation marks have been intentionally left off.

3　The policing of the border against unauthorized entry has a long history. We can trace it back to at least 1924. That is when Congress established the US Border Patrol, the first genuine mechanism designed to deal with illegal border crossings. Until the late 1970s, however, the policing of the border was for the most part a rather low-key affair.

4　The Commission, though, did not believe that border interdiction alone would stop the flow of illegal immigrants. More important for them was implementing sanctions related to employment.

5　Unless otherwise specified, the information in this paragraph is drawn from Dunn 1996: 35–61, 180–4.

6　The number of positions authorized by Congress is different from actual staffing levels. The INS has historically had a high turnover rate. So all positions are not always filled.

7　The Border Patrol is currently organized into twenty sectors. Nine of these are along the US–Mexico border. These are: San Diego, El Centro, Yuma, Tucson, El Paso, Marfa, Del Rio, Laredo, and McAllen.

8　At the time the thought also seemed to be that sealing off the border would be prohibitively expensive and thus not feasible (US GAO 1977).

9　Once an illegal entrant gained access to the "interior" of the country, the job of detecting such a person fell on the Investigations Division of the INS. For information of these tactics see Domestic Council Committee 1976.

10　Under voluntary departure, an alien admits to illegal status, waives his/her right to a hearing, and is removed under INS/CBP supervision. This practice is extensively used to expedite the removal of "ordinary" illegal aliens from the country. Repeat or aggravated offenders and criminal violators are held for prosecution and/or deportation proceedings.

11 Policy analysts and researchers generally acknowledged that a good percentage of undocumented immigrants were visa abusers as opposed to illicit border crossers.

12 Enforcing employer sanctions mainly entailed checking employer hiring practices.

13 It was generally believed that for every person who was apprehended two made it through.

14 Most Mexicans who attempt to cross the border illegally come from the interior of Mexico. By the time they get to the border they have already invested a lot of time and money. So many just keep trying to cross until they get through.

15 INS headquarters approved the operation and provided $300,000 for overtime pay.

16 A vast majority of illegal border crossings in the El Paso sector occurred along this stretch of border. Geographical and climatic conditions combine to funnel migrants into, rather than around, El Paso. The rugged terrain and desert conditions that surround El Paso provide little respite for weary foot travelers (Bean et al. 1994: 13).

17 These were not new agents. They were withdrawn from such other duties as employer sanctions, traffic checks, and support positions (Bean et al. 1994: 7).

18 Bean et al. (1994) suggest that when considering the impact of Operation Blockade one should distinguish between two different kinds of illegal border crossers: Those whose destination was El Paso (for shopping, work, etc.) and those who were headed to an interior destination. According to them, the operation's deterrent effect was mainly on the former group. The latter simply sought to cross into the United States through other places along the border.

19 Immigrants who successfully crossed in urban areas could easily mix in with the population. Those who attempted to cross through remote areas had a long way to go before they reached populated areas. This gave the Border Patrol more time to spot and catch them.

20 The stadium-style lights and new border fence were largely erected before Operation Gatekeeper was conceptualized. But they were incorporated as important components of the strategy. New roads were also constructed to allow easier access to and along the border.

21 During that time, Operation Gatekeeper was extended to encompass all 66 miles of the San Diego Border Patrol sector, while Operation Hold the Line was expanded into New Mexico.

22 The growth of policing resources was largely due to the Illegal Immigration Reform and Immigrant Responsibility Act of 1996 and the Violent Crime Control and Law Enforcement Act of 1994. Both of these Acts provided money to strengthen control of the border (Clinton 1994; US GAO 1999b: 26).

23 I should note here that not everyone agrees with the assessment that enhanced border policing has been a success. For criticism see Eschbach et al. 1999; Cornelius 2001; Nevins 2002.

24 See Cornelius 2001 for a discussion of the problems with using apprehension figures as a sign of the success or failure of the Border Patrol's policy.

25 The focus was on street-corner labor markets where undocumented laborers often congregate.

26 The Border Patrol, of course, expected this shift. However, they also expected people to be deterred.

27 There are no statistics on migrant deaths in Arizona and Texas prior to 1996.

28 The volume of unauthorized migration, if judged from apprehensions statistics, did rise during this period of course. So one would expect migrant deaths to go up. However, the yearly increases of migrant deaths are much higher than the increases in apprehensions. Moreover, the fatalities count is likely to be underestimated. The Ministry only counts actual bodies that were discovered. There are no doubt additional bodies that are never found.

29 In 1995, of course, Operation Gatekeeper was already in operation. However, it had not been fully implemented. So it can still be used as a basis for comparison.

30 The data for California here includes deaths that took place in Arizona west of Tucson. The reason these deaths are counted is because they are seen as part of the displacement effect of Operation Gatekeeper.

REFERENCES CITED

Abramovitz, Mimi
    2000   Under Attack, Fighting Back: Women and Welfare in the United States.
    New York: Monthly Review Press.
Andreas, Peter
    2000   Border Games: Policing the US–Mexico Divide. Ithaca, NY: Cornell
    University Press.
Appadurai, Arjun
    1996   Number in the Colonial Imagination. *In* Modernity at Large: Cultural
    Dimensions of Globalization. Pp. 114–35. Minneapolis: University of Min-
    nesota Press.
Ayres, B. Drummond, Jr.
    1994   Stepped-Up Border Patrols Halve Unlawful Crossings. New York Times,
    December 13: 22.
Barlett, Donald L., and James Steele
    2004   Who Left the Door Open? Time, September 20. Electronic document,
    webl.infotrac.galegroup.com/itw/infomark/553/582/52112127wl/
    purl=rcl_EAIM_0_A1218453208dyn=8!ar_ftm?sw_aep=vcsantabarbara, accessed
    October 3, 2004.
Bean, Frank D., Roland Chanove, Robert G. Cushing, Rodolfo de la Garza,
    Gary P. Freeman, Charles W. Haynes, and David Spener
    1994   Illegal Mexican Migration and the United States/Mexico Border: The
    Effects of Operation Hold the Line on El Paso/Juárez. Research Paper
    prepared for the US Commission on Immigration Reform. Washington, DC:
    Government Printing Office.
Bean, Frank D., Barry Edmonston, and Jeffrey S. Passel, eds.
    1990   Undocumented Migration to the United States: IRCA and the Experi-
    ence of the 1980s. Washington, DC: Urban Institute.
Berrick, Jill Duerr
    2001   Targeting Social Welfare in the United States: Personal Responsibility,
    Private Behavior, and Public Benefits. *In* Targeting Social Benefits: Interna-

tional Perspectives and Trends. Neil Gilbert, ed. Pp. 129–56. New Brunswick, NJ: Transaction Publishers.

Bersin, Alan
1996 Interviewed by David Nissman. United States Attorneys Bulletin 44(2).

Berstein, Dan
1994 Brown Aims to Beef Up Border Patrol. Orange County Register, September 14: Metro 7.

Blakely, Edward J., and Mary Gail Snyder
1997 Fortress America: Gated Communities in the United States. Washington, DC: Brookings Institute Press.

Briggs, Vernon M., Jr.
1984 Immigration Policy and the American Labor Force. Baltimore: Johns Hopkins University Press.

Calavita, Kitty
1992 Inside the State: The Bracero Program, Immigration, and the INS. New York: Routledge.

Caldeira, Teresa P. R.
2000 City of Walls: Crime, Segregation, and Citizenship in São Paulo. Berkeley: University of California Press.

California Rural Legal Assistance Foundation
2004a Stop Gatekeeper! Migrant Deaths. Electronic document, www.stopgatekeeper.org/English/deaths.htm, accessed November 13, 2004.
2004b Stop Gatekeeper! Maps. Electronic document, www.stopgatekeeper.org/English/maps.htm, accessed November 13, 2004.

Carrasco, Gilbert Paul
1997 Latinos in the United States: Invitation and Exile. In Immigrants Out! The New Nativism and the Anti-Immigrant Impulse in the United States. Juan F. Perea, ed. Pp. 190–204. New York: New York University Press.

Castel, Robert
1981 La gestion des risques: De l'anti-psychiatrie à l'après-psychanalyse. Paris: Editions de Minuit.

Castillo, Leonel J.
1978 Testimony of Leonel J. Castillo, Commissioner, Immigration and Naturalization Service. In Immigration to the United States, no. 5. Hearings before the Select Committee on Population. US House of Representatives. 95th Congress, Second Session. Pp. 497–504. Washington, DC: Government Printing Office.

Chapman, Leonard F.
1975a Illegal Aliens: A Growing Population. I & N Reporter 24: 15–18.
1975b Report of the Commissioner of Immigration and Naturalization. In Annual Report of the Immigration and Naturalization Service, 1974. Pp. iii–iv. Washington, DC: Government Printing Office.
1976a Illegal Aliens: Time to Call A Halt! Reader's Digest no. 109: 188–92.

1976b Statement of Leonard F. Chapman, Jr., Commissioner, Immigration and Naturalization Service. *In* Immigration 1976. Hearings before the Subcommittee on Immigration and Naturalization of the Committee on the Judiciary. United States Senate. 94th Congress, Second Session, on S. 3074. Pp. 22–58. Washington, DC: Government Printing Office.

Chavez, Leo R.
2001 Covering Immigration: Popular Images and the Politics of the Nation. Berkeley: University of California Press.

Chaze, William L.
1982 Will US Shut the Door on Immigrants? US News & World Report, April 12: 47–50.

Cleeland, Nancy
1994 Blockade at Border Hasn't Cut Births. San Diego Union-Tribune, February 20: A23.

Clinton, William J.
1994 Accepting the Challenge: The President's Report on Immigration. Washington, DC: Government Printing Office.

Coffey, Ruth
1994 Another "D-Day" Needed to End America's Immigration Invasion. Nationalist Times, July. Electronic document, www.anu.org/archives_anotherd-dayneeded.html, accessed July 10, 2004.

Cohen, Patricia Cline
1982 A Calculating People: The Spread of Numeracy in Early America. Chicago: University of Chicago Press.

Coleman, James
1994 Illegal Immigrants Are, by Definition, Criminals. Los Angeles Times, September 12: B11.

Congressional Research Service
1977 Illegal Aliens: Analysis and Background. Prepared for the Use of the Committee on the Judiciary. US House of Representatives. 95th Congress, First Session. Washington, DC: Government Printing Office.

Cornelius, Wayne A.
1989 Mexican Migration to the United States: An Introduction. *In* Mexican Migration to the United States: Origins, Consequences, and Policy Options. Wayne A. Cornelius and Jorge A. Bustamante, eds. Pp. 1–21. La Jolla: Center for US–Mexican Studies, University of California, San Diego.
1998 The Structural Embeddedness of Demand for Mexican Immigrant Labor: New Evidence from California. *In* Crossings: Mexican Immigration in Interdisciplinary Perspective. Marcelo M. Suárez-Orozco, ed. Pp. 115–44. Cambridge, MA: Harvard University Press.
2001 Death at the Border: Efficacy and Unintended Consequences of US Immigration Control Policy. Population and Development Review 27(4): 661–85.

Cornelius, Wayne A., Leo R. Chavez, and Jorge G. Castro
1982 Mexican Immigrants and Southern California: A Summary of Current Knowledge. Research Report Series, 36. La Jolla: Center for US–Mexican Studies, University of California, San Diego.

Corwin, Arthur F.
1982 The Numbers Game: Estimates of Illegal Aliens in the United States, 1970–1981. Law and Contemporary Problems 45(2): 223–97.

Coulson, Anthony W.
1994 Letter to the Editor: Hardworking or Not, Illegals Are a Burden to Social-Service Programs. Orange County Register, May 8: Commentary 5.

Crawford, Robert
1980 Healthism and the Medicalization of Everyday Life. International Journal of Health Services 10(3): 365–88.

Cruikshank, Barbara
1999 The Will to Empower: Democratic Citizens and Other Subjects. Ithaca, NY: Cornell University Press.

Dalton, Rex
1994 Births to Illegal Immigrants on the Rise: California Taxpayers Finance Soaring Number of Foreigners' Babies. San Diego Union-Tribune, February 20: A1.

Davis, Mike
1992 City of Quartz: Excavating the Future in Los Angeles. New York: Vintage Books.

Dean, Mitchell
1991 The Constitution of Poverty: Toward a Genealogy of Liberal Governance. New York: Routledge.
1995 Governing the Unemployed Self in an Active Society. Economy and Society 24(4): 559–83.
1999 Governmentality: Power and Rule in Modern Society. London: Sage Publications.

Defert, Daniel
1991 "Popular Life" and Insurance Technology. In The Foucault Effect: Studies in Governmentality. Graham Burchell, Colin Gordon, and Peter Miller, eds. Pp. 211–33. Chicago: University of Chicago Press.

De Genova, Nicholas P.
2002 Migrant "Illegality" and Deportability in Everyday Life. Annual Review of Anthropology 31: 419–47.

Deleuze, Gilles
1979 Foreword: The Rise of the Social. In The Policing of Families. Jacques Donzelot. Pp. ix–xvii. New York: Pantheon Books.

Dibble, Sandra
2000 Quest for New Life Ends in Death Near Border for Two. San Diego Union-Tribune, August 2. Electronic document, www.lexis-nexis.com/universe/printdoc, accessed March 30, 2005.

Domestic Council Committee on Illegal Aliens
1976   Preliminary Report. Washington, DC: Government Printing Office.

Donato, Katherine M., Jorge Durand, and Douglas S. Massey
1992   Stemming the Tide? Assessing the Deterrent Effects of the Immigration Reform and Control Act. Demography 29(2): 139–57.

Duerksen, Susan
1990   Medi-Cal Fraud Cases Soaring Here: State Probers Blame Mexicans Seeking Free Care. San Diego Union-Tribune, March 19: B1.

Dunn, Timothy J.
1996   The Militarization of the US–Mexico Border, 1978–1992: Low-Intensity Conflict Doctrine Comes Home. Austin, TX: CMAS Books.

Ellingwood, Ken
1999   Border Policy Violates Rights, Groups Charge. Los Angeles Times, February 11: A3, A28.

Erzen, Tanya
2001   Turnstile Jumpers and Broken Windows: Policing Disorder in New York City. In Zero Tolerance: Quality of Life and the New Police Brutality in New York City. Andrea McArdle and Tanya Erzen, eds. Pp. 19–49. New York: New York University Press.

Eschbach, Karl, Jacqueline Hagan, Nestor Rodriguez, Ruben Hernandez-Leon, and Stanley Bailey
1999   Death at the Border. International Migration Review 33(2): 430–54.

Escobar, Arturo
1995   Encountering Development: The Making and Unmaking of the Third World. Princeton, NJ: Princeton University Press.

Ewald, François
1986   L'état providence. Paris: Grasset.
1991   Insurance and Risk. In The Foucault Effect: Studies in Governmentality. Graham Burchell, Colin Gordon, and Peter Miller, eds. Pp. 197–210. Chicago: University of Chicago Press.

Ezell, Harold W.
1994   Letter to the Editor: We Need More Border Control. Orange County Register, September 26: Metro 7.

Fallows, James
1983   Immigration: How It's Affecting Us. Atlantic Monthly, November: 45–8, 99–106.

Farrell, Raymond F.
1972   Statement of Hon. Raymond F. Farrell, Commissioner, Immigration and Naturalization Service. In Illegal Aliens, part 5. Hearings before Subcommittee No. 1 of the Committee on the Judiciary. US House of Representatives. 92nd Congress, Second Session. Pp. 1307–54. Washington, DC: Government Printing Office.

Federation for American Immigration Reform (FAIR)
1989   Ten Steps to Securing America's Borders. Washington, DC: FAIR.

1997   Anchor Babies: Is Citizenship an Entitled Birthright? Electronic document, fairus.org/html/04139708.htm, accessed May 22, 2001.

2001   California: Social Policy Issues. Electronic document, fairus.org/html/042casoc.htm, accessed May 22, 2001.

2003   Breaking the Piggy Bank: How Illegal Immigration is Sending Schools Into the Red. Washington, DC: FAIR Horizon Press.

Ferguson, James, and Akhil Gupta

2006   Spatializing States: Toward an Ethnography of Neoliberal Governmentality. *In* Anthropologies of Modernity: Foucault, Governmentality, and Life Politics. Jonathan Xavier Inda, ed. Pp. 105–26. Malden, MA: Blackwell.

Fogel, Walter

1977   Illegal Alien Workers in the United States. Industrial Relations 16(3): 243–63.

1979   Mexican Illegal Alien Workers in the United States. Los Angeles: Institute of Industrial Relations, University of California.

Foucault, Michel

1988   The Political Technology of Individuals. *In* Technologies of the Self: A Seminar with Michel Foucault. Luther H. Martin, Huck Gutman, and Patrick H. Hutton, eds. Pp. 145–62. Amherst: University of Massachusetts Press.

1990   The History of Sexuality, vol. 2: The Use of Pleasure. New York: Vintage Books.

1991   Governmentality. *In* The Foucault Effect: Studies in Governmentality. Graham Burchell, Colin Gordon, and Peter Miller, eds. Pp. 87–104. Chicago: University of Chicago Press.

2000   The Subject and Power. *In* The Essential Works of Foucault, 1954–1984, vol. 3: Power. James D. Faubion, ed. Pp. 326–48. New York: The New Press.

Fraser, Nancy

1993   Clintonism, Welfare, and the Antisocial Wage: The Emergence of a Neoliberal Political Imaginary. Rethinking Marxism 6(1): 9–23.

Fraser, Nancy, and Linda Gordon

1994   A Genealogy of *Dependency*: Tracing a Keyword of the US Welfare State. Signs: Journal of Women in Culture and Society 19(2): 309–36.

García y Griego, Manuel

1980   El volumen de la migración de mexicanos no documentados a los Estados Unidos: Nuevas hipótesis. Mexico City: Centro Nacional de Información y Estadisticas del Trabajo.

1998   The Bracero Program. *In* Migration Between Mexico and the United States: Binational Study, vol. 3: Research Reports and Background Materials. Pp. 1215–21. Mexico City: Mexican Ministry of Foreign Affairs; Washington DC: US Commission on Immigration Reform.

Garland, David

1996   The Limits of the Sovereign State: Strategies of Crime Control in Contemporary Society. British Journal of Criminology 36(4): 445–71.

2001   The Culture of Control: Crime and Social Order in Contemporary Society. Chicago: University of Chicago Press.

Greco, Monica

1993   Psychosomatic Subjects and the "Duty to be Well": Personal Agency within Medical Rationality. Economy and Society 22(3): 357–72.

Greenhalgh, Susan

2003   Planned Births, Unplanned Persons: "Population" in the Making of Chinese Modernity. American Ethnologist 30(2): 196–215.

Greenwood, Peter W., C. Peter Rydell, Allan F. Abrahamse, Jonathan P. Caulkins, James Chiesa, Karyn E. Model, and Stephen P. Klein

1994   Three Strikes and You're Out: Estimated Benefits and Costs of California's New Mandatory-Sentencing Law. Santa Monica, CA: RAND.

Guss, Edward Jon

1977   "Even If You're on the Right Track, You'll Get Run Over If You Just Sit There." INS Reporter 25(4): 51–6.

Gutiérrez, David G.

1995   Walls and Mirrors: Mexican Americans, Mexican Immigrants, and the Politics of Ethnicity. Berkeley: University of California Press.

Hacking, Ian

1982   Biopower and the Avalanche of Printed Numbers. Humanities in Society 5(3–4): 279–95.

Hayes, Linda B.

1994   Letter to the Editor: California's Prop. 187. New York Times, October 15: 18.

Heer, David M.

1979   What is the Annual Net Flow of Undocumented Mexican Immigrants to the United States? Demography 16(3): 417–23.

Hing, Bill Ong

2004   Defining America through Immigration Policy. Philadelphia: Temple University Press.

Horn, David G.

1994   Social Bodies: Science, Reproduction, and Italian Modernity. Princeton, NJ: Princeton University Press.

Huddle, Donald

1993   The Costs of Immigration. Washington, DC: Carrying Capacity Network.

1994   The Net National Cost of Immigration in 1993. Washington, DC: Carrying Capacity Network.

Inda, Jonathan Xavier

2002   Biopower, Reproduction, and the Migrant Woman's Body. In Decolonial Voices: Chicana and Chicano Studies in the 21st Century. Arturo J. Aldama and Naomi H. Quiñonez, eds. Pp. 98–112. Bloomington: Indiana University Press.

Jackson, Robert L.

2001   Family Welfare Rolls Show Slight Drop. Los Angeles Times, September 6: A14.

Kalpagam, U.

2000 The Colonial State and Statistical Knowledge. History of the Human Sciences 13(2): 37–55.

2002 Colonial Governmentality and the Public Sphere in India. Journal of Historical Sociology 15(1): 35–58.

Keely, Charles B.

1977 Counting the Uncountable: Estimates of Undocumented Aliens in the United States. Population and Development Review 3(4): 473–81.

Kelly, Orr

1977 Border Crisis: Illegal Aliens Out of Control? US News & World Report, April 25: 33–9.

King, Desmond

1999 In the Name of Liberalism: Illiberal Social Policy in the United States and Britain. Oxford: Oxford University Press.

Kinsman, Gary

1996 "Responsibility" as a Strategy of Governance: Regulating People Living with AIDS and Lesbians and Gay Men in Ontario. Economy and Society 25(3): 393–409.

Krikorian, Mark

2004 Safety Through Immigration Control. Providence Journal, April 24. Electronic document, www.cis.org/articles/2004/mskoped042404.html, accessed October 22, 2004.

Lamm, Richard D., and Gary Imhoff

1985 The Immigration Time Bomb: The Fragmenting of America. New York: Truman Talley Books.

Lancaster, Clarice, and Frederick J. Scheuren

1978 Counting the Uncountable Illegals: Some Initial Statistical Speculations Employing Capture–Recapture Techniques. In 1977 Proceedings of the Social Statistics Section of the American Statistical Association, part 1. Pp. 530–5. Washington, DC: American Statistical Association.

Latour, Bruno

1986 Visualization and Cognition: Thinking with Eyes and Hands. Knowledge and Society 6: 1–40.

Lesko Associates

1976[1975] Final Report. Basic Data and Guidance Required to Implement a Major Illegal Alien Study During Fiscal Year 1976. In Immigration 1976. Hearings before the Subcommittee on Immigration and Naturalization of the Committee on the Judiciary. United States Senate. 94th Congress, Second Session, on S. 3074. Pp. 133–41. Washington, DC: Government Printing Office.

Los Angeles County Internal Services Department

1992 Impact of Undocumented Persons and Other Immigrants on Costs, Revenues, and Services in Los Angeles County. Report prepared for Los Angeles County Board of Supervisors. Los Angeles, CA: Board of Supervisors.

Luibhéid, Eithne

2002 Entry Denied: Controlling Sexuality at the Border. Minneapolis: University of Minnesota Press.

Lupton, Deborah

1995 The Imperative of Health: Public Health and the Regulated Body. London: Sage Publications.

1999a Risk. London: Routledge.

1999b Risk and the Ontology of Pregnant Embodiment. In Risk and Sociocultural Theory: New Directions and Perspectives. Deborah Lupton, ed. Pp. 59–85. Cambridge: Cambridge University Press.

McArdle, Andrea

2001 Introduction. In Zero Tolerance: Quality of Life and the New Police Brutality in New York City. Andrea McArdle and Tanya Erzen, eds. Pp. 1–16. New York: New York University Press.

McArdle, Andrea, and Tanya Erzen, eds.

2001 Zero Tolerance: Quality of Life and the New Police Brutality in New York City. New York: New York University Press.

Mallette, Pat

2004 America Is Changing and Not Necessarily for the Better. Immigration is Out of Control. Inland Valley Daily Bulletin, April 29. Electronic document, www.lexis-nexis.com/universe/printdoc, accessed October 17, 2004.

Martin, John L.

1993 Operation Blockade: Bullying Tactic or Border Control Model? Washington, DC: Center for Immigration Studies.

Martinez, Gebe, and Patrick J. McDonnell

1994 Prop. 187 Forces Rely on Message – Not Strategy. Los Angeles Times, October 30: A1, A36.

Martínez, Rubén

2001 Crossing Over: A Mexican Family on the Migrant Trail. New York: Metropolitan Books.

Mayer, Allan J., with Tom Joyce and Pamela Ellis Simons

1976 Immigration: The Alien Wave. Newsweek, February 9: 56–7.

MGT of America

2002 Medical Emergency: Costs of Uncompensated Care in Southwest Border Counties. Austin, TX: MGT of America.

Migdail, Carl J.

1977 Time Bomb in Mexico: Why There'll Be No End to the Invasion by "Illegals." US News & World Report, July 4: 27–8.

Miller, Peter, and Nikolas Rose

1990 Governing Economic Life. Economy and Society 19(1): 1–31.

Mink, Gwendolyn

1998 Welfare's End. Ithaca, NY: Cornell University Press.

Murray, Charles

1984 Losing Ground: American Social Policy, 1950–1980. New York: Basic Books.

Nevins, Joseph
2002   Operation Gatekeeper: The Rise of the "Illegal Alien" and the Making of the US–Mexico Boundary. New York: Routledge.
Ngai, Mae M.
1999   The Architecture of Race in American Immigration Law: A Re-examination of the Immigration Act of 1924. Journal of American History 86(1). Electronic document, www.historycooperative.org/journals/jah/86.1/ngai.html, accessed June 23, 2002.
2001   Making and Unmaking of Illegal Aliens: Deportation Policy and the Production of Nation-State Territoriality, 1925–1945. Unpublished MS. Department of History, University of Chicago.
N.d.   The Strange Career of the Illegal Alien: Immigration Restriction and Deportation Policy in the United States. Unpublished MS. Department of History, University of Chicago.
North, David S., and Marion F. Houstoun
1976   The Characteristics and Role of Illegal Aliens in the US Labor Market: An Exploratory Study. Washington, DC: Linton and Company, Inc.
Nunez, Peter K.
2004   Prepared Statement of the Honorable Peter K. Nunez. In Preventing the Entry of Terrorists into the United States. Hearing before the Subcommittee on International Terrorism, Nonproliferation, and Human Rights of the Committee on International Relations. US House of Representatives. 108th Congress, Second Session. Pp. 40–3. Washington, DC: Government Printing Office.
Oaks, Laury
2001   Smoking and Pregnancy: The Politics of Fetal Protection. New Brunswick, NJ: Rutgers University Press.
Office of Homeland Security (OHS)
2002   National Strategy for Homeland Security. Washington, DC: Office of Homeland Security.
Olson, W.
1994   Letter to the Editor: Hardworking or Not, Illegals Are a Burden to Social-Service Programs. Orange County Register, May 8: Commentary 5.
O'Malley, Pat
1991   Legal Networks and Domestic Security. Studies in Law, Politics, and Society 11: 171–90.
1992   Risk, Power, and Crime Prevention. Economy and Society 21(3): 252–75.
1996   Risk and Responsibility. In Foucault and Political Reason: Liberalism, Neo-Liberalism, and Rationalities of Government. Andrew Barry, Thomas Osborne, and Nikolas Rose, eds. Pp. 189–207. Chicago: University of Chicago Press.
1999   Social Justice After the "Death of the Social." Social Justice 26(2): 92–100.

2001 Policing Crime Risks in the Neo-Liberal Era. *In* Crime, Risk, and Justice: The Politics of Crime Control in Liberal Democracies. Kevin Stenson and Robert R. Sullivan, eds. Pp. 89–103. Portland, OR: Willan Publishing.

Ong, Aihwa
1995 Making the Biopolitical Subject: Cambodian Immigrants, Refugee Medicine, and Cultural Citizenship in California. Social Science and Medicine 40(9): 1243–57.
1999 Flexible Citizenship: The Cultural Logics of Transnationality. Durham, NC: Duke University Press.

Ong, Aihwa, and Stephen J. Collier, eds.
2005 Global Assemblages: Technology, Politics, and Ethics as Anthropological Problems. Malden, MA: Blackwell Publishing.

Ono, Kent A., and John M. Sloop
2002 Shifting Borders: Rhetoric, Immigration, and California's Proposition 187. Philadelphia: Temple University Press.

Osborne, Thomas, and Nikolas Rose
1999 Governing Cities: Notes on the Spatialization of Virtue. Environment and Planning D: Society and Space 17: 737–60.

O'Toole, Marion
1994 Letter to the Editor: Deport Criminal Illegals. Orange County Register, November 23: Metro 9.

Parker, Richard A., and Louis M. Rea
1993 Illegal Immigration in San Diego County: An Analysis of Costs and Revenues. Report to the California State Senate Special Committee on Border Issues. Sacramento, CA: Senate Publications.

Parrish, David
1994 Immigrant Tide Stemmed at Border: Beefed-Up Border Patrol Proves a Deterrent to Crossings. San Francisco Examiner, December 11: C4.

Passel, Jeffrey S.
1999 Undocumented Immigration to the United States: Numbers, Trends, and Characteristics. *In* Illegal Immigration in America: A Reference Handbook. David W. Haines and Karen E. Rosenblum, eds. Pp. 27–111. Westport, CT: Greenwood Press.

Passel, Jeffrey S., and Rebecca L. Clark
1994 How Much Do Immigrants Really Cost? A Reappraisal of Huddle's "The Cost of Immigrants." Washington, DC: Urban Institute.

Passel, Jeffrey S., Randy Capps, and Michael Fix
2004 Undocumented Immigrants: Facts and Figures. Washington, DC: Urban Institute.

Perea, Juan F., ed.
1997 Immigrants Out! The New Nativism and the Anti-Immigrant Impulse in the United States: New York: New York University Press.

Petersen, Alan R.
1996 Risk and the Regulated Self: The Discourse of Health Promotion as Politics of Uncertainty. Australian and New Zealand Journal of Sociology 32(1): 44–57.
Petersen, Alan R., and Deborah Lupton
1996 The New Public Health: Health and Self in the Age of Risk. London: Sage Publications.
Pinkerton, James
1996 Heat Gets the Blame for Deaths. Houston Chronicle, June 1. Electronic document, www.lexis-nexis.com/universe/printdoc, accessed March 30, 2005.
Poovey, Mary
1998 A History of the Modern Fact: Problems of Knowledge in the Sciences of Wealth and Society. Chicago: University of Chicago Press.
Porter, Theodore M.
1995 Trust in Numbers: The Pursuit of Objectivity in Science and Public Life. Princeton, NJ: Princeton University Press.
Portillo, Patricia G., and Mark Henry
1998 Immigrants Risked Heat of Desert for Work. Press Enterprise, August 19. Electronic document, www.lexis-nexis.com/universe/printdoc, accessed March 30, 2005.
Powell, Stewart
1979 Illegal Aliens: Invasion Out of Control? US News & World Report, January 29: 38–42.
Pratt, John
1999 Governmentality, Neo-Liberalism, and Dangerousness. In Governable Places: Readings on Governmentality and Crime Control. Russell Smandych, ed. Pp. 133–61. Aldershot: Ashgate/Dartmouth.
Press Enterprise
1994 State's Great Debate. Press Enterprise, November 6. Electronic document, www.lexis-nexis.com/universe/printdoc, accessed January 4, 2003.
Procacci, Giovanna
1993 Gouverner la misère: La question sociale en France, 1789–1848. Paris: Editions du Seuil.
Rabinow, Paul
1989 French Modern: Norms and Forms of the Social Environment. Cambridge, MA: MIT Press.
Reimers, David M.
1998 Unwelcome Strangers: American Identity and the Turn against Immigration. New York: Columbia University Press.
Romero, Philip J., and Andrew J. Chang
1994 Shifting the Costs of a Failed Federal Policy: The Net Fiscal Impact of Illegal Immigrants in California. Sacramento, CA: Governor's Office of Planning and Research.

Romero, Victor C.

2005   Alienated: Immigrant Rights, the Constitution, and Equality in America. New York: New York University Press.

Rose, Nikolas

1993   Government, Authority, and Expertise in Advanced Liberalism. Economy and Society 22(3): 283–99.

1996a   Governing "Advanced" Liberal Democracies. *In* Foucault and Political Reason: Liberalism, Neo-Liberalism, and Rationalities of Government. Andrew Barry, Thomas Osborne, and Nikolas Rose, eds. Pp. 37–64. Chicago: University of Chicago Press.

1996b   Psychiatry as a Political Science: Advanced Liberalism and the Administration of Risk. History of the Human Sciences 9(2): 1–23.

1996c   The Death of the Social? Re-Figuring the Territory of Government. Economy and Society 25(3): 327–56.

1998   Inventing Our Selves: Psychology, Power, and Personhood. Cambridge: Cambridge University Press.

1999a   Powers of Freedom: Reframing Political Thought. Cambridge: Cambridge University Press.

1999b   Inventiveness in Politics. Economy and Society 28(3): 467–93.

2000a   Governing Liberty. *In* Governing Modern Societies. Richard V. Ericson and Nico Stehr, eds. Pp. 141–76. Toronto: University of Toronto Press.

2000b   Government and Control. British Journal of Criminology 40: 321–39.

Rose, Nikolas, and Peter Miller

1992   Political Power Beyond the State: Problematics of Government. British Journal of Sociology 43(2): 173–205.

Rotella, Sebastian

1994   Border Patrol Masses by San Diego. Houston Chronicle, October 2: 24.

Rotstein, Arthur H.

2004   Trash Dumping Endemic in State with Flood of Illegal Immigration. Associated Press, July 11. Electronic document, www.lexis-nexis.com/universe/printdoc, accessed October 17, 2004.

Rouse, Bronwyn

2004   US Faces Silent Invasion. Deseret Morning News, June 27. Electronic document, www.lexis-nexis.com/universe/printdoc, accessed October 17, 2004.

Ruhl, Lealle

1999   Liberal Governance and Prenatal Care: Risk and Regulation in Pregnancy. Economy and Society 28(1): 95–117.

Sánchez, George J.

1993   Becoming Mexican American: Ethnicity, Culture, and Identity in Chicano Los Angeles, 1900–1945. New York: Oxford University Press.

Sanchez, Leonel

1994   Arrests Triple Along Border: Change in Tactics Viewed as Success. San Diego Union-Tribune, October 3: B1.

Sandia National Laboratories
1993   Systematic Analysis of the Southwest Border. Unpublished MS. Albuquerque, New Mexico.

Save Our State
1994a   Proposition 187: The "Save Our State" Initiative: The Questions and the Answers. Santa Ana, CA: Citizens for Legal Immigration Reform.
1994b   Proposition 187: The "Save Our State" Initiative: The Fiction and the Facts. Santa Ana, CA: Citizens for Legal Immigration Reform.

Schneiderman, Leonard, and Ellen Schneiderman
2001   Proposed Laws Don't Address Actual Issues. Los Angeles Times, July 8: M2.

Schram, Sanford F.
2000   After Welfare: The Culture of Postindustrial Social Policy. New York: New York University Press.

Scott, David
2006   Colonial Governmentality. In Anthropologies of Modernity: Foucault, Governmentality, and Life Politics. Jonathan Xavier Inda, ed. Pp. 23–49. Malden, MA: Blackwell.

Siegel, Jacob S., Jeffrey S. Passel, and J. Gregory Robinson
1981   Preliminary Review of Existing Studies of the Number of Illegal Residents in the United States. In US Immigration Policy and the National Interest. Appendix E to the Staff Report of the Select Commission on Immigration and Refugee Policy. Papers on Illegal Migration to the United States. Pp. 15–39. Washington, DC: Government Printing Office.

Silver, Jack
2004   What is Occurring in California is a Takeover Invasion of Lawbreakers. Inland Valley Daily Bulletin, July 1. Electronic document, www.lexis-nexis.com/universe/printdoc, accessed October 17, 2004.

Simon, Jonathan
1997   Governing Through Crime. In The Crime Conundrum: Essays on Criminal Justice. Lawrence M. Friedman and George Fisher, eds. Pp. 171–89. Boulder, CO: Westview Press.
2000   Megan's Law: Crime and Democracy in Late Modern America. Law and Social Inquiry 25(4): 1111–50.

Simon, Julian L.
1999   The Economic Consequences of Immigration. 2nd edition. Ann Arbor: University of Michigan Press.

Soja, Edward W.
2000   Postmetropolis: Critical Studies of Cities and Regions. Oxford: Blackwell Publishers.

Spagat, Elliot
2004   Migrants Mark Border-Crackdown Anniversary with Solemn March. Associated Press, October 2. Electronic document, www.lexis-nexis.com/universe/printdoc, accessed March 30, 2005.

Starr, Paul
  1987 The Sociology of Official Statistics. In The Politics of Numbers. William Alonso and Paul Starr, eds. Pp. 7–57. New York: Russell Sage Foundation.
Stenson, Kevin
  2000 Crime Control, Social Policy, and Liberalism. In Rethinking Social Policy. Gail Lewis, Sharon Gewirtz, and John Clarke, eds. Pp. 229–44. London: Sage Publications.
Stevenson, Mark
  2001 Global Economy Drew Mexican Men on Ill-Fated Trip North. Associated Press, June 1. Electronic document, www.lexis-nexis.com/universe/printdoc, accessed March 30, 2005.
Suro, Roberto
  1994 Border Patrol Beefed Up to "Stop the Bleeding." Chicago Sun-Times, September 25: 26.
Time
  1977 Immigration: Getting Their Slice of Paradise. Time, May 2: 26–32.
TRAC-DHS
  2002 Immigration and Naturalization Service Staff: 1975–2001. Electronic document, trac.syr.edu/tracins/findings/national/insStaff7501.html, accessed May 15, 2005.
Urla, Jacqueline
  1993 Cultural Politics in an Age of Statistics: Numbers, Nations, and the Making of Basque Identity. American Ethnologist 20(4): 818–43.
US Border Patrol
  1994 Border Patrol Strategic Plan: 1994 and Beyond, National Strategy. Washington, DC: US Border Patrol.
US Commission on Immigration Reform
  1994 US Immigration Policy: Restoring Credibility. Washington, DC: Government Printing Office.
US Customs and Border Protection (CBP)
  2003 Performance and Annual Report: Fiscal Year 2003. Washington, DC: US Customs and Border Protection.
  2004a Factsheet: US Customs and Border Protection Actions Taken Since 9/11. Electronic document, www.cbp.gov/xp/cgov/newsroom/press_releases/09172004.xml, accessed October 3, 2004.
  2004b Overview of the Immigration Inspections Program. Electronic document, www.cbp.gov/xp/cgov/enforcement/port_activities/overview.xml, accessed November 11, 2004.
US Department of Health and Human Services (DHHS)
  2000 Change in TANF Caseloads Since Enactment of New Welfare Law. Electronic document, www.acf.hhs.gov/news/stats/aug-dec.htm, accessed June 30, 2004.

US Department of Homeland Security (DHS)

2004a   Yearbook of Immigration Statistics, 2003. Washington, DC: Government Printing Office.

2004b   Immigration Monthly Statistics Report, August 2004. Washington, DC: Government Printing Office. Electronic document, uscis.gov/graphics/shared/aboutus/statistics/msraug04/SWBORD.HTM, accessed October 16, 2004.

2004c   Securing Our Homeland: US Department of Homeland Security Strategic Plan. Washington, DC: Department of Homeland Security.

2004d   US-VISIT: Keeping America's Doors Open and Our Nation Secure. Washington, DC: Department of Homeland Security.

2004e   US-VISIT: How Does US-VISIT Work? Electronic document, www.dhs.gov/dhspublic/display?theme=91&content=4071&print=true, accessed November 11, 2004.

2004f   US-VISIT: Fact Sheet. Washington, DC: Department of Homeland Security.

2004g   Fact Sheet: Department of Homeland Security Appropriations Act of 2005. Electronic document, www.dhs.gov/dhspublic/display?theme=43&content=4065&print=true, accessed November 7, 2004.

2004h   Southwest Border Apprehensions. Electronic document, uscis.gov/graphics/shared/aboutus/statistics/msrsep04/SWBORD.HTM, accessed November 13, 2004.

US Department of Justice (DOJ)

1998   Operation Gatekeeper: An Investigation Into Allegations of Fraud and Misconduct. Electronic document, www.usdoj.gov/oig/special/9807/gkp01.htm#P118_6319, accessed May 15, 2005.

2002   FY2002 Budget Summary: Immigration and Naturalization Service Budget Authority, 1993–2002. Electronic document, www.usdoj.gov/jmd/2002summary/html/ins_budget_authority.htm, accessed May 15, 2005.

US General Accounting Office (GAO)

1977   Illegal Entry at United States–Mexico Border: Multiagency Enforcement Efforts Have Not Been Effective in Stemming the Flow of Drugs and People. Washington, DC: Government Printing Office.

1980   Illegal Aliens: Estimating Their Impact on the United States. Washington, DC: Government Printing Office.

1991   Border Patrol: Southwest Border Enforcement Affected by Mission Expansion and Budget. Washington, DC: Government Printing Office.

1993   Illegal Aliens: Despite Data Limitations, Current Methods Provide Better Population Estimates. Washington, DC: Government Printing Office.

1994a   Illegal Aliens: Assessing Estimates of Financial Burden on California. Washington, DC: Government Printing Office.

1994b   Border Control: Revised Strategy is Showing Some Positive Results. Washington, DC: Government Printing Office.

1995a   Illegal Aliens: National Net Cost Estimates Vary Widely. Washington, DC: Government Printing Office.

1995b   Border Control: Revised Strategy is Showing Some Positive Results. Washington, DC: Government Printing Office.

1997a   Illegal Aliens: Extent of Welfare Benefits Received on Behalf of US Citizen Children. Washington, DC: Government Printing Office.

1997b   Undocumented Aliens: Medicaid-Funded Births in California and Texas. Washington, DC: Government Printing Office.

1997c   Illegal Immigration: Southwest Border Strategy Results Inconclusive; More Evaluation is Needed. Washington, DC: Government Printing Office.

1999a   Illegal Immigration: Status of Southwest Border Strategy Implementation. Washington, DC: Government Printing Office.

1999b   US–Mexico Border: Issues and Challenges Confronting the United States and Mexico. Washington, DC: Government Printing Office.

2001   INS' Southwest Border Strategy: Resource and Impact Issues Remain After Seven Years. Washington, DC: Government Printing Office.

2003   Land Border Ports of Entry: Vulnerabilities and Inefficiencies in the Inspections Process. Washington, DC: Government Printing Office.

2004a   Undocumented Aliens: Questions Persist about Their Impact on Hospitals' Uncompensated Care Costs. Washington, DC: Government Printing Office.

2004b   Illegal Alien Schoolchildren: Issues in Estimating State-by-State Costs. Washington, DC: Government Printing Office.

US Immigration and Naturalization Service (INS)

1971   Annual Report of the Immigration and Naturalization Service, 1970. Washington, DC: Government Printing Office.

1978   Annual Report of the Immigration and Naturalization Service, 1976. Washington, DC: Government Printing Office.

1991   Statistical Yearbook of the Immigration and Naturalization Service, 1990. Washington, DC: Government Printing Office.

1994   Statistical Yearbook of the Immigration and Naturalization Service, 1993. Washington, DC: Government Printing Office.

1996a   Building a Comprehensive Southwest Border Enforcement Strategy. Washington, DC: INS Public Affairs.

1996b   Meeting the Challenge Through Innovation. Washington DC: US Immigration and Naturalization Service.

2002   Statistical Yearbook of the Immigration and Naturalization Service, 2000. Washington, DC: Government Printing Office.

2003a   Statistical Yearbook of the Immigration and Naturalization Service, 2001. Washington, DC: Government Printing Office.

2003b   Executive Summary: Estimates of the Unauthorized Immigrant Population Residing in the United States: 1990 to 2000. Washington, DC: INS Office of Policy and Planning.

US Select Commission on Immigration and Refugee Policy

1981   US Immigration Policy and the National Interest. Washington, DC: Government Printing Office.

Van Hook, Jennifer, and Frank D. Bean
1998   Estimating Unauthorized Mexican Migration to the United States: Issues and Results. *In* Migration Between Mexico and the United States: Binational Study, vol. 2: Research Reports and Background Materials. Pp. 511–50. Mexico City: Mexican Ministry of Foreign Affairs; Washington, DC: US Commission on Immigration Reform.
Wacquant, Loïc
2001   Deadly Symbiosis: When Ghetto and Prison Meet and Mesh. Punishment and Society 3(1): 95–134.
Walker, Dennis
1994   Letter to the Editor: Proposition 187 Is a Step Forward. Orange County Register, September 29: Metro 9.
Walters, William
2000   Unemployment and Government: Genealogies of the Social. Cambridge: Cambridge University Press.
Warren, Robert
1994   Estimates of the Unauthorized Immigrant Population Residing in the United States, by Country of Origin and State of Residence: October 1992. Unpublished MS. Washington, DC: US Immigration and Naturalization Service.
Weintraub, Daniel M.
1994   Wilson Sues US Over Immigrants' "Invasion." Los Angeles Times, September 23: A3, A37.
Weir, Lorna
1996   Recent Developments in the Government of Pregnancy. Economy and Society 25(3): 372–92.
Welch, Michael
2002   Detained: Immigration Laws and the Expanding INS Jail Complex. Philadelphia: Temple University Press.
2003   Ironies of Social Control and the Criminalization of Immigrants. Crime, Law, and Social Change 39: 319–37.
West, Bill
2004   Prepared Statement of Bill West, Consultant, The Investigative Project. *In* Preventing the Entry of Terrorists into the United States. Hearing before the Subcommittee on International Terrorism, Nonproliferation, and Human Rights of the Committee on International Relations. US House of Representatives. 108th Congress, Second Session. Pp. 45–6. Washington, DC: Government Printing Office.
Wilson, Peter
1994   Letter to the Editor: Washington Must Act Now on Immigrants. Washington Post, May 6: A25.
Woodrow, Karen A.
1991   Preliminary Estimates of Undocumented Residents in 1990: Demographic Analysis Evaluation Project D2. Preliminary Research and Evaluation Memorandum No. 75. Washington, DC: US Bureau of the Census.

INDEX

Numbers in *italic* refer to illustrations.

Made in the USA
Lexington, KY
03 September 2013